★ FOR PATRICK, WITH LOVE. –KK ★

Library of Congress Cataloging-in-Publication Data is available.
ISBN 978-1-5235-1586-8

Design by John Passineau and Galen Smith
Cover illustration by Monique Steele

Interior illustrations by Monique Steele except where noted
Spot illustrations by Lourdes Ubidia: pages V; VI; VII; VIII; 30; 31; 36; 37; 48; 54; 61; 68; 76; 77; 81; 84; 104; 109; 113; 117; 119; 122; 126; 181; 191; 192; 195; 205; 207; 214; 216; 219; 225; 226; 227; 230
Map illustrations by Andy Wang: pages 25; 33; 41; 50; 51; 58; 62; 103; 106; 114; 121; 159; 180; 193; 197; 209
Art assistance by Amit Tayal

Workman books are available at special discounts when purchased in bulk for premiums and sales promotions as well as for fundraising or educational use. Special editions or book excerpts can also be created to specification. For details, please contact special.markets@hbgusa.com.

Workman Publishing Co., Inc.,
a subsidiary of Hachette Book Group, Inc.
1290 Avenue of the Americas
New York, NY 10104

workman.com

WORKMAN is a registered trademark of Workman Publishing Co., Inc.,
a subsidiary of Hachette Book Group, Inc.

Printed in Malaysia on responsibly sourced paper.
First printing September 2023
10 9 8 7 6 5 4 3 2 1

CONTENTS

★ ★ INTRODUCTION ★ ★

This book tells you about the forty-five people who have been president of the United States. "Just forty-five?" you ask. "Isn't Joe Biden the forty-sixth president?" Yes—but Grover Cleveland was the twenty-second president and the twenty-fourth. Two presidencies, one person. Thanks for throwing our count off, Grover.

The president heads the executive branch, one of the three branches of government. **The presidency** has become more powerful in recent decades, but the Constitution set it up to be equal to the legislative branch (which is **Congress**— made up of both the House of Representatives and the Senate) and the judicial branch **(the Supreme Court).** Checks and balances make sure that no branch gains too much power. For example, the president can veto acts of Congress, but Congress can override a veto and it can impeach the president. And while the Supreme Court can rule something the president has done to be unconstitutional, it's the president who appoints Supreme Court justices.

The president is the most powerful person in the government and leads the country, and their priorities often become policy. That affects not just the United States, but the entire world.

Article II of the Constitution sets up the executive branch. That's the presidency. Article II tells us how presidents are to be elected, gives their oath of office, and talks about how to impeach them if they do something wrong. To remove a president, the House of Representatives draws up the articles of impeachment, the Senate hears the trial, and the Chief Justice of the Supreme Court presides. If two-thirds of senators vote guilty, the president is removed from office and can still be tried in criminal courts; if impeached and found not guilty, the president stays in office.

What else does the Constitution say about presidents? It requires them to be at least thirty-five years old, be a natural-born citizen of the United States, and have lived in the United States for at least fourteen years. (See US Constitution, Article 2, Section 1.) Each term is four years long and begins at noon on January 20 of the year following the election. (Though they used to begin on March 4.) The Twenty-Second Amendment (1951) limits a president to two terms in office. When a vice president takes office after the death of a president, they can have two terms of their own if they served less than two years of their predecessor's unfinished term. (If they were in office for more than two years of their predecessor's term, they can only serve one term of their own.) The Twenty-Second Amendment was proposed because Franklin Roosevelt ran for—and won—the presidency four times. Although Roosevelt was popular, many people felt that a long-term presidency could lead to a dictatorship.

The American presidency is sometimes called the hardest job in the world. Not everyone has done it well.

The president is in charge of both **domestic policy** (plans for things inside the United States, like the economy) and **foreign policy** (relations with other nations). The president also appoints ambassadors, or ministers, to represent US interests, negotiate treaties, and help American citizens in other countries.

The president has a vice president and a cabinet (a group of people, made up of the heads of federal departments, to give advice), but the president decides whether to veto each law or allow it to go into effect. In addition, the president is the commander in chief of the armed forces. That means that although Congress has the power to declare war, the president heads the military. They don't have to lead the army into battle personally, though—only George Washington ever has.

Historians usually rank Abraham Lincoln as the greatest of American presidents. George Washington and Franklin Delano Roosevelt also get high marks. The presidents right before the Civil War, Franklin Pierce and James Buchanan, are usually ranked at or near the bottom. Those in the 1920s, the decade after World War I—Warren G. Harding and Calvin Coolidge—rank low, too. But those are general observations and you may disagree. A person who might have done a fine job in different circumstances may rank low because they didn't do well with the actual challenges they faced. An example of that would be Herbert Hoover, who was in office when the Great Depression started. And while historians may consider a given president to be *good*, only those who faced extraordinary difficulties were *great*.

When you look back on the forty-five people who've done the job over the past two hundred-plus years, how do you know who did a good job or a bad job, or even what's true? You use good sources and you find the information in more than one place; good history writing is based on documents and evidence. You'll find primary sources in every entry of this book. You can read them and draw your own conclusions about how they help tell us what each president did.

Primary sources are direct. That

means there's no filter between you and the subject, no one else telling you what it means. Examples of primary sources are letters, troop enlistment rosters, and firsthand accounts. A school lunch menu is a primary source—it tells you things about diet and food availability. Your brother's or sister's diary is a primary source; is that why you've been reading it? You're ensuring historical accuracy? Good for you.

Secondary sources have someone between you and the subject. Most books about history are secondary sources. Examples include a biography or an account of a battle written by someone who wasn't there. The writer will have looked at primary sources, and with any luck, they'll be a trained historian.

Tertiary (TERSH-ee-air-ee) **sources** have two layers between you and the subject. Encyclopedias, textbooks, and Wikipedia are examples of tertiary sources. The author read a bunch of secondary sources (layer 2) based on primary sources (layer 1) to write the entry you read. Tertiary sources increase the chances of an error. In general, the farther you get from a primary source, the easier it is to use that source—but the more likely it is to be wrong. Historians refer to tertiary sources as "bird vomit"—someone else has already digested the information and is spitting it back to you. Gross. That's why

you'll find primary sources in every single entry in this book.

There are a few things to remember as you look at primary sources in this book and in the wild:

1 **Words have changed over time.** For example, today we think of the First Lady as the wife of a president, but it used to mean the White House hostess. A number of presidents were widowed or had wives who were sick, and for some of them, a different woman took on the role of First Lady; that doesn't mean she married the president, just that she made sure there was enough crab salad for the next state dinner.

2 **Documents were written differently in different time periods.** For example, the way people begin and end a letter is typically less formal today, and some spellings are different now. You know what was hard about choosing sources from the early presidents for this book? Reading their handwriting! (Zachary Taylor's is a mess.) Once people started using typewriters, it got a lot easier. But if you come across a document dated 1776 and it is typewritten—well, you should be suspicious. In addition, staples have changed in size. During World War II they got teeny-tiny because metal was needed for the war effort, not for keeping papers tidy. And you know what? Those pint-sized staples did the trick. If you find a document dated 1944 (that's during World War II) with a big staple, your spidey sense should tingle.

3 **You can tell a surprising amount from an original document,** and it's always a good idea to look at one when you can. Today, many historical documents are available online, and even if there's a transcription—which is somebody else writing down what the document says—it's still smart to look at the original yourself. For example, Dwight Eisenhower, the thirty-fourth president, was the general in charge of D-Day during World War II. The day before his troops stormed the beaches of Normandy, France, Eisenhower handwrote an "in case of failure" message. It's what he would have released if German forces beat his men. You can find a picture of it online.

The first draft says, "Our landings in the Cherbourg-Havre area have failed to gain a satisfactory foothold and the troops have been withdrawn." But Ike, as he was known, struck through "have been withdrawn" and rewrote the text so that he himself would take responsibility for the retreat, should it occur. The final draft reads, "Our landings in the Cherbourg-Havre area have failed to gain a satisfactory foothold and I have withdrawn the troops." Eisenhower was in charge, and the decisions were his to make. His edits show that he wanted to make that clear.

You can see something else from looking at the original, too—it's misdated as July 5. If you just read about it, you would be told that Eisenhower wrote the message on June 5, the day before the D-Day invasion. And that's true.

But when you look at the document yourself, you see that even Eisenhower had nerves the night before battle.

As you read through the entries in this book, remember that history moves in only one direction. Presidents didn't know what was going to happen next. Sometimes they led with courage and wisdom, and sometimes they really messed up. Either way, presidents represent all the people of the nation, including those who didn't vote for them. And as you look back on the people who led the country, think about what kind of qualifications each had. What seems most important to you? Military service, like Washington, Grant, and Eisenhower had? A long history of government service, like that of John Quincy Adams and George H. W. Bush? What do you feel made each president a success— or a failure?

They're important questions because presidents have great power—and huge responsibilities. They have to turn the office over safely to the next person, even if they disagree with them. They take an oath to defend the Constitution and to protect the right of the people to have a say in their own government— to make certain that the next generation also enjoys the blessings of liberty. To ensure, as President Lincoln said, that "government of the people, by the people, for the people, shall not perish from the earth."

So are you ready to decode a presidency . . . or forty-five? Forty-six? (Still a problem, Grover. Still a problem.)

UNITED STATES PRESIDENTS

GEORGE WASHINGTON
1789–1797

JOHN ADAMS
1797–1801

THOMAS JEFFERSON
1801–1809

JAMES MADISON
1809–1817

JAMES MONROE
1817–1825

JOHN QUINCY ADAMS
1825–1829

ANDREW JACKSON
1829–1837

MARTIN VAN BUREN
1837–1841

WILLIAM H. HARRISON
1841

JOHN TYLER
1841–1845

JAMES K. POLK
1845–1849

ZACHARY TAYLOR
1849–1850

MILLARD FILLMORE
1850–1853

FRANKLIN PIERCE
1853–1857

JAMES BUCHANAN
1857–1861

ABRAHAM LINCOLN
1861–1865

ANDREW JOHNSON
1865–1869

ULYSSES S. GRANT
1869–1877

RUTHERFORD B. HAYES
1877–1881

JAMES A. GARFIELD
1881

CHESTER A. ARTHUR
1881–1885

GROVER CLEVELAND
1885–1889

BENJAMIN HARRISON
1889–1893

GROVER CLEVELAND
1893–1897

WILLIAM MCKINLEY
1897–1901

THEODORE ROOSEVELT
1901–1909

WILLIAM H. TAFT
1909–1913

WOODROW WILSON
1913–1921

WARREN G. HARDING
1921–1923

CALVIN COOLIDGE
1923–1929

HERBERT HOOVER
1929–1933

FRANKLIN D. ROOSEVELT
1933–1945

HARRY S TRUMAN
1945–1953

DWIGHT D. EISENHOWER
1953–1961

JOHN F. KENNEDY
1961–1963

LYNDON B. JOHNSON
1963–1969

RICHARD M. NIXON
1969–1974

GERALD FORD
1974–1977

JAMES E. CARTER
1977–1981

RONALD REAGAN
1981–1989

GEORGE H. W. BUSH
1989–1993

WILLIAM J. CLINTON
1993–2001

GEORGE W. BUSH
2001–2009

BARACK OBAMA
2009–2017

DONALD TRUMP
2017–2021

JOSEPH R. BIDEN, JR.
2021–PRESENT

BORN: 1732

DIED: 1799

IN OFFICE: 1789–1797

FROM: Virginia; his home was known as Mount Vernon

VICE PRESIDENT: John Adams

PARTY: Tried to avoid political parties, but became a Federalist

GEORGE ★★★★★★ WASHINGTON

DID YOU KNOW?

- Washington is the only president to have been elected by a unanimous vote in the electoral college.

- At only 135 words, Washington's second inaugural address (given in 1793) is the shortest in US history.

- Washington is the only president never to live in Washington, DC, even though he helped choose the location for the nation's capital. He took his first oath of office in New York. When he took the oath for his second term, the capital had moved to Philadelphia, where it remained for ten years.

Life Before the Presidency

George Washington was born in Virginia. When he was eleven, his father died and his older half brother, Lawrence, became his guardian. Lawrence Washington died when George was twenty, and George later became the owner of the family's Mount Vernon estate. He was very interested in farming and livestock, and although he disapproved of slavery, he enslaved people.

At this time, the North American colonies were still under European rule. Britain and France both wanted to expand their holdings in North America and the French and Indian War (1754–1763) soon broke out.

Washington served in the British army, and in one battle he had two horses shot out from under him and four bullets hit his coat—but not him. His military experience would serve him well later.

In 1774, Washington was a delegate to the First Continental Congress, which tried to unite colonists against what they saw as increasingly unfair treatment by Great Britain. When relations with Britain didn't improve, the Second Continental Congress met in Philadelphia in 1775. Washington was again a delegate, and the Second Continental Congress chose him to be the general of the colonial troops that fought against the British in the American Revolution.

Letter to Martha Washington, June 18, 1775

Philadelphia June 18, 1775

My Dearest

I am now set down to write you on a subject which fills me with inexpressible concern—and this concern is greatly aggravated and Increased, when I reflect upon the uneasiness I know it will give you—It has been determined in Congress that the whole Army raised for the defence of the American Cause shall be put under my care, and that it is necessary for me to proceed immediately to Boston to take upon me the command of it. You may believe me my dear Patcy, when I assure you, in the most solemn manner, that, so far from seeking this appointment I have used every endeavor in my power to avoid it, not only from my unwillingness to part with you and the Family, but from a consciousness of its being a trust too great for my Capacity.

DECODED This letter that Washington sent to his wife, Martha, shows his concern over being chosen to lead American troops against King George III's British troops. Washington enclosed a new will with the letter, indicating just what a serious moment it was for the couple—they both knew that he might not survive the assignment.

Serving together in the army helped give men from different colonies a common identity as Americans. They were always underdogs, though, and in many ways it's surprising that they won the Revolution.

They were helped by a bold decision Washington made. It wasn't on a battlefield—and the enemy was a disease.

Letter to William Shippen Jr., February 6, 1777

Head Qurs Morristown February 6th 1777.

Dear Sir

Finding the Small pox to be spreading much and fearing that no precaution can prevent it from running through the whole of our Army, I have determined that the troops shall be inoculated. This Expedient may be attended with some inconveniences and some disadvantages, but yet I trust in its consequences will have the most happy effects. Necessity not only authorizes but seems to require the measure, for should the disorder infect the Army in the natural way and rage with its usual virulence we should have more to dread from it than from the Sword of the Enemy.

DECODED Smallpox was a dangerous disease with a high death rate. When a smallpox epidemic started in North America during the Revolutionary War, British troops had an advantage. More of them had been exposed to it before, so they had a higher immunity rate, while more American troops would die or become blind because of the disease. Washington made the bold decision to have the Continental Army troops inoculated against the disease. It's unlikely that the Continental Army could have won the Revolution with significantly fewer troops—Washington's decision to protect his men from disease may have won the war.

After the Revolution, Washington returned home to Mount Vernon. In 1787, he was chosen as president of the Constitutional Convention, whose members wrote the US Constitution. Washington was greatly respected, and most people assumed he'd win the first presidential election. They were right. He received every vote.

Mr. President

One of George Washington's biggest problems was that no one had been president before him. The Constitution set up the office of the president and said that the president should enforce the laws, command the armed forces, and make treaties with the advice and consent of the Senate. Beyond that, it was vague. Washington didn't have any examples to look to for how to do the job—no one in the world had been an elected president before. People didn't know what to call him at first; it was Washington himself who chose the title "Mr. President."

The French Revolution (1789–1799) started while Washington was in office. It sparked a series of wars in Europe that involved many countries, including France and Britain. That was dangerous for the United States. The young country had just been through a major war and needed to recover. But Americans traded with both countries, and some people (like Secretary of State Thomas Jefferson) favored France's interests, while others (like Vice President John Adams) favored Britain's interests. Events in Europe could wind up pulling America apart.

President Washington didn't want the United States to get involved in the war between France and Great Britain. He sent John Jay, an American statesman and diplomat, to talk with the British, hoping to solve the problems between the countries and make it easier to stay out of the war. Jay negotiated a treaty, or agreement, with British king George III. But almost everyone in the United States disliked the treaty, and it hurt Washington's popularity.

On the domestic front, farmers in western Pennsylvania refused to pay a new tax on whiskey they made from the grain they grew; their revolt was called the Whiskey Rebellion. They threatened to pull their counties out of the young country. Washington responded strongly to that threat. He saddled up and rode after them himself. After all, he was the commander in chief of the armed forces. Though no one quite knew what that meant yet, Washington was the general who'd won the Revolutionary War. He thought he should lead the troops who put down the Whiskey Rebellion, and he commanded more troops during that time than at any point during the Revolutionary War.

EXCERPT FROM JAY'S TREATY, NOVEMBER 19, 1794

ARTICLE 12 OF JAY'S TREATY SAID:

Provided always that the said American vessels do carry and land their Cargoes in the United States only, it being expressly agreed and declared that during the Continuance of this article, the United States will prohibit and restrain the carrying any Melasses, Sugar, Coffee, Cocoa or Cotton in American vessels, either from His Majesty's Islands or from the United States, to any part of the World, except the United States, reasonable Sea Stores excepted. Provided also, that it shall and may be lawful during the same period for British vessels to import from the said Islands into the United States, and to export from the United States to the said Islands, all Articles whatever being of the Growth, Produce or Manufacture of the said Islands, or of the United States respectively, which now may, by the Laws of the said States, be so imported and exported. And that the Cargoes of the said British vessels, shall be subject to no other or higher Duties or Charges, than shall be payable on the same articles if so imported or exported in American Vessels.

DECODED Article 12 was one of the parts of the treaty that most outraged Americans. The measure looked like Great Britain wasn't restricting American trade with the West Indies until you actually read it. It said that American ships were free to trade with the West Indies (which were much closer to the United States than Great Britain), *but* that American ships traveling there had to be small, which limited the amount of cargo they could carry. It also said that American ships couldn't take their cargoes to other countries. And they couldn't transport molasses, sugar, coffee, cocoa, or cotton, which were precisely the goods they wanted to get from the West Indies. The trade was important to the US economy.

No president since Washington has led troops while being president.

WHISKEY REBELLION PROCLAMATION

PHILADELPHIA, SEPT. 25, 1794

. . . Now therefore I George Washington President of the United States, in obedience to that high and irresistible duty consigned to me by the Constitution "to take care that the laws be faithfully executed"; . . .

And I do moreover exhort all individuals . . . to call to mind, that as the people of the United States have been permitted under the divine favor, in perfect freedom, after solemn deliberation, and in an enlightened age, to elect their own Government; so will their gratitude for this inestimable blessing be best distinguished by firm exertions to maintain the Constitution and the Laws.

DECODED In this proclamation, Washington quotes the Constitution Article II, Section 3 which says that the president's job is "to take care that the laws be faithfully executed." That means that if the people don't follow the law, he's supposed to do something about it. He goes on to remind people that they choose their own government through elections and so they need to obey the laws it makes. Americans had won a revolution and written a constitution that gave them broad rights, but if they wanted to keep their democracy, they couldn't dabble in armed insurrection. Political changes are made by voting, not attacking government officials, laws, or buildings. Washington moved swiftly against the uprising, understanding that it was a threat to the country.

One of the big problems Washington faced was building the economy at home. Midwestern farmers couldn't use the Mississippi River to get their goods to market. At that time, Spain owned New Orleans, which is where the Mississippi River empties into the Gulf of Mexico. If Midwestern farmers couldn't ship their crops downriver and out through the Gulf, their rich farmland would never be very profitable. Washington sent a diplomat to negotiate, and Spain agreed to let American farmers ship through New Orleans. Opening New Orleans to American exports made the middle of the country prosperous and helped keep the young country together at a delicate time.

At the same time that Washington was opening New Orleans and staying neutral in Europe, he signed the Fugitive Slave Act of 1793, which Congress had passed. It allowed enslavers to recapture enslaved people who had escaped to free states by hunting for them there. The practice of enslaving people created a division between states. Americans worried about the effect that would have on the country in the future.

Legacy

Washington's leadership on the battlefield, at the Constitutional Convention, and then as the first president was critical to the stability of the young republic. He had the greatest prestige of anyone in the country, allowing him to navigate tricky foreign policy issues and major domestic challenges. His legacy is setting the precedent for those who followed him in office and leaving the United States prosperous and peaceful.

Washington strongly believed that one person should not stay in power for a long time. He published a farewell address as a way of announcing that he wouldn't try to get a third term in office. He thought stepping down after two terms was an important part of the job.

When he left office, Washington went back to Virginia to manage his estate, Mount Vernon. He died there in December 1799. As the first president, Washington established important precedents; in many ways he shaped not only the presidency but the entire executive branch. He used his personal prestige and popularity to create a strong executive authority and active presidency. Although a soldier, he worked for peace; although an easterner, he tried to make the west profitable; and although a farmer himself, he fielded an army to put down an agrarian uprising in order to preserve the country and the authority of its government. Each new president is evaluated, ultimately, against the standards that Washington set.

WASHINGTON'S FAREWELL ADDRESS, 1796

. . . The unity of government which constitutes you one people . . . is a main pillar in the edifice of your real independence, the support of your tranquility at home, your peace abroad; of your safety; of your prosperity; of that very liberty which you so highly prize. But as it is easy to foresee that, from different causes and from different quarters, much pains will be taken, many artifices employed to weaken in your minds the conviction of this truth; as this is the point in your political fortress against which the batteries of internal and external enemies will be most constantly and actively (though often covertly and insidiously) directed, it is of infinite moment that you should properly estimate the immense value of your national union to your collective and individual happiness. . . .

[DECODED] Washington warned the people that national unity was the key to their safety and liberty. He also warned that America's enemies, both inside and outside the country, would attack the idea that Americans should stick together. He went on to foresee that regional differences could drive the country apart if people valued their own area's needs over those of the country as a whole. And Washington was right; less than seventy years later, the South seceded from the Union and the North and South fought a bloody civil war.

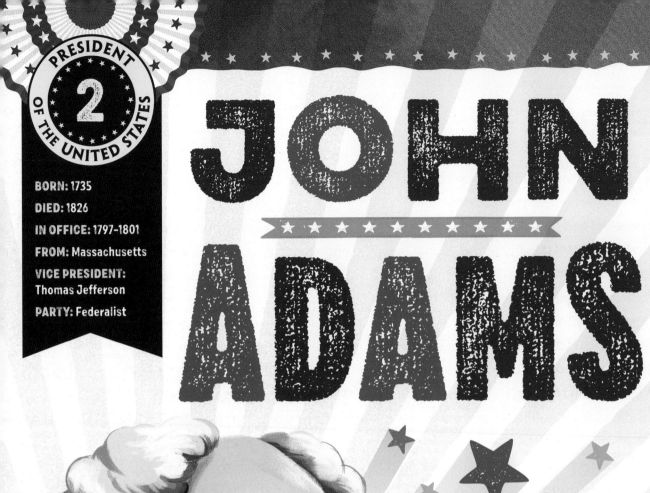

JOHN ADAMS

★ ★ ★ ★ ★ ★ ★ ★ ★ ★ ★ ★

BORN: 1735

DIED: 1826

IN OFFICE: 1797–1801

FROM: Massachusetts

VICE PRESIDENT: Thomas Jefferson

PARTY: Federalist

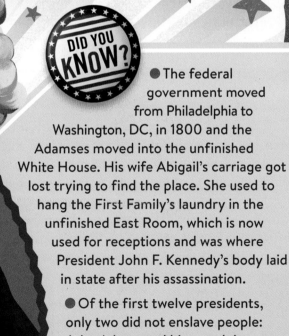

DID YOU KNOW?

● The federal government moved from Philadelphia to Washington, DC, in 1800 and the Adamses moved into the unfinished White House. His wife Abigail's carriage got lost trying to find the place. She used to hang the First Family's laundry in the unfinished East Room, which is now used for receptions and was where President John F. Kennedy's body laid in state after his assassination.

● Of the first twelve presidents, only two did not enslave people: John Adams and his son, John Quincy Adams.

Life Before the Presidency

John Adams was born near Boston, Massachusetts, and grew up on a farm. He enrolled in Harvard College at the age of sixteen, and when he graduated he became a teacher, a job he didn't much like. He began to study law in the evenings and opened his own law practice in 1758. In 1764, he married Abigail. They had six children, including John Quincy Adams, who would become the sixth president. In 1768, Adams moved his family to Boston to be closer to the anti-British protests occurring in the years leading up to the American Revolution.

Adams thought Great Britain was unfair to the colonies, and he was angry about it, but in 1770, he defended some British soldiers in court. British troops stationed in Boston had opened fire on local residents after being pelted with ice balls; five colonists died. This event became known as the Boston Massacre, and it resulted in murder charges against some British soldiers. Adams wanted to make sure that the trial was fair.

Adams was a delegate to the First Continental Congress in 1774, and then the Second Continental Congress in 1775. It was at that convention where Adams nominated George Washington to be commander of the Continental Army, and he served on the five-person committee that was supposed to write a declaration of independence. (Thomas Jefferson wound up doing most of the writing.)

During the Revolutionary War, Adams sailed to France to try to get the French to help the Americans. French entry into the War in 1778 proved decisive. After the war, Adams became ambassador to Great Britain. He was the first of the Founders of the American republic to meet King George III.

When George Washington was elected as the first president, John Adams had the second highest vote total, so he became the first vice president. He didn't have much to do and didn't like the job.

Washington stepped down after two terms and Adams ran for president in 1796. He ended up winning the presidency, but his opponent, Thomas Jefferson, who was from a different political party, wound up with the second highest vote total. Only twice has the United States had a president of one party and a vice president of the other party. Adams's presidency was the first, and the other was Abraham Lincoln's.

Letter to Abigail Adams, December 20, 1796

Dec. 20, 1796: It is supposed to be certain that Mr. Jefferson cannot be P[resident]. and a narrow Squeak it is as the Boys say, whether he or P[inckney]. shall be Daddy Vice: a Character that I shall soon relinquish whether I am or not the Person whom they now toast under the Title of "The President elect." I have been Daddy Vice long enough.

DECODED The sealed electoral college votes came to Adams, as vice president, and he desperately hoped that the ballots inside were marked for him. He wrote to his wife, Abigail, every couple of days through December 1796, alternating between claiming that he didn't mind if he wasn't elected and agonizing over who might be voting against him. Adams had a prickly personality, and the uncertainty was hard on him. Note that he calls the vice president "Daddy Vice."

Mr. President

Adams was the first president to take over from another president, and George Washington was a tough act to follow.

The wars of the French Revolution were still going on. President Washington had said that the United States wouldn't take sides. But American opinion was split. President Adams favored Britain, while others, like Vice President Jefferson, favored France. Worse, neither France nor Britain wanted to let Americans be neutral. The problem was that battles were happening on the seas—with both nations targeting American ships. President Adams needed to do something.

Adams sent diplomats to France to try to prevent a war. The French foreign minister refused to meet with them or even start talks unless the United States paid him a huge bribe and gave France a loan. He sent three of his aides to explain this to the US diplomats. When President Adams told the public about it, he replaced the French agents' names with the letters X, Y, and Z, so it became known as the XYZ Affair.

Americans were furious, and many wanted to go to war with France. Adams thought that would be a mistake and continued to negotiate, although the United States and France fought at sea for the next couple of years.

On the domestic front, the Federalist-controlled Congress passed four measures in 1798, which together were known as the Alien and Sedition Acts, and President Adams signed them. ("Aliens" meant people in the United States who weren't US citizens.) The Alien Enemies Act allowed the president to deport citizens of an enemy nation during times of war. The Alien Friends Act allowed the president to deport anyone who wasn't a US citizen and was suspected of plotting against the United States during peacetime. The Alien Enemies and Alien Friends Acts were a response to the undeclared war with France, the Quasi-War. The Naturalization Act required people to live in the United States for fourteen years before they could be citizens, which effectively put off the point at which these people could vote. New immigrants were more likely to vote for the Federalists' opponents; the Act kept them from voting for an additional nine years. The last and most unpopular measure was the Sedition Act, which made it illegal to criticize the government or the president. The Sedition Act was by far the most important of the four measures and a direct attack on free speech. It outlawed criticism of the president—but not the vice president, Thomas Jefferson, who was from the opposition party.

SEDITION ACT, 1798

And be it farther enacted, That if any person shall write, print, utter or publish . . . scandalous and malicious writing or writings against the government of the United States, or either house of the Congress of the United States, or the President of the United States, with intent to defame . . . or to bring them . . . into contempt or disrepute . . . then such person, being thereof convicted before any court of the United States having jurisdiction thereof, shall be punished by a fine not exceeding two thousand dollars, and by imprisonment not exceeding two years.

[DECODED] The Sedition Act made it a crime to criticize the president but not the vice president. Critics thought it was a clear violation of the right to free speech.

The Federalists who controlled Congress were pro-British. Many were upset that Adams tried so hard to avoid a war with France and that issue would cost him the 1800 election. Vice President Jefferson, a strong defender of free speech, argued that the Sedition Act violated the First Amendment's protection of free speech. Twenty-five people, mostly journalists, were arrested under the Sedition Act, including Benjamin Franklin's grandson, Benjamin Bache, who used Franklin's old printing equipment and was a vocal critic of the Federalists, which was Adams' party. Franklin, who had died eight years before, would have been appalled. He supported free speech and didn't want the United States to be a country where "a Man cannot call his Tongue his own."

Adams hadn't asked Congress for a sedition act, but he did sign it into law. Many historians consider it the lowest point of his presidency.

Legacy

Adams became the first president to lose reelection. His departure from office was the first test of the peaceful transfer of power for which America is justly famous. And he stepped down, transferring power to the other party for the first time in American history.

We remember John Adams for his long service to his country, beginning before the Revolution. He was president when complex European wars affected, and endangered, the United States. Adams put his country's best interests ahead of those of his party or his own career, establishing an important precedent even if it cost him reelection.

After he left office, Adams returned to his farm in Massachusetts. In 1825, he got to see the inauguration of his son, John Quincy Adams, as the sixth president. Adams died on July 4, 1826—the same day as his sometimes friend, sometimes enemy, Thomas Jefferson. His last words reportedly were, "Thomas Jefferson still survives." Adams didn't know that Jefferson had died in Virginia a few hours before.

THOMAS ★ JEFFERSON

PRESIDENT
3
OF THE UNITED STATES

BORN: 1743

DIED: 1826

IN OFFICE: 1801–1809

FROM: Virginia; his home was known as Monticello

VICE PRESIDENT: Aaron Burr (first term), George Clinton (second term)

PARTY: Democratic-Republican

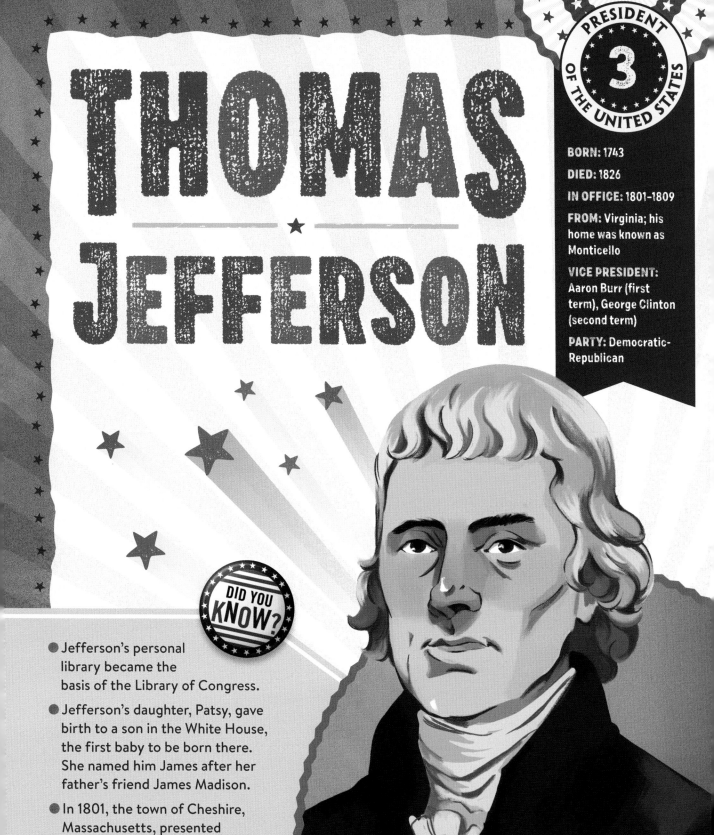

DID YOU KNOW?

- Jefferson's personal library became the basis of the Library of Congress.

- Jefferson's daughter, Patsy, gave birth to a son in the White House, the first baby to be born there. She named him James after her father's friend James Madison.

- In 1801, the town of Cheshire, Massachusetts, presented Jefferson with a 1,235-pound ball of cheese.

Life Before the Presidency

Thomas Jefferson was born in Virginia. He was shy but read extensively and was an excellent violinist. He became a lawyer and was an outstanding writer, but he was a poor public speaker. Jefferson inherited land and money from his father, a successful planter who died when Jefferson was fourteen. In 1768, he began building his home, Monticello, on a Virginia hill with a tremendous view of the surrounding countryside.

Jefferson served in the House of Burgesses (the Virginia state legislature) until 1774. He was a delegate to the Second Continental Congress, where, in 1775, he was chosen to write a justification for the colonists having taken up arms against the British king. This was the Declaration of Independence. As Congress debated the draft, they edited Jefferson's words, which offended him. Worse than that, though, they struck his entire passage condemning the slave trade, which would have tragic consequences for enslaved people—and for the country. (Although Jefferson attacked the slave trade, he also enslaved people and had several children with Sally Hemings, a woman whom he enslaved.)

DECLARATION OF INDEPENDENCE,
JULY 1776

We hold these truths to be self-evident, that all men are created equal, that they are endowed by their Creator with certain unalienable Rights, that among these are Life, Liberty and the pursuit of Happiness.

DECODED This line states American political principles and is one of the most famous sentences in US history.

Jefferson returned to Virginia in late 1776, and he again served in the state legislature. Among other bills that he worked on, he secured passage of a bill establishing a state library. Jefferson loved books. He spent more than he could afford on books sent from Europe—but he never could resist them. He also wrote a bill on religious freedom, an issue he always cared about. Jefferson strongly opposed mixing religion and government. He became governor of Virginia in 1779, while the Revolutionary War was raging. He had to flee when British troops invaded, and he was almost captured.

Jefferson served as secretary of state (1790–1793) under George Washington, and as vice president (1797–1801) under John Adams before being elected president.

Mr. President

Thomas Jefferson won the first sharply contested presidential election. He ran against President John Adams. The two men had become bitter adversaries. Adams lost when his party, the Federalists, didn't unite behind him. It was the first peaceful transfer of power from one party to another and set an important precedent.

JEFFERSON'S FIRST INAUGURAL ADDRESS, 1801

Let us, then, fellow-citizens, unite with one heart and one mind. . . . [E]very difference of opinion is not a difference of principle. We have called by different names brethren of the same principle. We are all Republicans, we are all Federalists.

DECODED In 1800, political parties had already formed—Democratic-Republicans (Jefferson's party) and Federalists (John Adams's party). People had sharp differences of opinion coming into the 1800 election, and in his inaugural address, Jefferson tried to unite people and remind them that they could disagree on issues and still love their country, and democracy.

As president, Jefferson's domestic policies were more successful than his foreign policies. In 1803, he made the Louisiana Purchase, buying a huge chunk of land in the middle of the current United States from France. It cost $15 million, or four cents per acre. With a stroke of the pen, Jefferson doubled the size of the country.

LOUISIANA PURCHASE AGREEMENT, 1803

ARTICLE III

The inhabitants of the ceded territory shall be incorporated in the Union of the United States and admitted as soon as possible according to the principles of the federal Constitution to the enjoyment of all these rights, advantages and immunities of citizens of the United States, and in the mean time they shall be maintained and protected in the free enjoyment of their liberty, property and the Religion which they profess.

DECODED When the United States bought the huge territory of the Louisiana Purchase from France, there were already people living on the land. The United States promised to honor treaties France had made with Indigenous nations (found in Article VI of the agreement). Here in Article III, the United States agreed that these people would have constitutional rights and be able to keep their religion.

But the Louisiana Purchase opened the territory to white settlers, and conflict—and the loss of Indigenous rights and culture—followed.

BRITISH NORTH AMERICA

LOUISIANA PURCHASE

UNITED STATES

SPANISH POSSESSIONS

Jefferson sent Meriwether Lewis and William Clark west to explore the continent. He had never been more than a few miles west of his house, but he was fascinated with the reports of the landscape, plants, and animals that Lewis and Clark sent back.

Meriwether Lewis

William Clark

In foreign affairs, American shipping faced danger from the four Barbary states, Morocco, Algiers, Tunis, and Tripoli, which lined the Mediterranean Sea on the African coast. Pirates attacked ships and stole cargoes unless they were paid off. European nations made treaties with the Barbary states that required them to make an annual tribute payment. President Adams had made tribute payments, too, to protect American shipping in the Mediterranean. But three months after his inauguration, President Jefferson dispatched the US navy to the Mediterranean, wanting to make a show of force in the waters where several American ships and crews had been seized. The leader of Tripoli declared war on the United States after Jefferson refused to pay more, but American victories at sea allowed Jefferson to settle things with Tripoli on terms that were

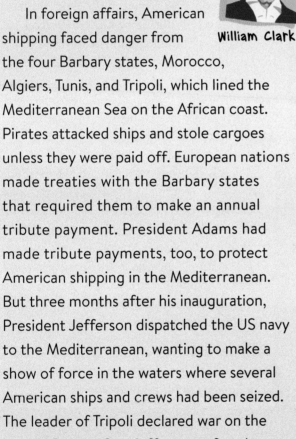

good for the United States and reduced the pirate threat.

The most complicated foreign policy issue Jefferson faced was still the fighting between France and Britain. As they jockeyed for position in their ongoing wars, the French often seized American ships and the British stopped American ships and impressed some of their crew, which means they made American sailors become sailors on British ships. Those practices violated Americans' rights as a neutral nation—one that wasn't fighting for one side or the other.

At Jefferson's urging, Congress passed the Embargo Act in 1807, which prohibited overseas trade with Britain and France until they recognized American neutrality. But this act, which was meant as a punishment for Britain and France, badly hurt the American economy. It was worst for New England, whose economy relied on shipping. By the time Congress overturned the Embargo Act in 1809, American exports had fallen from $108 million a year to $22 million. While the measure was meant to keep the United States out of war, Jefferson noted that the country could have waged a war for less money. The Embargo Act hurt Jefferson's popularity, especially because the impact was felt unevenly throughout the country. New Englanders were furious that the South, where Jefferson was from, escaped the brunt of the impact.

Jefferson continued to think and write about liberty as president. One of his most famous phrases, the separation of church and state, didn't come from his work during the American Revolution but instead was found in a letter written while he was president.

Letter to the Danbury Baptist Association of Connecticut, January 1, 1802

Believing with you that religion is a matter which lies solely between Man & his God, that he owes account to none other for his faith or his worship, that the legitimate powers of government reach actions only, & not opinions, I contemplate with sovereign reverence that act of the whole American people which declared that their legislature should "make no law respecting an establishment of religion, or prohibiting the free exercise thereof," thus building a wall of separation between Church & State.

DECODED The First Amendment to the Constitution contains the words that Jefferson uses here in quotation marks—that Congress shall make no law respecting an establishment of religion, or prohibiting the free exercise thereof. In other words, the government can't make you practice any religion or stop you from doing so if you want. This built a wall between church and state—that is, it separated them. Early Americans had different religious views, and the country's Founders didn't want that to become the basis of discrimination.

Legacy

Jefferson is best known for his work at the time of the American Revolution, and especially for writing the Declaration of Independence. But he was an important president, too.

His legacy there is the Louisiana Purchase, in which he doubled the size of the country inexpensively and without war. This vast new territory would provide resources and opportunities for many Americans but eventually led to the forced removal of Indigenous people from their ancestral homelands.

Jefferson had mixed results as president. He made American ships safer in Barbary waters, but France and Britain continued to threaten American commerce, and his Embargo Act was wildly unpopular. And while he wanted to end slavery, he himself enslaved people.

In his post-presidential period Jefferson founded the University of Virginia in 1819. He struggled with debt and eventually had to sell his enormous book collection—the largest private collection in the country—to the United States. His books restarted the Library of Congress after the British burned it during the War of 1812. The sale helped Jefferson a little financially, but he used the money to buy more books.

BORN: 1751

DIED: 1836

IN OFFICE: 1809–1817

FROM: Virginia; his home was known as Montpelier

VICE PRESIDENT: George Clinton (first term), Elbridge Gerry (second term)

PARTY: Democratic-Republican

JAMES
★★★★★★★★
MADISON

DID YOU KNOW?

● Madison had a frostbite scar on his nose. He got it walking for miles in the winter campaigning against James Monroe.

● Both of Madison's vice presidents died in office. George Clinton was the first and Elbridge Gerry was the second.

● At five feet four inches tall and a hundred pounds, Madison was the smallest president. He was nicknamed "Little Jemmy."

● Dolley Madison was the first First Lady to attend her husband's inauguration.

● The first inaugural ball was held after Madison's inauguration.

● Madison was the first wartime president.

Life Before the Presidency

James Madison grew up on a wealthy plantation in Virginia. He got his early education from his parents and a nearby school, then enrolled in what was later named Princeton University. He began to study law and became involved in Virginia state politics in 1776.

Madison was elected to the Second Continental Congress in 1779. He wasn't yet thirty years old and was the youngest delegate. The Constitutional Convention was held in the summer of 1787 to replace the Articles of Confederation, which hadn't proven strong enough to keep the country together. Madison wrote to his friend, Thomas Jefferson, who was in France, that the hardest problem the Framers of the Constitution dealt with was how many members of Congress each state would get. Madison proposed a plan which would give the more populous states (like Virginia) more delegates in Congress. This was known as the Virginia Plan. Eventually the Constitution reflected this idea in the House of Representatives, which gives more representatives to more populous states. (The compromise between large and small states on how to calculate congressional representation is called the Great Compromise. It was a critical piece in writing a constitution that was acceptable to enough people that it could be ratified. Each state has two senators regardless of their population.)

The Constitution had to be ratified, or approved, by nine states before it would go into effect, and it wasn't certain the states would approve it. Madison, along with Alexander Hamilton and John Jay, wrote newspaper essays under a pseudonym, trying to persuade people to ratify the Constitution. These essays together are known as the Federalist Papers, and they are important documents in American history.

FEDERALIST NO. 51, FEBRUARY 8, 1788

If men were angels, no government would be necessary. If angels were to govern men, neither external nor internal controls on government would be necessary. In framing a government which is to be administered by men over men, the great difficulty lies in this: you must first enable the government to control the governed; and in the next place oblige it to control itself.

DECODED Federalist Number 51 is one of the most famous of the essays Madison wrote to defend the new Constitution and persuade the states to ratify it. Here Madison explains the need for checks and balances within a government and for the separation of powers, so that one branch of government doesn't become too powerful.

Madison was a member of the very first group in the House of Representatives (1789) and proposed the Bill of Rights, the first ten amendments to the Constitution that contain many important freedoms. He had been hesitant to put specific rights in the Constitution because he was afraid that if they listed some rights but not others, people might think they meant to *exclude* the rights they had left out. Many people were upset that the Constitution didn't clearly list freedoms, and Madison agreed to propose a Bill of Rights after he won office.

Mr. President

When James Madison was elected president, France's wars were still going on. The French Revolution had spanned a decade, and then Napoleon Bonaparte came to power and invaded many other European countries, starting another set of wars. France and Britain were still fighting, and that caused problems for American shipping. Madison backed passage of Macon's

Bill No. 2, a congressional bill that said the United States would start trading again with either Britain or France—whichever one first agreed to stop capturing American ships and sailors. France jumped first, saying it would respect American neutrality. When American ships reached French ports, however, Napoleon confiscated them. He'd tricked Madison.

Meanwhile, the British continued to seize sailors off American ships, including a US naval ship, which outraged Americans. That, combined with the more pro-French position of Madison's party, the Democratic-Republicans, meant that when the United States went to war, it would fight against Great Britain.

Madison knew better than anyone that the Constitution gives Congress, not the president, the power to decide whether to go to war. Madison addressed Congress on June 1, 1812, asking for a declaration of war against Great Britain. On June 17, Congress granted it. This began the War of 1812. It was sometimes called "Mr. Madison's War," and Madison became the first president to be in office when the country was at war.

MADISON'S WAR MESSAGE, JUNE 1, 1812

[T]he conduct of [the British] government presents a series of acts hostile to the United States as an independent and neutral nation. British cruisers have been in the continued practice of violating the American flag on the great highway of nations, and of seizing and carrying off persons sailing under it. . . .

We behold . . . on the side of Great Britain, a state of war against the United States, and on the side of the United States a state of peace toward Great Britain.

[Whether to go to war] is a solemn question which the Constitution wisely confides to the legislative department of the government. In recommending it to their early deliberations I am happy in the assurance that the decision will be worthy the enlightened and patriotic councils of a virtuous, a free, and a powerful nation.

DECODED President Madison lists British violations of American neutral rights, including impressment, or "seizing and carrying off persons" on American ships and forcing them to sail on British ships. Madison goes on to note that the Constitution gives Congress the power to declare war, and he suggests that they'd better start talking about it.

When the War of 1812 began, Britain had a much bigger and better navy. The United States couldn't challenge Britain on the seas, so instead it invaded Canada, which was a British possession. The initial battles went badly for the Americans. On top of that, Britain had Indigenous allies.

A few years earlier, Shawnee chief Tecumseh had tried to unite Indigenous nations in the Ohio and Indiana territories. Indiana Territory governor William Henry Harrison (later the ninth president) attacked Tecumseh's forces at the Battle of Tippecanoe in 1811. Harrison won the battle, but afterward Tecumseh joined forces with the British.

In 1814, a British force landed in Maryland and marched to Washington, DC, where it burned the White House. James Madison fled. His wife, Dolley, saved a portrait of George Washington and a copy of the Declaration of Independence on her way out the door.

Letter to Dolley Madison, August 28, 1814

Should the fort have been taken, the British Ships with their barges will be able to throw the City again into alarm, and you may be again compelled to retire from it, which I find would have a disagreeable effect. Should the Ships have failed in their attack, you can not return too soon.

DECODED This letter was sent after the British had set fire to the White House during the War of 1812. James and Dolley Madison wound up being separated as the British approached Washington, DC. His letter shows his lack of information about the attack and his concern for Dolley. The fort in question was probably Fort Warburton, which American defenders blew up to keep out of the hands of the British. Clearly Madison didn't know that yet.

A month later the British attacked Baltimore, Maryland, a strategic point defended by Fort McHenry, but they were repelled. The British failure there was a turning point in the war and helped lead to the end of the war by a peace treaty, known as the Treaty of Ghent.

Legacy

When his second term as president was over, Madison returned to his plantation in Virginia. We remember him for his work in writing the Constitution and the Bill of Rights. His presidency was important, too, though. In the War of 1812, the young United States proved that it was strong enough to fight a major power. In some ways the War of 1812 was a second act of the American Revolution—it cemented the victories of the earlier war. And the War of 1812 gave America important symbols: the White House became a symbol of the nation and the future national anthem was written.

FRANCIS SCOTT KEY'S POEM, WRITTEN DURING THE SIEGE OF FORT MCHENRY, SEPTEMBER 1814

O say can you see, by the dawn's early light,
What so proudly we hail'd at the twilight's last
    gleaming,
Whose broad stripes and bright stars through the
    perilous fight
O'er the ramparts we watch'd were so gallantly
    streaming?
And the rocket's red glare, the bomb bursting in air,
Gave proof through the night that our flag was
    still there,
O say does that star-spangled banner yet wave
O'er the land of the free and the home of the brave?

DECODED Francis Scott Key wrote this poem while he waited to see whether the American defenders would hold Fort McHenry or whether British forces would take the fort during the War of 1812. Key watched through the night to see if the American flag continued to fly over the fort. Imagine squinting into the distance through the dark, trying to see which flag was flying—and then suddenly everything is bright for a moment, like it is when lightning strikes. Those were the rockets' red glare, the bombs bursting in air that lit up the sky long enough for Key to see that the American flag still flew.

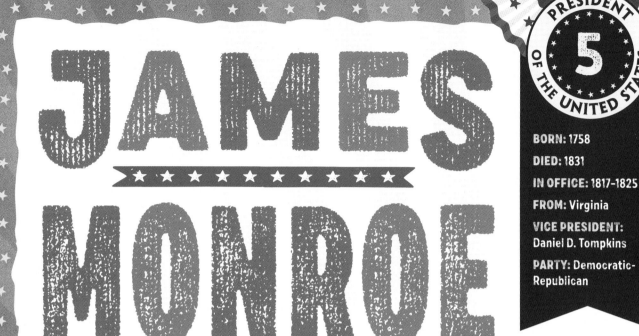

JAMES ★★★★★★★★★ MONROE

PRESIDENT 5 OF THE UNITED STATES

BORN: 1758

DIED: 1831

IN OFFICE: 1817–1825

FROM: Virginia

VICE PRESIDENT: Daniel D. Tompkins

PARTY: Democratic-Republican

DID YOU KNOW?

- Three of the first five presidents died on July 4; Monroe was the third (after Thomas Jefferson and John Adams).

- Monroe was the last of the Founders to be president.

- Monroe was the last president who wore a tricorn hat.

- Monroe was the last president never to be photographed.

- The American Colonization Society (founded in 1817) wanted to free enslaved people and send them to Africa, although most of them had never seen the continent. The society bought land in Africa for the purpose, named it Liberia, and established a capital of Monrovia—named for President James Monroe.

Life Before the Presidency

James Monroe grew up in a moderately wealthy Virginia family, the fourth of the first five presidents to be from Virginia. He attended the College of William and Mary but the Revolutionary War was beginning, and so he enrolled in the Virginia infantry. The early fighting did not go well for the Americans, and when General Washington crossed the Delaware River in 1776 to attack the British forces in the Battle of Trenton, Monroe was there. He led a company that captured two cannons, which was a turning point in the battle. Monroe was promoted, but he wasn't able to raise a regiment of troops (something he had to do on his own) so was unable to stay in the army. He went back to college and began to study law. The Virginia governor, Thomas Jefferson, tutored him and they became good friends.

When the state of Virginia voted on whether to adopt the Constitution, Monroe voted against it. Among other objections, Monroe thought the Constitution should contain a Bill of Rights (which was added later, after the document was ratified), and that the president and senators should be elected directly by the people. (Senators were originally elected by state legislatures but are now elected by voters.)

Monroe served as governor of Virginia from 1799 through 1802 and then again in 1811. He was governor during Gabriel's Rebellion of 1800. Gabriel was an enslaved blacksmith who planned an uprising that he hoped would end slavery in Virginia. Gabriel was betrayed, however. Seventy-two of his fellow rebels were tried. Twenty-six were found guilty and hanged; another thirteen were found guilty, but Monroe pardoned them.

Under President Madison, Monroe became secretary of state, and oversaw the talks that ended the War of 1812. The Federalist Party collapsed after the War of 1812 and didn't even field a candidate in the 1816 election. That meant the Democratic-Republican Party was the only one left. Once the Democratic-Republicans nominated Monroe to be their presidential candidate, he won easily.

Mr. President

Monroe's presidency was a pivotal point for the country. His terms served as an end to the period following the American Revolution and began the lead-up to the Civil War. As soon as he took office, President Monroe went on a tour of the northern states. He was greeted warmly, even though New England had been where his old opponents in the Federalist Party had been strongest. A Boston newspaper, the *Columbian Centinel*, said the United States had entered an "era of good feelings," lending a name to the age. The young nation was proud to have held off the British in the War of 1812, and although Monroe didn't have the intellect of presidents like

Jefferson and Madison, he was very likable. He traveled as far west as Detroit, helping to unify the country through his presence and force of personality. During this Era of Good Feelings, the nation became even more closely tied together when the Erie Canal was constructed (1817–1825), linking Albany and Buffalo. Now ships could move from New York Harbor to the Great Lakes.

Conflict flared in Florida during Monroe's presidency. The Seminole nation that lived there gave shelter to enslaved people who had escaped. Since Florida wasn't part of the United States, once people were over the border, they had some safety. The Seminoles also raided American settlements. President Monroe sent Andrew Jackson, a national hero after winning the Battle of New Orleans at the end of the War of 1812, to attack the Seminole nation. Jackson's orders were vague. Because of that, he interpreted them very widely and actually *invaded* Florida. This was a big problem because Florida was owned by Spain. On top of that, Jackson hanged two British citizens while he was there, then took a fort in Pensacola. Secretary of State John Quincy Adams argued that the orders were vague

and Jackson had done what he needed to do. Jackson's actions in Florida allowed President Monroe to negotiate the Adams-Onís Treaty, in which Spain gave Eastern Florida to the United States in exchange for the United States agreeing that Texas belonged to Spain.

Monroe was so popular at the end of his first term that in his reelection, he won all the electoral college votes—except for one. Only George Washington had ever won unanimously in the electoral college, and it's possible that the elector who voted against Monroe wanted to keep it that way.

In 1817, Missouri petitioned to be admitted to the Union as a state where enslaving people was allowed. At that time, the balance between free states and slave states was equal, at eleven each. If Missouri was admitted, that count would be thrown off and would upset the balance of power in Congress. In order to keep the balance, Maine was brought in as a free state, and Missouri was brought in as a slave state. This was the Missouri Compromise. It included allowing slavery in western territories that were south of the southern border of Missouri, and not allowing it in territories that lay north of that line. Linking the admission of states that did or did not allow slavery wouldn't work forever, though. Congress was kicking the problem down the road for now.

CONGRESSIONAL RECORD
APRIL 4, 1818

Mr. Livermore submitted the following resolution [an amendment to the Constitution, which said]: "No person shall be held to service or labor as a slave, nor shall slavery be tolerated in any State hereafter admitted to the Union, or made one of the United States of America." The resolution was read and, on the question of proceeding to its consideration, it was decided in the negative.

DECODED In 1818, Representative Arthur Livermore of New Hampshire proposed a bill to end slavery. It wouldn't even get discussion in Congress. Today, we sometimes act as though slavery wasn't an issue until shortly before the Civil War, but there were efforts to abolish it from below, meaning by enslaved people, working on their own or together (in periodic uprisings like Gabriel's Rebellion). There were also efforts to abolish it from above, meaning by people in positions of power.

Monroe also made one of the most famous and important foreign policy speeches as president. In 1823, he put forward what has come to be called the Monroe Doctrine, which warned European nations to stay out of the affairs of nations in North and South America.

Legacy

After serving as president, Monroe returned to his home in Virginia, and after his wife died, he moved in with his daughter in New York City.

Monroe is remembered today for being president in the Era of Good Feelings, when American power was on the rise. He issued the Monroe Doctrine, setting limits on European intrusion, and presided over the Missouri Compromise, which didn't resolve the slavery issue but postponed the crisis.

Letter From Thomas Jefferson to John Holmes, April 22, 1820

Referring to the "Missouri question"—whether Missouri should be admitted as a state where holding enslaved people was allowed, and thus if slavery would expand westward—Jefferson wrote:

this momentous question, like a fire bell in the night, awakened and filled me with terror.

DECODED Congress had passed the Missouri Compromise by the time Jefferson wrote to Holmes. In his letter, Jefferson added, "this is a reprieve only, not a final sentence." He was right—the issue of slavery and its expansion would go on to rip the country apart. Monroe had bought the country time, but the Civil War would settle the issue in the 1860s.

JOHN
Q ★ U ★ I ★ N ★ C ★ Y
ADAMS

PRESIDENT
6
OF THE UNITED STATES

BORN: 1767

DIED: 1848

IN OFFICE: 1825–1829

FROM: Massachusetts

VICE PRESIDENT:
John C. Calhoun

PARTY: Federalist
as a young man;
Democratic-
Republican as
president; Whig post-
presidency

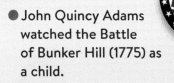

DID YOU KNOW?

- John Quincy Adams watched the Battle of Bunker Hill (1775) as a child.

- Adams persuaded Congress to end dueling in Washington, DC, after Representative William Graves of Kentucky killed Representative Jonathon Cilley of Maine in a duel in 1838.

- Adams was the first president whose father was also a president. (George W. Bush was the second.)

Life Before the Presidency

John Quincy Adams was the second child and oldest son of John and Abigail Adams. He grew up in the Boston area, where many events leading up to the American Revolution took place. John Quincy learned a great deal from his father, John Adams, both in lessons and informally, watching his interactions with other revolutionary leaders.

By the time John Quincy Adams entered Harvard College, he had crossed the Atlantic several times and visited a number of countries. He served as minister to even more countries under Presidents Washington and Madison. He spoke several languages, an advantage for a diplomat. He was also a lawyer and served as a senator from Massachusetts (1803–1808). And as James Monroe's secretary of state, John Quincy Adams was the main writer of the Monroe Doctrine, which aimed to keep European nations out of the Americas.

In 1820, John Quincy Adams had the worst electoral college loss in US history, when James Monroe got every electoral vote but one. This was a tough break for Adams, particularly because he wasn't even running for president at that time.

When John Quincy Adams actually ran for president in 1824, he ended up being chosen by the House of Representatives. Five candidates ran in that election: Adams, Secretary of the Treasury William H. Crawford, Speaker of the House Henry Clay, Senator Andrew Jackson, and Secretary of War John C. Calhoun, who eventually dropped out to run for vice president. With four candidates running, none of them got more than half the votes. The Constitution says that if that happens, the House of Representatives chooses a president from among the three candidates with the highest vote totals (see US Constitution Article II, Section I). In 1824, those were Adams, Crawford, and Jackson. After a serious stroke, Crawford was very unlikely to win. Henry Clay, the fourth candidate, who had no path to winning, persuaded Crawford's supporters to help John Quincy Adams. When the House chose Adams to be president, Adams turned around and appointed Henry Clay to be his secretary of state. Jackson's supporters were outraged.

ANDREW JACKSON
Electoral Votes: 99
Popular Votes: 151,271

✓ JOHN QUINCY ADAMS
Electoral Votes: 84
Popular Votes: 113,122

WILLIAM H. CRAWFORD
Electoral Votes: 41
Popular Votes: 40,856

They said it had been a "corrupt bargain"—that Clay had sold his support in exchange for the appointment.

Mr. President

John Quincy Adams is known more for the way he came to office and for his impressive career in the House after he left the presidency than for anything he did as president.

In his single term in office, Adams supported Henry Clay's "American System." This proposal advocated for the construction of roads and canals to help farmers get their crops to market, a national bank to help commerce, and a tariff to help protect industry. Clay—and Adams—had uneven success in getting measures of the American System passed. Adams also tried to advance education and the arts and sciences. He even proposed building an astronomical observatory.

FIRST ANNUAL MESSAGE TO CONGRESS, DECEMBER 6, 1825

Roads and canals, by multiplying and facilitating the communications and intercourse between distant regions and multitudes of men, are among the most important means of improvement. But moral, political, intellectual improvement are duties assigned by the Author of Our Existence to social no less than to individual man.

Connected with the establishment of an university, or separate from it, might be undertaken the erection of an astronomical observatory, with provision for the support of an astronomer, to be in constant attendance of observation upon the phenomena of the heavens, and for the periodical publication of his observances. It is with no feeling of pride as an American that the remark may be made that on the comparatively small territorial surface of Europe there are existing upward of 130 of these light-houses of the skies, while throughout the whole American hemisphere there is not one.

[DECODED] Adams wanted to see improvements in the country's educational institutions. His call for an American astronomical observatory—and the phrase "light-houses of the skies"—was mocked by his opponents, who painted him as an elitist when he ran for reelection.

The nation already had regional differences based on how people made a living. Congress passed the Tariff Act of 1828, raising the tax on imported goods like wool and iron, which would help Northern industries. Southerners feared it would cause other countries to raise taxes on agricultural products exported from America—goods mostly produced in Southern states, like cotton and rice. Most Southerners were upset with the tariff. They thought it would cost them money, and they felt that their economic interests were being hurt to help another part of the country. They didn't think that was fair. When President John Quincy Adams signed the bill, they were furious.

In 1828, John Quincy Adams ran for reelection. So did his vice president, John C. Calhoun—but this time he ran on Andrew Jackson's ticket. When Adams lost to Jackson, Calhoun stayed on as vice president. At the end of 1828, which was Adams's last full year in office, Calhoun anonymously wrote a pamphlet called *South Carolina Exposition and Protest*. He suggested that South Carolina should nullify the Tariff of 1828—that is, say it simply didn't apply in South Carolina. The idea of nullification would almost split the country during Andrew Jackson's presidency.

Legacy

After his presidency ended, Adams was elected to the House of Representatives and remained there for the rest of his life.

His career was divided into three periods—those of the successful young diplomat, the not-very-successful president, and the brilliant orator railing against slavery. We remember Adams most because he was a president, but he probably served the United States better as a member of the House.

He may have been the most important ex-president. Representative Adams worked tirelessly against slavery. In 1839, fifty-three enslaved Africans, including several children, were shipped to Cuba on the Spanish ship *Amistad*. Cuba was a Spanish colony at the time. The Africans took over the ship and tried to return home, but the *Amistad* was seized by a US warship. Martin Van Buren, who was president at the time, decided to hand the Africans over to Spanish officials in Cuba, which would have led to their enslavement. But because there was an international law against the slave trade, a trial was held to decide what to do. The case eventually went to the Supreme Court, and ex-president Adams gave closing arguments.

JOHN QUINCY ADAMS'S CLOSING ARGUMENT IN *UNITED STATES V. THE AMISTAD,*
FEBRUARY 24, 1841

The Constitution of the United States recognizes the slaves, held within some of the States of the Union, only in their capacity of persons—persons held to labor or service in a State under the laws thereof—persons constituting elements of representation in the popular branch of the National Legislature—persons, the migration or importation of whom should not be prohibited by Congress prior to the year 1808. The Constitution nowhere recognizes them as property.

DECODED Southern pro-slavery forces insisted on language in the Constitution that protected slavery and the slave trade until 1808 (see US Constitution Article I, Section 9, and Article V)—but they didn't use the word *slave* or *slavery* anywhere in the document. The word wasn't used until the Thirteenth Amendment (1865), which ended slavery (see US Constitution Amendment 13). Here John Quincy Adams turns that on its head, pointing out that the Constitution nowhere calls enslaved people property—so how could it give enslavers property rights?

The court ruled for the Africans in 1841. President Van Buren's successor, John Tyler, refused to provide money to return them to Africa, so private funds had to be raised. They arrived home in January 1842.

Congress received large numbers of petitions asking them to restrict slavery. Because the First Amendment says that people have a right to petition the government, Congress had to deal with all of those petitions, which slowed down their work. In 1836, Congress passed a "gag rule" that automatically kept anti-slavery petitions from being reviewed. John Quincy Adams led the attack on the gag rule as a violation of civil liberties and helped shift the debate on slavery in the 1830s and '40s.

Adams remained in the House of Representatives for the rest of his life. In fact, he died in the Capitol building, where Congress meets, two days after having a stroke on the House floor.

CONGRESSIONAL RECORD
HOUSE OF REPRESENTATIVES, FEBRUARY 21, 1848

The Clerk, at the request of several gentlemen, again read the resolutions for their information. The SPEAKER then rose to put the question, but he was interrupted by—Mr. HUNT, who desired him to stop, and by several gentlemen, who sprang from their seats, to the assistance of the venerable JOHN QUINCY ADAMS, who was observed to be sinking from his seat in what appeared to be the agonies of death.

DECODED John Quincy Adams had a stroke on the floor of the House of Representatives in 1848. He was carried first to the Rotunda, then to the Speaker of the House's room, where he died two days later, without ever having left the Capitol building.

BORN: 1767

DIED: 1845

IN OFFICE: 1829–1837

FROM: Carolina

VICE PRESIDENT: John C. Calhoun (first term), Martin Van Buren (second term)

PARTY: Democratic

ANDREW ★ ★ ★ JACKSON

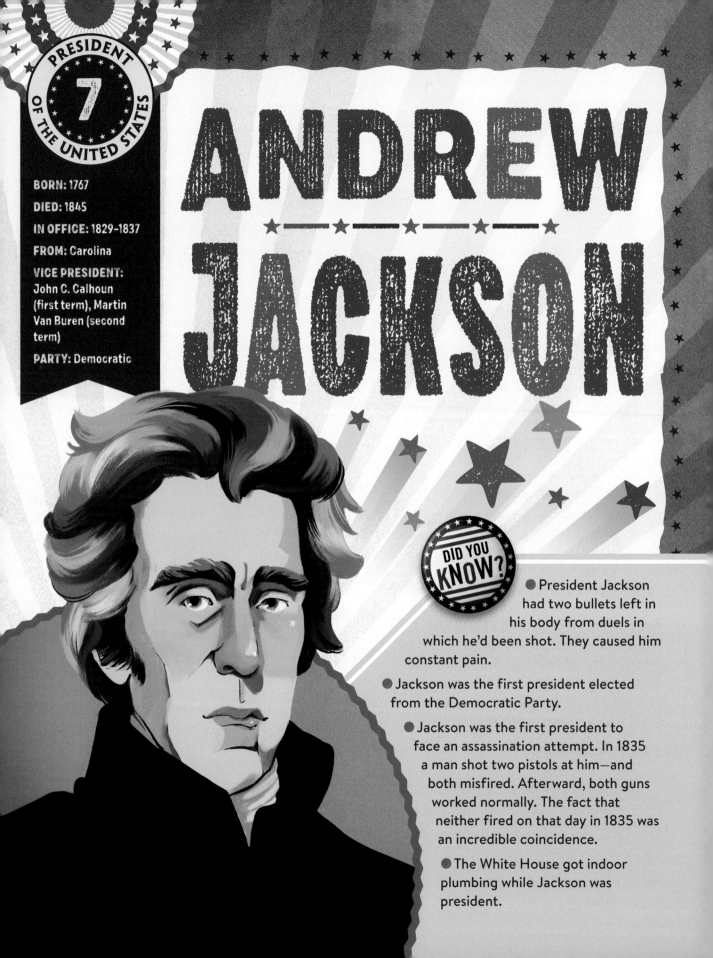

DID YOU KNOW?

● President Jackson had two bullets left in his body from duels in which he'd been shot. They caused him constant pain.

● Jackson was the first president elected from the Democratic Party.

● Jackson was the first president to face an assassination attempt. In 1835 a man shot two pistols at him—and both misfired. Afterward, both guns worked normally. The fact that neither fired on that day in 1835 was an incredible coincidence.

● The White House got indoor plumbing while Jackson was president.

Life Before the Presidency

Andrew Jackson was born in Carolina—we're not exactly sure where. His father died before he was born, and his mother went to stay with relatives. One set of relatives was in North Carolina and one in South Carolina; we're not sure who she stayed with. He fought in the American Revolution as a young teenager and was captured. He lost two brothers and his mother in the Revolution. He was alone in the world, a veteran and smallpox survivor all by fourteen years old.

Jackson studied law and went west to what is now Tennessee in 1788. He helped draft the Tennessee constitution and was Tennessee's first member of the House of Representatives.

After the US declared war on Great Britain in 1812, Jackson raised a militia unit and led it hundreds of miles toward New Orleans to defend the city, as ordered. The government then decided the militia wasn't needed and sent them home. Jackson was furious. Later, Jackson was told his men were needed to fight a part of the Muscogee nation, who had massacred settlers in Alabama. He led a five-month campaign in 1813–1814, winning at the Battle of Horseshoe Bend—after preventing his own men from deserting by threatening them at gunpoint. He marched to New Orleans when the British sent an army to take the city, and won a major victory at the Battle of New Orleans, which made him a national hero.

In 1817, Jackson moved into West Florida on vague orders from Secretary of War John C. Calhoun. A group of people from the Seminole nation were raiding across the border from Spanish Florida into US territory. Jackson interpreted his orders very broadly and invaded Florida, even capturing Pensacola. Spain protested, but then Secretary of State John Quincy Adams defended Jackson in Washington.

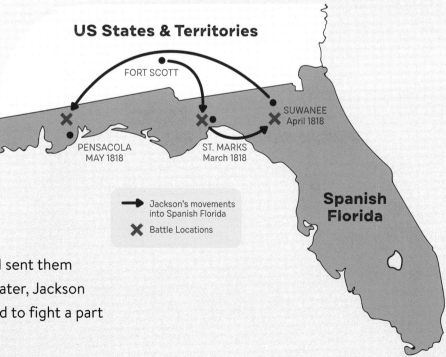

US States & Territories

FORT SCOTT

SUWANEE
April 1818

PENSACOLA
MAY 1818

ST. MARKS
March 1818

➤ Jackson's movements into Spanish Florida

✖ Battle Locations

Spanish Florida

And President Monroe signed a treaty that gave Eastern Florida to the US in exchange for the US agreeing that Texas belonged to Spain.

In 1824, Jackson ran for president. He got the most popular votes and the most electoral college votes, but because four candidates were running, he didn't get a majority. The choice went to the House of Representatives, and it chose John Quincy Adams. Jackson's supporters were outraged.

Jackson ran for president again in 1828, and again he ran against John Quincy Adams. The 1828 campaign was a dirty one in which both sides hurled personal insults at their opponent. One of the things Adams's supporters gossiped about was Jackson's marriage to Rachel Robards Jackson. Rachel had gotten divorced from her first husband, and it turned out that the divorce hadn't been finalized. Neither she nor Jackson knew that. As soon as they found out, they started living separately, got the divorce papers straightened out, and then remarried. But Adams's supporters charged Andrew and Rachel Jackson with adultery, which means a married person having a romantic relationship with someone who isn't their spouse. Jackson ended up winning the election, beating President Adams, but the victory came at a cost. Rachel was humiliated by all the gossip. She had a massive heart attack and died. Jackson buried her on Christmas Eve in the dress she'd bought

to wear at the inaugural ball. The grieving president wore a miniature picture of Rachel on a chain around his neck for the rest of his life.

Mr. President

Jackson campaigned as a man of the people, and so when he was elected president, the people showed up at his inauguration. After he took the oath, a crowd walked down to the White House and crammed into the building.

They stood on the furniture and knocked over a punch bowl, and Jackson was almost crushed. At least a few people climbed out the windows to escape the crowd and a White House official resorted to dragging large tubs of an alcoholic punch onto the lawn to get people to go outside.

One of Jackson's first problems as president was the "Petticoat Affair." Washington society shunned Peggy Eaton, the wife of Secretary of War John Eaton, because the Eatons had married quickly after her first husband died. That reminded Jackson of the criticism his wife had faced, and it caused the executive branch to grind to a halt.

Two things came out of this. First, to help Jackson, Secretary of State Martin Van Buren resigned. That gave Jackson a chance to reorganize his cabinet, which he needed to do in order to get things moving again. The second thing was that Jackson turned to a "Kitchen Cabinet," an informal group of advisers that he talked issues over with instead of the department heads of government agencies.

Of more substance—and great national danger—was the issue of nullification, which arose in 1832–1833. Near the end of John Quincy Adams's term, Congress had passed the Tariff Act of 1828. That prompted then Vice President John C. Calhoun to come up with the theory of nullification—the idea that a state could ignore federal laws within its borders. In 1832, South Carolina nullified the tariff and threatened to secede, or withdraw, from the Union over the issue.

Toast by President Andrew Jackson, April 1830

Our federal Union! It must be preserved.

DECODED At a dinner honoring the late president Thomas Jefferson's birthday, Andrew Jackson took a glass to make a toast. Jackson had spoken forcefully for states' rights in the past, but now that nullification threatened the existence of the Union, he strongly opposed the principle of nullification.

Toast by Vice President John C. Calhoun, in Response to Andrew Jackson, April 1830

The Union—next to our liberty, most dear.

DECODED As soon as Jackson gave his toast, Vice President Calhoun replied with his own toast—making it clear that he thought "our liberty" was more important than the country. In other words, he was in favor of nullification so that the states could do what was best for them.

Calhoun resigned as Jackson's vice president after he won a Senate seat, and he led the nullification faction against the president. Jackson responded by saying he would send federal troops into South Carolina if he had to. In early 1833, Congress passed the Force Bill, which authorized the use of the armed forces in collecting import duties. (Import duties are a tax on goods brought into the country for sale.) In this tense atmosphere, Congress lowered the tariff, hoping to satisfy the South, but the South Carolina Nullification Convention got in one final shot—it nullified the Force Bill.

STATEMENT ON NULLIFICATION BY ANDREW JACKSON, DECEMBER 10, 1832

I consider, then, the power to annul a law of the United States, assumed by one State, *incompatible with the existence of the Union, contradicted expressly by the letter of the Constitution, unauthorized by its spirit, inconsistent with every principle on which It was founded, and destructive of the great object for which it was formed.* . . . Their object is disunion, [b]ut be not deceived by names; disunion, by armed force, is TREASON.

DECODED Andrew Jackson spoke against nullification in the strongest terms—and held the Union together for another generation.

South Carolina eventually backed down in the face of the president's tough stand. Jackson had kept the Union together. It would be another thirty years before secession would be tried again, and when it was, it would again be South Carolina in the lead.

Another major issue for Jackson was the national bank, which helped control the flow of currency. (The president didn't control the bank's functioning, but he could help determine whether it existed.) Jackson strongly opposed the bank because he felt that wealthy private interests controlled it

and it wasn't responsive to average people. He vetoed a bill that would allow it to keep operating. When Jackson won reelection in 1832, he pulled government money out of the national bank and sent it to several state banks. It was not clear whether Jackson was acting within his constitutional authority. Congress was furious and the Senate and House of Representatives together censured him, which means they publicly criticized him through a vote. Jackson is the only president to have been censured.

Jackson's destruction of the bank had far-reaching effects for the economy. It helped cause a recession at the end of his term that resulted in bank failures and mass unemployment, all of which lasted until about 1843–1844.

While he was in office, Jackson also signed the Indian Removal Act in 1830, which resulted in the forced relocation of Indigenous nations in the southeast to lands west of the Mississippi. The land was nothing like what they were used to. It was hard to adapt and earn a living because the climate, soil, and vegetation were different, and many nations fought back. The Second Seminole War, in 1835, began in Florida under Seminole leader Osceola, and in the Midwest, Black Hawk led the Sauk in the Black Hawk War. These resistance efforts were unable to stop forced relocations in the southeast or other regions.

INDIAN REMOVAL ACT, SIGNED MAY 28, 1830

Be it enacted by the Senate and House of Representatives of the United States of America, in Congress assembled, That it shall and may be lawful for the President of the United States to cause so much of any territory belonging to the United States, west of the river Mississippi, not included in any state or organized territory, and to which the Indian title has been extinguished, as he may judge necessary, to be divided into a suitable number of districts, for the reception of such tribes or nations of Indians as may choose to exchange the lands where they now reside, and remove there. . . .

And be it further enacted, That in the making of any such exchange or exchanges, it shall and may be lawful for the President solemnly to assure the tribe or nation with which the exchange is made, that the United States will forever secure and guaranty to them, and their heirs or successors, the country so exchanged with them. . . .

DECODED Jackson didn't think that Indigenous people and white people could live in peace and thought that separating them was the best option. The choice indicated in the first paragraph wasn't a choice at all: Indigenous nations were forced from their lands. And the guarantee made in the second paragraph didn't last. The Indian Removal Act said that the United States would guarantee that the Indigenous nations could keep the land they swapped for their homelands, but in later years, there were further demands on Indigenous lands west of the Mississippi. The Indian Removal Act led to tragedy for Indigenous people in the southeastern US.

Legacy

After he left office, Jackson went back to Tennessee. He used his political clout to pick Martin Van Buren to be his successor, and he lived long enough to help an old ally, James K. Polk, beat his old adversary, Henry Clay, in the 1844 election.

Jackson was a more active president than any who came before him, using the power of the presidency more than anyone else had up to that time. He opposed keeping politics in the hands of a few wealthy families. In the 1830s, democracy spread as more people were able to vote and took advantage of the opportunity, energized by the wild elections of 1824 and 1828. They expected the government to address their needs, and Andrew Jackson tried to do that. He came from a more humble background than any previous president had and was the first president to be seen as a man of the people. Jackson's legacy is complex. He fought the bank, but his face is now found on the twenty-dollar bill. He advocated for greater democracy yet he enslaved people. He preserved the nation, while his policies caused great harm to Indigenous nations. Perhaps no president has simultaneously caused more harm and had more major accomplishments than Andrew Jackson.

PRESIDENT **8** OF THE UNITED STATES

BORN: 1782

DIED: 1862

IN OFFICE: 1837–1841

FROM: Kinderhook, New York

VICE PRESIDENT: Richard M. Johnson

PARTY: Democratic

MARTIN VAN BUREN

DID YOU KNOW?

● Van Buren was the first president who was born after the Declaration of Independence was written and the first to be born a citizen of the United States (and therefore was never a British subject).

● Van Buren is the only president whose native language wasn't English. He spoke Dutch at home, including in the White House.

● Van Buren was nicknamed "Old Kinderhook" after his birthplace. Van Buren often signed documents in Washington with the initials "OK." That's how the term *O.K.* or *okay* entered the language.

Life Before the Presidency

Martin Van Buren grew up in New York, the descendant of indentured servants from the Netherlands and the son of a tavernkeeper. He was a lawyer with a reputation for having a keen mind. His wife died when he was thirty-six, years before he was elected president, and he never remarried. He had a more modest background than most of the earlier presidents, who were wealthier and more politically connected. After being elected to the New York state legislature in 1812, Van Buren called for an end to jailing people simply because they were poor, which was a common practice at the time. He wanted to see democracy widen and more power go to common people, and in the 1830s more people did get the right to vote.

Van Buren became an ally of Andrew Jackson, and in 1829, he became Jackson's secretary of state. During the Petticoat Affair (1829–1831), Van Buren resigned to let Jackson rearrange his cabinet, and increasingly became a favorite of Jackson's. Van Buren became vice president after Jackson won reelection in 1832. And when Jackson left office, he handpicked Van Buren to be the Democratic nominee for president. Van Buren won the 1836 election.

VAN BUREN'S INAUGURAL ADDRESS, MARCH 4, 1837

Unlike all who have preceded me, the Revolution that gave us existence as one people was achieved at the period of my birth; and whilst I contemplate with grateful reverence that memorable event, I feel that I belong to a later age and that I may not expect my countrymen to weigh my actions with the same kind and partial hand.

DECODED Van Buren notes that the previous presidents all took part in the American Revolution. Even Andrew Jackson, who was a child when war broke out, fought, was captured, wounded, and lost family members. Van Buren is acutely aware that he is the first president of the post-Revolutionary era. As a new generation took over leadership, politics was becoming a rougher sport, and Van Buren clearly knew it.

Mr. President

As president, Van Buren continued most of Andrew Jackson's policies, and his single term is seen as an extension of the age of Jackson. Van Buren even kept most of Jackson's cabinet members. An economic depression hit when he had been in office for just a few weeks, however; this was known as the Panic of 1837. (*Panic* is an old term for an economic depression.) This panic began when British banks tightened their credit and stopped investing in the United States. American banks responded by calling in loans (that is, demanding repayment) because they now had less money on hand. It was made worse because Jackson had shifted money from the national bank to state banks; many of the state banks that had benefited from Jackson's policy now failed and bankrupted their customers. Van Buren set up an independent treasury system to control the money supply through the US Treasury, hoping to fix the problem. This system was used until Woodrow Wilson set up the Federal Reserve in 1913. The economic problems hurt Van Buren's popularity, however, because voters blamed him for the downturn.

In 1837, Texas petitioned to be annexed, or taken over, by the United States. Mexico threatened war if the United States claimed the area. In addition, Texas was a huge slave territory, and annexation would upset the balance of free and slave states in the Union. Van Buren denied the annexation petition and the issue of Texas—and the Mexican-American War—would wait a decade.

Van Buren continued Jackson's policy of forcibly relocating Indigenous nations from the southeastern United States to areas west of the Mississippi. The Second Seminole War, which had begun in 1835 when Jackson was still president, lasted until 1842, after Van Buren left office. The Seminoles, under leader Osceola, fought to stay in Florida. They ambushed US troops in December 1835 and fought successfully through 1836, attacking plantations and army supply lines. In late 1837, Osceola and some followers were captured under a false flag of truce. (A truce is when both sides agree not to fight for a short time, often so they can talk or exchange injured soldiers. A false flag of truce means that one side claims they're not going to fight—but then they do anyway.) The major battles were over by the end of 1838. Smaller fights continued until 1842, at which point the great majority of people from the Seminole nation had been forced from their land.

Around the same time, the Aniyunwiya (Cherokee) people were forced to move to Oklahoma in a brutal march that today is called the Trail of Tears. About a quarter of the Aniyunwiya died on the way.

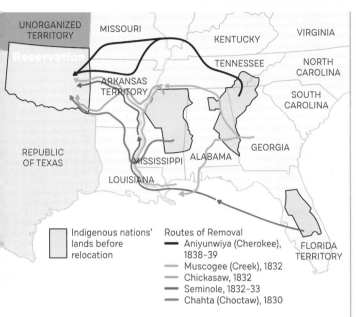

UNORGANIZED TERRITORY

Reservation

MISSOURI

KENTUCKY

VIRGINIA

ARKANSAS TERRITORY

TENNESSEE

NORTH CAROLINA

SOUTH CAROLINA

REPUBLIC OF TEXAS

MISSISSIPPI   ALABAMA

GEORGIA

LOUISIANA

FLORIDA TERRITORY

Indigenous nations' lands before relocation

Routes of Removal
— Aniyunwiya (Cherokee), 1838–39
— Muscogee (Creek), 1832
— Chickasaw, 1832
— Seminole, 1832–33
— Chahta (Choctaw), 1830

Van Buren was important in labor history, too: He signed an executive order limiting the workday for federal employees to ten hours. He came from more humble circumstances than most of his predecessors and was sympathetic to the plight of average workers.

Any political gain from that decision, though, was lost by his refusal to annex Texas, an unpopular move in an era where most people wanted to see the country expand. In 1840, Van Buren lost his bid for reelection, the first incumbent who wasn't an Adams to do so.

Legacy

Van Buren ran for the presidency again in 1840, 1844, and 1848. But after failing three times—and getting no electoral college votes in his final attempt—he stopped trying. He is best remembered for harsh policies toward Indigenous people and, to a lesser extent, as the first president whom voters held accountable for a bad economy.

EXECUTIVE ORDER LIMITING THE WORKDAY FOR FEDERAL EMPLOYEES, MARCH 31, 1840

The President of the United States, finding that different rules prevail at different places as well in respect to the hours of labor by persons employed on the public works under the immediate authority of himself and the Departments as also in relation to the different classes of workmen, and believing that much inconvenience and dissatisfaction would be removed by adopting a uniform course, hereby directs that all such persons, whether laborers or mechanics, be required to work only the number of hours prescribed by the ten-hour system.

DECODED Early industrialization was often brutal. Hours were long, pay was low, and factories were dangerous. Van Buren here creates a ten-hour workday for federal employees, an early effort to improve the lives of workers. Legislation to help workers would come in bits and pieces—almost a hundred years later Franklin D. Roosevelt ended many remaining abuses, such as child labor in the textile industry.

BORN: 1773

DIED: 1841

IN OFFICE: 1841

FROM: Charles City County, Virginia

VICE PRESIDENT: John Tyler

PARTY: Whig

WILLIAM HENRY HARRISON

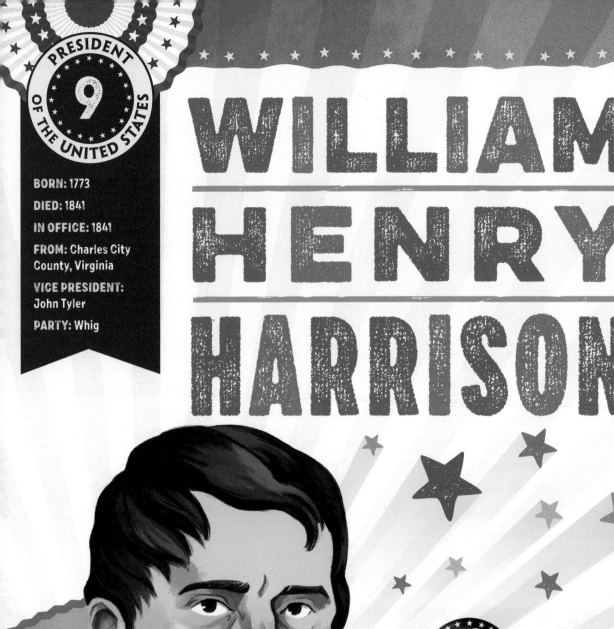

DID YOU KNOW?

● William Henry Harrison's father, Benjamin, signed the Declaration of Independence, and his parents were good friends with George and Martha Washington. When Harrison was eight years old, the British surrendered at Yorktown, just thirty miles from his family's plantation.

● Harrison was the first president to die in office.

Life Before the Presidency

William Henry Harrison was the youngest of seven children. His father wanted him to be a doctor and Harrison studied medicine, but when his father died he joined the army. It's what he'd wanted to do, anyway. Harrison went to the Northwest Territory (the present-day Midwest) when he was eighteen and spent many years there with the army.

When the Northwest Territory split into the Ohio Territory and Indiana Territory in 1800, Harrison became the governor of the Indiana Territory. (This is roughly modern Indiana, Illinois, Michigan, Minnesota, and Wisconsin.) He improved roads, but he also tried to get as much land from Indigenous nations as possible, taking advantage of them and using unfair tactics. That angered Tecumseh, a chief of the Shawnee nation. Tecumseh tried to get British military help and started a confederacy of Indigenous nations to regain their lost lands. He also went to talk to Harrison to explain the problem, but it ended in a standoff with swords drawn.

SPEECH FROM TECUMSEH TO WILLIAM HENRY HARRISON, AUGUST 20, 1810

Brother, do not believe that I came here to get presents from you. If you offer us anything we will not take it. By taking goods from you, you will hereafter say that with them you purchased another piece of land from us.

DECODED Experience had made Tecumseh careful. In 1809, Harrison had signed the Treaty of Fort Wayne, which forced Indigenous nations to sell to the United States almost three million acres of land for two cents an acre. Many Indigenous people objected, but because some of their leaders had signed the treaty, the United States considered it to be binding. The Treaty of Fort Wayne—and Harrison's attack on an Indigenous settlement in the Battle of Tippecanoe in 1811—ended a peace in the area that had lasted since George Washington was in office.

In 1811, Tecumseh was away trying to recruit more people to his resistance movement, and Harrison took advantage of his absence to attack a group of Indigenous people on the banks of the Tippecanoe Creek. His victory there made him popular with frontier settlers who were worried about raids, which had only increased because of Harrison's combative policies. Harrison had almost single-handedly brought war to the Indiana Territory, and his actions caused Tecumseh to side with the British during the War of 1812. In 1824, Harrison won a US Senate seat, and in 1840, he ran for president. A newspaper that favored his opponent, President Martin Van Buren, said of Harrison,

"Give him a barrel of hard cider and settle a pension of two thousand a year on him, and take my word for it, he will sit the remainder of his days in his log cabin." The insult backfired. Harrison's people painted Van Buren as a fancy aristocrat whereas Harrison was a plain man of the people. The 1840 campaign became the "Log Cabin Campaign," with pro-Harrison voters using the log cabin as a symbol, and it worked. Harrison beat President Van Buren and became president.

Mr. President

Harrison gave the longest inaugural speech in US history—almost two hours. He stood outside in cold, wet weather without a coat and then attended inaugural events without changing his clothes. He got pneumonia and was sick throughout his presidency, dying on April 4, 1841, one month to the day after his inauguration.

WILLIAM HENRY HARRISON'S INAUGURAL ADDRESS, MARCH 4, 1841

> . . . Under no circumstances will I consent to serve a second term.

DECODED Harrison said in his inaugural address that he thought the Constitution shouldn't allow someone to run for a second term. He wanted a constitutional amendment to make the presidency one term only and promised that he wouldn't run for a second term. That wasn't a problem because he died a month later.

Anna Harrison never made it to Washington to be First Lady. She was still packing when her husband died. Ironically, at the end of his life, Harrison's desperate doctors tried some Indigenous remedies, but they didn't save him.

Legacy

William Henry Harrison is best remembered for sparking war on the frontier before he was president and dying promptly after taking office. But he also sparked a succession crisis, the first in US history. What happens when a president dies in office? It had never happened before, and the Constitution wasn't entirely clear. There were three presidents in 1841—Van Buren ended his term in March, when Harrison was sworn in. Harrison died in April 1841, and his vice president, John Tyler, became the third president in five weeks.

Harrison was the first president to die in the period of the "Twenty-Year Curse." For 120 years, the president elected every twenty years died in office. (You can also look at it as every president in that period elected in a year ending with 0.) Harrison: elected in 1840, died; Lincoln: elected in 1860, assassinated; Garfield: elected in 1880, assassinated; McKinley: elected in 1900, assassinated; Harding: elected in 1920, died; Franklin Roosevelt: elected in 1940, died; Kennedy: elected in 1960, assassinated.

JOHN TYLER

BORN: 1790

DIED: 1862

IN OFFICE: 1841–1845

FROM: Charles City County, Virginia

VICE PRESIDENT: none

PARTY: Whig

DID YOU KNOW?

- Tyler was the first president to get married while president (although he didn't get married in the White House). He and his second wife, Julia Gardiner, got married on June 26, 1844. Tyler's first wife, Letitia, had died in September 1842; she was the first First Lady to die in the White House.

- Tyler was the first president to have impeachment proceedings started against him (after he vetoed a tariff bill).

Life Before the Presidency

John Tyler held hardline pro-slavery and states-rights views. As a member of the US House of Representatives, he strongly opposed the Missouri Compromise (1820) because he felt slavery should be allowed everywhere. As a senator in early 1833, during the Nullification Crisis, Tyler gave an angry speech blasting President Jackson's hardline policy with South Carolina, and he was the only senator to vote against the Force Bill. He thought the bill gave the president too much power and was unconstitutional.

Democracy expanded in the 1820s and 1830s. More people got the right to vote and more people were participating in politics. Andrew Jackson wanted to end the electoral college and have the people choose the president instead of the electors choosing. (Individual voters cast their ballots for electors, who then vote for the president. These electors form the "electoral college," which is a layer between the people and the choice of president. See the US Constitution Article II, Section 1.) Tyler, however, wanted to keep the electoral college.

When President Harrison died after only one month in office, Vice President John Tyler was there to assume the role.

Mr. President

A president had never died in office before and so when President Harrison passed, no one quite knew what to do. Was Vice President Tyler now the president, or was he just the acting president, doing the job until a real president could be put back in power?

Tyler announced that he was really president even though the Constitution wasn't clear, and many people felt that he was seizing power. (The Constitution was changed in 1967 by the Twenty-Fifth Amendment to confirm that the vice president becomes the real president in that situation.)

Tyler demanded the privileges of the office: He returned letters addressed to him as "Acting President" without opening them, and his wife started the custom of playing "Hail to the Chief" when he arrived at official events.

HAIL TO THE CHIEF

As president, he made an enemy of Henry Clay, a powerful senator from Kentucky who was famous for compromising. He also upset Secretary of State Daniel Webster of Massachusetts. That Clay and Webster were Whigs, and therefore in Tyler's party, was a bad sign—Tyler couldn't even get along with his own side. And on top of that, most of Congress was outraged that Tyler simply arranged an inauguration for himself. His presidency was marked by tension and arguments and he was not well-liked.

When he had the chance to sign Whig bills into law, Tyler didn't really want to. With a Whig president in the White House and a majority in Congress, the Whig Party assumed that they would be able to pass plenty of legislation. But President Tyler vetoed bill after bill.

CONGRESSIONAL RECORD

DISCUSSION OF A TYLER VETO, REPRESENTATIVE ALEXANDER STUART OF VIRGINIA, JUNE 30, 1842

[T]he President's objections, when divested of their unintelligible verbiage, did not turn on constitutional grounds. . . .

DECODED The House discussed Tyler's use of the veto, which angered the Whigs—his own party—because Tyler kept vetoing major parts of their program. *Unintelligible* means "can't be understood"; *verbiage* means "words," especially "a lot of words." Representative Stuart is saying that if you cut through a lot of bad writing, you figure out that the president isn't following the Constitution.

After Tyler vetoed a bank bill, Congress passed it again over his veto, and he vetoed that bill, too. Everyone in his cabinet except for the secretary of state resigned in protest. Tyler immediately appointed replacements for them, which enraged Whig leaders, who finally kicked him out of the Whig Party.

Tyler also vetoed several tariff bills, and in July 1842, Representative John Botts of Virginia—Tyler's home state—filed impeachment charges against him, the first against any president. The House investigated and decided that Tyler was guilty of "gross abuse of constitutional power" but didn't go ahead with impeachment. Anti-Tyler protests were common and included burning him in effigy at the White House. (Burning someone in effigy means making a straw figure to look like them and then burning it. It indicates extreme dislike.)

Tyler did have some successes. They included invoking the Monroe Doctrine to keep European nations from claiming Hawaii and signing the Webster-Ashburton Treaty with Great Britain, which settled boundary disputes between Maine and Canada. The United States got more than half of the disputed forestland in that negotiation, and both sides agreed to monitor the African coast to try to disrupt the transatlantic slave trade, which was illegal but still occurring.

But Texas remained a problem. The Republic of Texas claimed to be an independent state, and the United States and some European nations recognized it as one. Mexico claimed that Texas was Mexican territory. Some Americans wanted to annex Texas, which carried external and internal dangers, including both starting a war with Mexico and bringing in a large new slave territory that would upset the balance of slave and free states. In 1837, President Martin Van Buren had refused to annex Texas. But President

Tyler went ahead and started the annexation process, causing the last member of his original cabinet, his secretary of state, Daniel Webster, to resign. Tyler replaced Webster with John C. Calhoun, a pro-slavery Southerner who had led the nullification movement during Andrew Jackson's time in office.

Tyler signed the Texas annexation treaty in April 1844, and it went to the Senate, which has to ratify, or agree to, all treaties. But the Senate didn't ratify the annexation. Secretary of State Calhoun had publicly said that the United States needed Texas in order to protect slavery. That made it harder for people to agree to take over Texas and shifted the debate from expansion to slavery.

By the time of the 1844 election, the Whig Party was still so frustrated by Tyler's actions as president that it nominated Henry Clay as its candidate. It's very unusual for the incumbent not to be nominated for another term. Tyler tried to run as a third-party candidate even though he had no chance of winning, but he dropped out after the Democrats promised to annex Texas. They were worried that Tyler would pull votes away from their candidate, James K. Polk. Polk won. Before he left office, Tyler asked Congress to vote on annexation again. This time Congress passed the bill and Tyler signed it, three days before he left office.

Legacy

After serving as president, Tyler returned to Virginia. He was a member of the Virginia Secession Congress (1861) that voted to secede from the United States and was a member of the Confederate Provisional Congress, making him the only president who clearly committed treason after his presidency. Congress didn't provide a marker for Tyler's grave until 1915 because he helped the Confederacy. Tyler is best remembered for taking over as president after Harrison's death, although it was unclear that he had the authority to do so, and for being so unpopular that his own party kicked him out. He has not grown more popular with time.

JOHN TYLER
PRESIDENT
OF THE
UNITED STATES

BROOKLYN DAILY EAGLE, JANUARY 21, 1862

"DEATH OF EX-PRESIDENT TYLER"

By telegraph we learn that ex-President John Tyler died at Richmond on Friday last after a brief illness. . . . Harrison's death, a month after his inauguration, placed Mr. Tyler in the Presidential chair. As is well known, he repudiated many of the cherished schemes of his party and his administration gave little satisfaction to either party. . . . His beautiful residence has been occupied by Union soldiers, his magnificent State has been ravaged by war, and the country so prosperous when he administered its affairs, is rent with civil war. John Tyler did perhaps as little as any man to prevent these evils.

DECODED That is one scorching summary of a life.

JAMES K ★ N ★ O ★ X POLK

BORN: 1795

DIED: 1849

IN OFFICE: 1845–1849

FROM: born in Mecklenburg County, North Carolina; lived in Tennessee

VICE PRESIDENT: George M. Dallas

PARTY: Democratic

DID YOU KNOW?

- Polk's inauguration was the first to be reported by telegraph— the news was sent personally by Samuel F. B. Morse, for whom Morse code is named.

- Polk's postmaster general started the use of postage stamps in the United States. The Stamp Act of 1765 had helped cause the American Revolution, and it took until the Polk administration for Americans to get past their anti-stamp bias. When they began using stamps, they had two options: a stamp with Benjamin Franklin's picture or one with George Washington's.

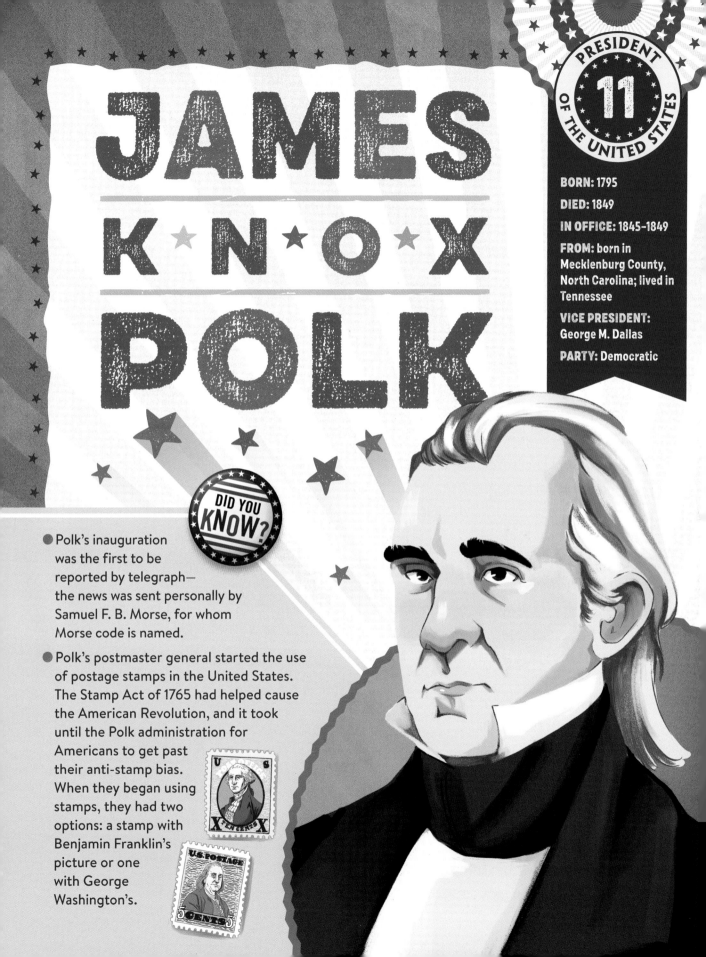

Life Before the Presidency

James Knox Polk was frequently ill as a child and young man. His formal education started late, but he was bright and learned Latin and Greek. He graduated from the University of North Carolina before studying law. As a US Representative, he tried (and failed) to get a law passed to end the electoral college and choose the president based on the popular vote. Polk held the House's most powerful position, the Speaker of the House, from 1835 to 1839. He was elected president in 1844.

He wasn't expected to win that presidential race. He wasn't even expected to run. The Democratic Convention couldn't pick a candidate—and Polk wasn't mentioned as a possibility for the first seven ballots. But former president Andrew Jackson liked Polk and eventually suggested him as a compromise candidate (someone both sides could agree on if they couldn't get their first choice). Polk was the second president (after Van Buren) to get the nomination because of Andrew Jackson's influence.

Mr. President

During his presidential campaign, Polk had suggested that the United States might go to war with Great Britain over the Oregon Territory, which both countries claimed. The issue was where the line between the United States and British Canada should be drawn. Polk claimed western Canada all the way to the southern border of Alaska. Americans had been traveling to Oregon on the Oregon Trail, looking for economic opportunities on the West Coast, assuming it would become American territory. Because so many more people were there, settling the border became a pressing issue.

Polk and the British went back and forth and eventually settled the border on the forty-ninth parallel. (Parallels are imaginary lines that run east to west across the world. Longitude lines run north to south. Together they help mapmakers locate things.)

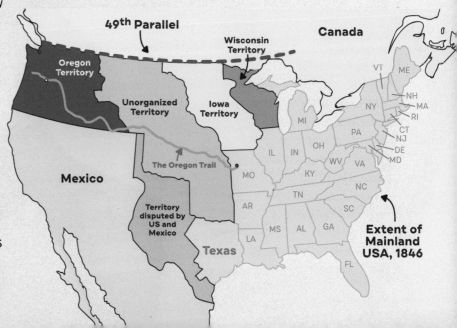

In 1845, Texas became a US state, but Mexico and Texas didn't agree on where the border between them lay. Negotiations failed and President Polk ordered General Zachary Taylor into the area, hoping to provoke a war. In April 1846, Mexican forces attacked an American patrol, setting off the Mexican-American War. In his message to Congress on May 11, Polk said that Mexico had shed American blood on American soil. Illinois representative Abraham Lincoln later pointed out that the attack had not been on soil previously claimed as American, and he demanded that Polk name the spot on which blood had been shed.

WAR MESSAGE TO CONGRESS, MAY 11, 1846

Upon the pretext that Texas, a nation as independent as herself, thought proper to unite its destinies with our own she has affected to believe that we have severed her rightful territory, and in official proclamations and manifestoes has repeatedly threatened to make war upon us for the purpose of reconquering Texas. In the meantime we have tried every effort at reconciliation. . . .

DECODED Polk lists what he sees as Mexican insults to the United States and says that a state of war already exists because Mexico invaded "our territory"—a claim Mexico would strongly disagree with. Polk had already sent General Zachary Taylor to the area. Taylor would go on to win the Mexican-American War and become popular enough to win the presidency, too.

The Mexican-American War, which lasted from 1846 into 1848, caused sharp disagreements in the United States. Many Northerners worried that it would bring in more territory where slavery was allowed and upset the balance of states. When the Treaty of Guadalupe Hidalgo (1848) ended the war, Mexico gave up California, New Mexico, and its claim to Texas in return for $15 million, which was less than it had been offered before the war. In addition, the United States agreed to take over financial claims American citizens had against the Mexican government.

Polk expanded US territory more than any other president, including even Thomas Jefferson, who bought the Louisiana Purchase. The Southwest, California, and the Pacific Northwest came in under Polk, giving the United States roughly its current shape.

While he is best known for the Mexican-American War and the Oregon settlement, Polk also lowered tariffs and reformed the treasury system. He had announced that he wouldn't seek a second term in office, and he didn't. He also didn't need one, as he'd accomplished all his goals in one term. Polk was one of the most successful presidents, and one of the hardest workers.

Legacy

Polk had the shortest post-presidential period of anyone who survived their term in office. He left in March 1849—and died in June. But he got a lot done while he was in office, and he was one of the most successful presidents in terms of accomplishing his aims. The nation had expanded dramatically during his term, but slavery was increasingly dividing Americans.

James K. Polk Diary Entry, February 13, 1849

It is four years ago this day since I arrived in Washington, preparatory to entering on my duties as President of the U.S. on the 4th of March following. They have been four years of incessant labour . . . and of great responsibility. . . . I am heartily rejoiced that my term is so near its close. . . . As a private citizen I will have no one but myself to serve.

DECODED Polk's diaries detail constant cabinet meetings, official receptions, and orders read and sent. He worked incredibly hard, and most historians feel that he worked himself to death. He left office exhausted and died three months later.

ZACHARY
★ ★ ★ ★ ★ ★ ★
TAYLOR

PRESIDENT
12
OF THE UNITED STATES

BORN: 1784

DIED: 1850

IN OFFICE: 1849–July 9, 1850

FROM: born in Virginia; grew up in Kentucky; lived in Louisiana

VICE PRESIDENT: Millard Fillmore

PARTY: Whig

DID YOU KNOW?

- Historians think that Taylor was the last president to bring enslaved people with him to the White House.

- Taylor's daughter, Sarah Knox ("Knoxie"), was the first wife of Jefferson Davis, who would be president of the Confederate States of America during the Civil War.

- Taylor's son, Richard, was a Confederate officer in the Civil War. Many documents and letters from Taylor's presidency were stored on his plantation, which was ransacked by Union troops during the war, and some items were destroyed.

- Taylor was the last president to have been born before the Constitution was written.

Life Before the Presidency

Zachary Taylor was born in Virginia but grew up in Kentucky. His father served as an officer under George Washington in the Revolutionary War, and Taylor had a career in the army, too. He fought in the War of 1812 and was promoted for gallant conduct in what was considered the first American victory on land during that war. He fought in the Second Seminole War in Florida and was largely responsible for winning the Mexican-American War.

Despite his military success, Taylor thought of himself as a farmer and liked to talk about his plantation. In 1848, he got the Whig nomination for president although he wasn't very interested in politics. He had never even voted, yet he won the election for president.

Mr. President

The biggest issue during Zachary Taylor's presidency was whether slavery should expand into the newly acquired western territories. Taylor enslaved a large number of people, but he opposed the expansion of slavery into new areas—something that surprised many of the people who had voted for him. Southern states began to talk about secession, and Taylor said he would personally lead an army into any state that seceded.

Taylor was deeply offended by Southern threats to secede, and he wasn't going to budge. His tough stance made it hard to reach a compromise. Senator Henry Clay from Kentucky still tried to find common ground. In January 1850, Clay proposed putting five different issues facing Congress into one bill:

1. **California would come into the Union as a free state.**

2. **The rest of the territory acquired from Mexico after the Mexican-American War would be divided up into the territories of New Mexico and Utah, without deciding on whether they would allow slavery or not.**

3. **The border between Texas and New Mexico would be set.**

4. **Selling enslaved people in Washington, DC, would end.**

5. **A new, tougher fugitive law would go into effect, making it harder for people who escaped slavery to stay free, and punishing anyone who helped them.**

This five-part bill would become the Compromise of 1850. The fifth point—known as the Fugitive Slave Act—produced a tremendous backlash in the North, turning many people into abolitionists.

Taylor suggested that he would veto the bill if Congress ever passed it. He refused to allow slavery to expand into new territories and wouldn't cave to secession threats.

In the meantime, President Taylor was able to make a treaty with Great Britain over a proposed canal across the isthmus of Panama.

CLAYTON-BULWER TREATY WITH GREAT BRITAIN, 1850

A canal across the Isthmus of Panama had been proposed, and the United States and Great Britain, both of which were interested in a Panama canal, agreed that neither nation would take "for itself any exclusive control over the said ship-canal."

DECODED At this time ships sailing from the East Coast to the West Coast of the United States had to go all the way around the bottom of South America. It was an expensive, dangerous, and time-consuming trip. Many people wanted to construct a canal across a narrow part of Central America to allow ships to pass directly between the Atlantic and Pacific Oceans. It took several decades before construction began, and it wouldn't be successful until Theodore Roosevelt was in the White House in 1903, but Zachary Taylor helped lay the diplomatic foundation for the canal.

In 1850, Taylor went to a Fourth of July picnic and caught a bad stomach bug, which killed him a few days later. He was the second president to die while in office and the second president to die in the White House.

Legacy

Taylor is remembered most for his victories in the Mexican-American War before running for office. He was president for a little more than a year, and although he was a Southerner and an enslaver, he dug in his heels against the expansion of slavery into western territories. He was a straightforward man without much education, but he had both personal and political courage.

Abraham Lincoln's Eulogy for Zachary Taylor, Chicago City Hall, July 25, 1850

His rarest military trait, was a combination of negatives—absence of excitement and absence of fear. He could not be flurried, and he could not be scared.

DECODED A eulogy is a speech about a person who has died, and it's often given at their funeral. Here Lincoln notes Taylor's calm, straightforward personality, one which impressed many young officers who served under him in the Mexican-American War—and went on themselves to be generals in the Civil War.

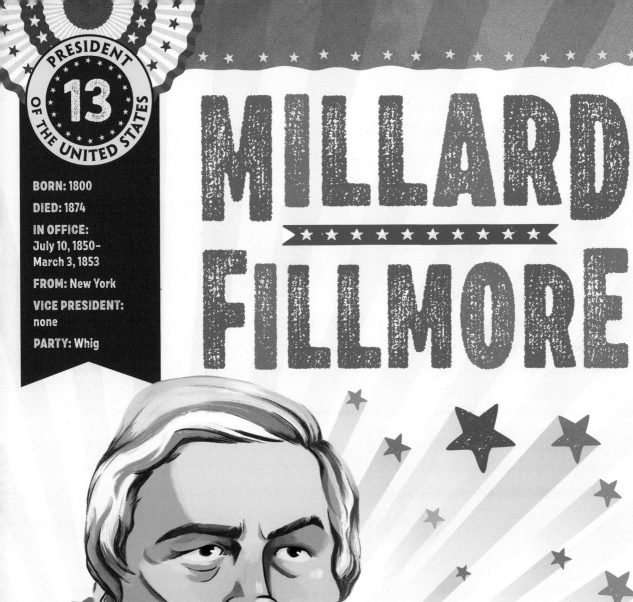

PRESIDENT
13
OF THE UNITED STATES

MILLARD ★★★★★★★ FILLMORE

BORN: 1800

DIED: 1874

IN OFFICE:
July 10, 1850–
March 3, 1853

FROM: New York

VICE PRESIDENT:
none

PARTY: Whig

DID YOU KNOW?

● Abigail Fillmore was the first First Lady who had a job after she got married. She was a teacher. She also started a library in the White House.

● When the Fillmores moved into the White House, the kitchen staff was still cooking over an open fire. Abigail Fillmore ordered a stove.

Life Before the Presidency

Millard Fillmore was born in New York State and grew up on his family's farm, working hard to help his parents, who struggled to get by. Fillmore worked hard to get an education, too. He learned to read at home by studying the family Bible, and enrolled in school at the age of nineteen, taking every opportunity to learn. Years later he married his teacher, who was almost his same age. He became a lawyer and served in the New York state legislature (1829–1831), where he focused especially on laws to end debtors' prisons (the practice of jailing people for being poor and unable to pay bills or fines). In 1832, Fillmore was elected to the US House of Representatives and was reelected several times. He resigned from the House to run for governor of New York in 1844 and lost, but in 1849 he became Zachary Taylor's vice president.

Mr. President

When Zachary Taylor died, Fillmore suddenly became president, and he had one big issue on his hands. It was the most important decision of his presidency: whether to sign the Compromise of 1850. These five bills, which Senator Henry Clay had proposed in an attempt to smooth over the differences dividing the nation, included the new, tougher Fugitive Slave Act.

FUGITIVE SLAVE ACT OF 1850

And be it further enacted, That any person who shall knowingly and willingly obstruct . . . such claimant . . . from arresting such a fugitive from service or labor . . . or shall rescue, or attempt to rescue, such fugitive . . . or shall aid . . . such person . . . to escape . . . shall, for either of said offences, be subject to a fine not exceeding one thousand dollars, and imprisonment not exceeding six months

And be it further enacted, That . . . in all cases where the proceedings are before a commissioner, he shall be entitled to a fee of ten dollars in full for his services in each case, upon the delivery of the said certificate to the claimant, his agent or attorney; or a fee of five dollars in cases where the proof shall not, in the opinion of such commissioner, warrant such certificate and delivery. . . .

DECODED The Fugitive Slave Act of 1850 said that helping an enslaved person escape carried a fine of up to $1,000 and a jail term of up to six months. When the enslaver, or someone sent in their place, caught a fugitive from slavery (or any free Black person they claimed to own, because they didn't have to provide any proof)—the judge who heard the case was paid $10 if they ruled for the enslaver, but only $5 if they ruled against them.

President Taylor had been a Southerner who enslaved people, but he opposed the Compromise of 1850 and the expansion of slavery. Fillmore was a Northerner who opposed slavery and did not enslave people, but he wanted to keep the Union together. So he signed the Compromise of 1850 even though it contained the Fugitive Slave Act. Many people in the North never forgave him—even his wife tried to convince him not to sign it.

The nation continued to divide on the issue of slavery. Abolitionists wanted to abolish it. The Fugitive Slave Act of 1850 increased abolitionist sentiment because it showed more people in the North what slavery was like and how brutal and unjust the process of capturing fugitives from slavery really was. Harriet Beecher Stowe's 1852 novel, *Uncle Tom's Cabin*, increased Northern disgust with slavery.

A civil war had been postponed in 1820 by the Missouri Compromise, in 1833 by Andrew Jackson's forceful action against nullification, and now by Millard Fillmore, who signed the Compromise of 1850. The war would come a decade later, though—and the North spent that decade increasing its industrial capacity and railroad lines.

During his presidency, Fillmore also sent naval officer Commodore Matthew Perry to Japan to discuss the possibility of trade with the United States. Up to this point, Japan had refused to trade with other nations. Perry's mission would eventually result in the 1854 Treaty of Kanagawa, an agreement that opened trade between the two nations made during Franklin Pierce's presidency. And two days before leaving office, Fillmore signed the bill splitting the very large Oregon Territory to create the Washington Territory out of northern Oregon. Washington would become a state in 1889.

Harriet Beecher Stowe

Washington Territory

Oregon Territory

Unorganized Territory

Utah Territory (semi-independent)

California

Fillmore finished Zachary Taylor's term in office, but the Whig Party passed over Fillmore for reelection in 1852.

FREDERICK DOUGLASS SPEECH TO THE NATIONAL FREE SOIL CONVENTION, AUGUST 11, 1852

The man who is right is a majority. He who has God and conscience on his side, has a majority against the universe. Though he does not represent the present state, he represents the future state. If he does not represent what we are, he represents what we ought to be.

DECODED Black abolitionist Frederick Douglass spoke against the Fugitive Slave Act at the Free Soil Party's convention in Pittsburgh. The Free Soil Party opposed slavery and wanted new territories that entered the United States to be free states. Delegates met there to choose candidates for president and vice president. The Free Soil Party had no real chance to elect a candidate in the 1852 election, and most of its members merged into the new Republican Party at the end of the 1850s.

Legacy

Fillmore had a tragic start to his post-presidential life. His wife got sick at his successor's inauguration and died at the end of the month. The next summer, his only daughter died at the age of twenty-two. Fillmore ran for president again in 1856 as the candidate for the Know-Nothing Party. The Know-Nothings were an anti-immigrant, anti-Catholic party that had significant success electing candidates in the mid-1850s, then faded very quickly. Fillmore thought that they might be able to unite the nation, which was dividing sharply on slavery. He lost badly to Democrat James Buchanan.

Fillmore remarried to wealthy widow Caroline McIntosh, and when the Civil War broke out he helped with enlistment drives and efforts to finance the Union's war effort. But he was always remembered as the president who signed the Fugitive Slave Act. When Lincoln was assassinated, a mob smeared black paint on Fillmore's house, angry that he hadn't put up mourning swags; fifteen years after the Compromise of 1850, public anger still burned hot. In his partial term Fillmore did more than sign the Compromise, but for people at the time it defined his presidency. That's still true.

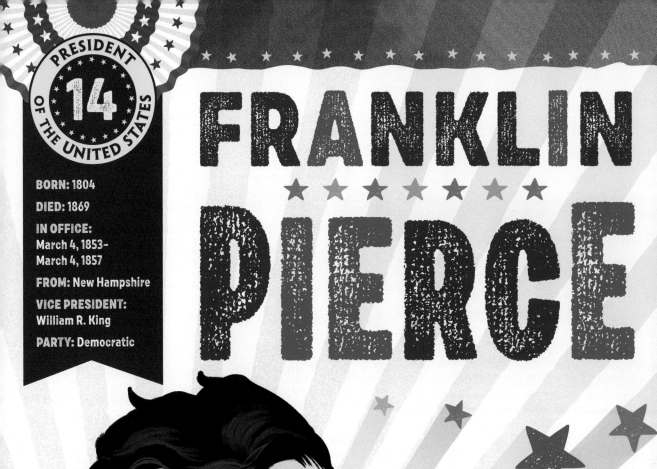

FRANKLIN PIERCE

BORN: 1804

DIED: 1869

IN OFFICE:
March 4, 1853–
March 4, 1857

FROM: New Hampshire

VICE PRESIDENT:
William R. King

PARTY: Democratic

DID YOU KNOW?

- Franklin Pierce is the only president who used the word *affirm* instead of *swear* in his oath of office.

- Pierce was the first president to have a full-time bodyguard. The Secret Service, which guards the president today, wasn't established until 1865, however.

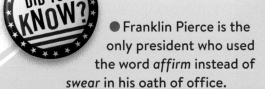

- Pierce is the only president who never changed any of his cabinet officers. No one resigned, died, or was replaced.

Life Before the Presidency

Franklin Pierce was born in New Hampshire and spent his childhood exploring the countryside, hunting, and fishing. Pierce was well educated and a close friend of poet Henry Wadsworth Longfellow and author Nathaniel Hawthorne. (Hawthorne even wrote a short sketch of Pierce's life for his campaign to use.) Pierce was a lawyer and well connected. His father, who had fought in the Revolutionary War, had been New Hampshire's governor and helped his son get into politics. Pierce was elected to the New Hampshire legislature in 1829, then to the US House of Representatives in 1833.

He was elected to the US Senate in 1837 but resigned before finishing his term because his wife disliked life in Washington and didn't support his political ambitions. They returned to New Hampshire, and a few years later he turned down an invitation to be President Polk's attorney general. When the Mexican-American War started, Pierce enlisted in the army.

In 1852, the Democrats nominated Pierce for the presidency, surprising everyone, including Pierce. Pierce was considered a "doughface"—a Northerner who favored Southern positions. He never enslaved people, but he thought that each state should decide whether or not to allow slavery. And he thought that slavery was protected by the Constitution because it protected property rights and enslavers considered enslaved people to be their property. At a time when abolitionist feeling was growing in the North, Pierce was anti-abolitionist.

Pierce won the presidency, but he lost his last remaining child before taking the oath. Franklin and Jane Pierce had had three sons. The first died as an infant, the second as a four-year-old, and the third, Benny, was killed in a railroad accident at the age of eleven, after his father was elected but before he was inaugurated. The Pierces were in the same train car as their son when an axle broke under them and the car plummeted off the track and down an incline, breaking up as it went. Benny was killed instantly—in front of his parents. Because the Pierces were in mourning, no inaugural ball was held, and Mrs. Pierce didn't attend the inauguration. She wore black throughout her years in the White House.

Mr. President

Pierce had a foreign policy blunder early in his presidency. Spain was about to free enslaved people in Cuba. Pro-slavery Americans thought that might cause an uprising of enslaved people in the United States. Pierce decided to buy Cuba to make sure that didn't happen. He implied that he would go to war against Spain if it refused to sell the island. When the Ostend Manifesto—the document containing details about the US proposal to buy Cuba—became public, it caused an international outcry. Spain and other nations felt the threat of war was unfair and Pierce had to back off.

Pierce supported expansion and tried to annex Hawaii and Alaska, though he wasn't able to get either one. He had more success with the Gadsden Purchase of 1853, in which the United States bought parts of Arizona and New Mexico from Mexico for $10 million. That gave the continental United States its current shape.

One of the biggest successes of the Pierce administration was the Kanagawa Treaty, which established trade between the United States and Japan. Former president Millard Fillmore had sent Commodore Matthew Perry off to Japan in 1853 to negotiate, and that mission served as the basis for the agreement Pierce signed.

TREATY OF KANAGAWA BETWEEN THE UNITED STATES AND JAPAN, MARCH 31, 1854

The United States of America and the empire of Japan, desiring to establish firm, lasting and sincere friendship between the two nations, have resolved to fix, in a manner clear and positive by means of a treaty or general convention of peace and amity, the rules which shall in future be mutually observed in the intercourse of their respective countries. . . .

 The Treaty of Kanagawa was Japan's first treaty with a Western nation.

When Pierce took office, the North and South were sharply divided over the issue of slavery. In January 1854, Senator Stephen Douglas of Illinois introduced the Kansas-Nebraska Bill, which would split the Kansas Territory into two territories—and eventually two states, Kansas and Nebraska. Douglas's bill said that slavery in the territories would be decided by popular sovereignty—that is, by a vote of the people living there. The Kansas-Nebraska Bill would undo the delicate balance of the 1820 Missouri Compromise by allowing territory that had been guaranteed to be free to become slave territory if the local residents voted that way. Congress—and the country—erupted over the bill. It was by far the biggest issue of Pierce's presidency. Southerners in Congress demanded that the Missouri Compromise be repealed, and President Pierce agreed with them.

KANSAS-NEBRASKA ACT
MAY 30, 1854

That the Constitution, and all laws of the United States which are not locally inapplicable, shall have the same force and effect within the said Territory of Kansas as elsewhere within the United States, except the eighth section of the act preparatory to the admission of Missouri into the Union, approved March sixth, eighteen hundred and twenty, which, being inconsistent with the principle of non-intervention by Congress with slavery in the States and Territories, as recognized by the legislation of eighteen hundred and fifty, commonly called the Compromise Measures, is hereby declared inoperative and void; it being the true intent and meaning of this act not to legislate slavery into any Territory or State, nor to exclude it therefrom, but to leave the people thereof perfectly free to form and regulate their domestic institutions in their own way, subject only to the Constitution of the United States. . . .

DECODED The Kansas-Nebraska Act repealed the Missouri Compromise, which had prohibited slavery above the 36°30' line (the southern border of Missouri). This meant that Northern territory that had been guaranteed as free could become slave territory.

Popular sovereignty in Kansas led to violence. When an election was held for a territorial legislature, a step on the way to statehood, hundreds of pro-slavery Missourians flooded over the border and illegally voted for pro-slavery candidates, resulting in a fraudulent pro-slavery legislature. Outraged that their election was stolen, abolitionist forces formed another government, leaving Kansas with two fiercely opposed legislatures. Franklin Pierce recognized the fraudulent pro-slavery legislature but not the other one, deepening the national divide. Pro-slavery riders ripped up a Kansas town that opposed them and there were a number of murders. Popular sovereignty in the territory had allowed national politicians to avoid taking on the issue of the expansion of slavery. Residents of the territory were supposed to figure it out on their own, but that didn't work, and led to "Bleeding Kansas," as it became known.

As the nation fractured, Pierce became more unpopular. After a term in which he accomplished little, Pierce was not renominated. The Democrats chose another Northerner doughface, James Buchanan, and the Union would split by the time his term ended.

Legacy

Franklin Pierce had entered the White House grief-stricken and was unable to cope with the increasingly sharp divisions in American society. He mishandled most of the issues in his single term, most notably the Kansas-Nebraska Act, which helped lead to the Civil War. He was a harsh critic of Abraham Lincoln during the Civil War, and after his wife's death in 1863, he withdrew almost entirely from the outside world. The country began to fall apart under Franklin Pierce, and he did nothing to stop it.

JAMES
BUCHANAN

BORN: 1791

DIED: 1868

IN OFFICE:
March 4, 1857–
March 4, 1861

FROM: Cove Gap,
Pennsylvania

VICE PRESIDENT:
John C. Breckenridge

PARTY: Democratic

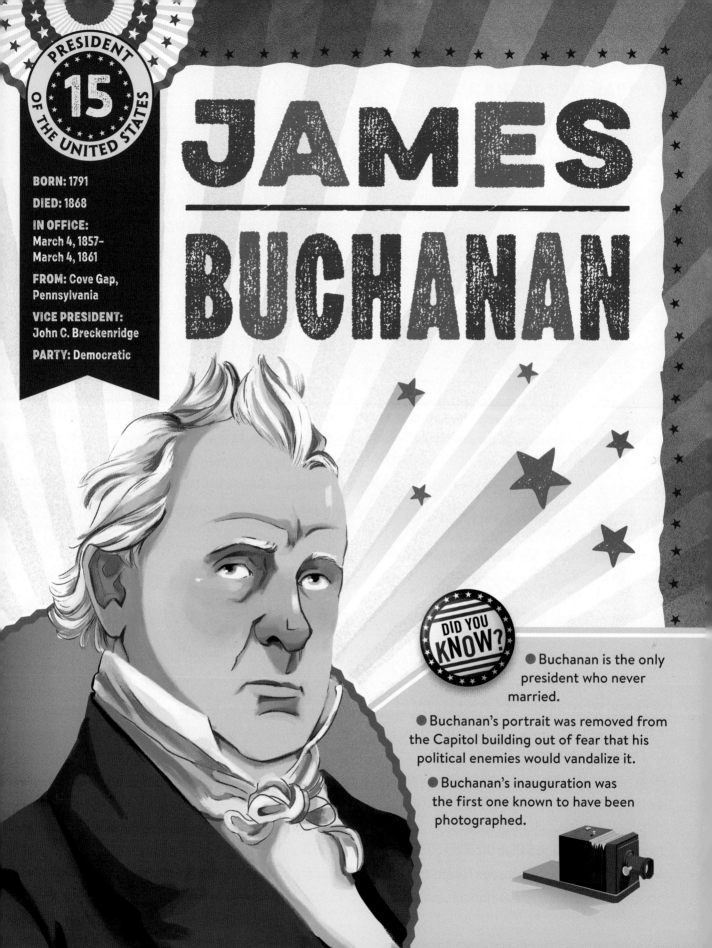

DID YOU KNOW?

- Buchanan is the only president who never married.

- Buchanan's portrait was removed from the Capitol building out of fear that his political enemies would vandalize it.

- Buchanan's inauguration was the first one known to have been photographed.

Life Before the Presidency

James Buchanan was the second of eleven children. He went to college, was kicked out for bad behavior, apologized, and was readmitted. He became a lawyer and served in a reserve unit in the War of 1812 but saw no action. He was a legislator at the state and federal levels and had extensive foreign policy experience—but his term was dominated by domestic crises.

In 1856, Buchanan got the Democratic nomination for the presidency. The Democratic Party was splitting on regional lines over the issue of slavery. Buchanan was considered a doughface—a Northerner who agreed with the South—and was a compromise candidate who might appeal to both regions.

Mr. President

Buchanan was the last president to serve before the Civil War began. His term began with a Supreme Court decision that inflamed the country, and it ended with seven states (South Carolina, Mississippi, Florida, Alabama, Georgia, Louisiana, and Texas) seceding from the Union. Buchanan opposed slavery, but he didn't think it was unconstitutional. He saw abolitionists as dangerous because efforts to free enslaved people could lead to unrest or uprisings.

Buchanan wanted the Supreme Court to decide on whether slavery could be expanded into the western territories, and whether it should be—or could be—limited. Americans differed sharply on whether, and where, slavery should be allowed to expand. Buchanan expected that no matter what the Supreme Court decided, people would accept the decision when it came down.

Letter from Justice John Catron to James Buchanan, February 19, 1857

The Dred Scott case has been before the Judge several times since last Saturday, and I think you may safely say in your Inaugural,

'That the question involving the constitutionality of the Missouri Compromise line is presented to the appropriate tribunal to decide; to wit, to the Supreme Court of the United States. It is due to its high and independent character to suppose that it will decide & settle a controversy which has so long and seriously agitated the country, and which *must* ultimately be decided by the Supreme Court. . . .'

DECODED Here Supreme Court Justice John Catron and Buchanan are clearly working together both on the wording of Buchanan's inaugural address and on the *Dred Scott* decision. Buchanan's hope that the issue of slavery could be peacefully settled by the Supreme Court was misguided and naive.

Two days after Buchanan took the oath of office, the Supreme Court released its decision in *Dred Scott v. Sandford* (1857), which is often considered the worst decision in Supreme Court history. Dred Scott was an enslaved man whose enslaver had taken him to free territory. When his enslaver took him back to slave territory, Scott sued, saying that his residence in free territory made him free. If it didn't—if slavery was allowed in free territory—what exactly did free territory mean?

Buchanan seems to have pressured the Supreme Court to make a sweeping ruling. The Court had declared that Scott did not have the legal right to sue, and it could have stopped there. If he didn't have standing, there was no reason to decide the case. The Court went on anyway, which was a terrible mistake.

DRED SCOTT DECISION 1857

Chief Justice Taney, for the Court: Thus the rights of property are united with the rights of person, and placed on the same ground by the fifth amendment to the Constitution, which provides that no person shall be deprived of life, liberty, and property, without due process of law. And an act of Congress which deprives a citizen of the United States of his liberty or property, merely because he came himself or brought his property into a particular Territory of the United States, and who had committed no offence against the laws, could hardly be dignified with the name of due process of law.

Upon these considerations, it is the opinion of the court that the act of Congress which prohibited a citizen from holding and owning property of this kind in the territory of the United States north of the line therein mentioned, is not warranted by the Constitution, and is therefore void; and that neither Dred Scott himself, nor any of his family, were made free by being carried into this territory; even if they had been carried there by the owner, with the intention of becoming a permanent resident.

Justice Daniel's concurring opinion: It may be assumed as a postulate, that to a slave, as such, there appertains and can appertain no relation, civil or political, with the State or the Government. He is himself strictly *property*. . . . Hence it follows, necessarily, that a slave, the *peculium* or property of a master, and possessing within himself no civil nor political rights or capacities, cannot be a CITIZEN.

Dred Scott

DECODED Justices Roger B. Taney (pronounced "Tawney") and Peter V. Daniel both sided with the majority in an appalling decision that hurt both free and enslaved Black people. A concurring opinion (like Daniel's) is written by a justice who agrees with the majority.

It ruled that no Black person, enslaved or free, could be a US citizen and that living in free territory didn't make Scott free. The *Dred Scott* decision also declared the Missouri Compromise of 1820 unconstitutional. The decision suggested that slavery could be allowed in northern territories—but not prohibited. The North was outraged.

As the country continued to divide over slavery, one possible solution was popular sovereignty—letting the people who lived in a particular area decide for themselves whether they would have slavery in that area. The 1854 Kansas-Nebraska Act had repealed the 1820 Missouri Compromise, divided up the Kansas Territory into two parts, and allowed for popular sovereignty. Buchanan thought that admitting Kansas as a state, as quickly as possible, would end the conflict over slavery in the territory. It sounded like a good solution to many people, including the president, but it didn't work. Arguments over slavery didn't end, and by the time Kansas became a state, the Union was already dissolving.

Buchanan had a foreign policy background and he negotiated two treaties while in office—one with Mexico and one with Nicaragua. But as Congress became consumed by the slavery question, the Senate refused to ratify either treaty and turned its attention away from foreign policy.

And in 1857, in response to conflict between Mormon leaders and the federal government, Buchanan sent federal troops to Utah. Mormons in the area were afraid the troops would attack them and prepared to defend themselves. About 150 people were killed during the Utah War (1857–1858), most of them migrants headed to California who were killed by Mormon militia, for reasons that remain unclear. Not long after, in October 1859, abolitionist leader John Brown raided Harper's Ferry, Virginia, hoping to free the enslaved people there. Brown was quickly captured and later hanged, but the South—and the president—were appalled by the raid.

Still, as events spun out of control, Buchanan failed to act, in part because he was afraid that any action would spark a dangerous reaction. When the 1860 election rolled around, Buchanan didn't think he'd be nominated—and he was right. A sitting president's party normally nominates him for reelection, so this was unusual, and it indicates how unpopular Buchanan had become, and how much trouble the parties were having deciding who to run for president while everything was falling apart.

The Democrats met in Charleston, South Carolina, in 1860—probably the worst possible choice. Not only did the city lack adequate facilities for hosting a national convention, but it was also a hotbed of anti-Northern sentiment. Northern

Democrats attended the convention, not yet understanding that their party had split on sectional lines. They met with a hostile reception and the convention split. In 1860, the Democrats wound up nominating two candidates: John C. Breckenridge, the vice president and a pro-slavery extremist, and Stephen Douglas, the senator from Illinois who had proposed the Kansas-Nebraska Act that had caused so much trouble. In addition, the short-lived Constitutional Union Party nominated John Bell, and the Republicans chose Abraham Lincoln.

James Buchanan gave only one speech to the general public before the 1860 election. He spoke from the portico of the White House and argued that enslaved people were property and that slavery should be allowed in the territories.

Abraham Lincoln was elected in November 1860, and in the four months before he took office, seven states seceded, led by South Carolina in December 1860. Buchanan's secretary of war, John B. Floyd of Virginia, took arms from northern arsenals and sent them south to help future Confederate states once fighting started.

Floyd wasn't the only federal official who stole military equipment from the United States and sent it to the enemy. Those actions made the Civil War longer and more expensive. And Buchanan did nothing to stop them.

Legacy

When his term ended, Buchanan went back to his estate in Pennsylvania. He wrote a book detailing the origins of the Civil War and blamed it on abolitionists and Republicans. The book came out a year after the war had ended and Lincoln had been killed. It didn't do well. Having just lived through the war, most people didn't want to read about it.

BUCHANAN'S IDEAS

Buchanan hesitated as the country split. He not only failed to meet the challenges posed by secession, he was strangely passive about the crisis. When historians rank presidents, most put James Buchanan at or near the very bottom.

ABRAHAM LINCOLN

PRESIDENT 16 OF THE UNITED STATES

BORN: 1809

DIED: 1865

IN OFFICE: March 4, 1861– April 15, 1865

FROM: born in Hodgenville, Kentucky; moved to Indiana in 1816; moved to Illinois in 1830

VICE PRESIDENT: Hannibal Hamlin (first term), Andrew Johnson (second term)

PARTY: Republican

DID YOU KNOW?

- Lincoln is the only president who got a patent for an invention. In 1849, Lincoln received US Patent No. 6,469 for a way to use air chambers to lighten a steamboat and help it get through shallow water.

- Lincoln was an excellent wrestler. He competed about three hundred times and lost only one match—to another soldier in the Black Hawk War. He is in the National Wrestling Hall of Fame.

- Lincoln's dog, a yellow Lab mix, was named Fido (the name means "faithful" in Latin). That's where we get "Fido" as a generic name for a dog. Fido Lincoln was the first dog of a president to be photographed.

Life Before the Presidency

Abraham Lincoln was born in a one-room log cabin with dirt floors in Hodgenville, Kentucky. His parents moved the family to Indiana in 1816. His mother died when he was nine years old and his father, Thomas Lincoln, remarried to Sarah Bush Johnston, whom young Lincoln liked. She encouraged his education, and although he had little formal schooling he studied hard, working through the day and reading at night by firelight.

As a young man he operated a ferry across a river and piloted a flatboat down the Mississippi River. He moved to New Salem, Illinois, on his own, and there he co-owned a general store.

In 1832, Lincoln enlisted as a soldier for the Black Hawk War but saw no action. He became postmaster at New Salem, and in 1834, he was elected to the Illinois state legislature. Four years later Lincoln won a seat in the US House of Representatives (1847–1849).

In May 1856, Lincoln was asked to speak at the Illinois Republican Party's first convention. He gave a stirring speech against slavery—so stirring that none of the reporters present remembered to take notes and we have no record of what he said.

Lincoln ran against Stephen Douglas for a US Senate seat in 1858. The two candidates met in seven Illinois towns to publicly debate the issues in a carnival-like atmosphere, which included parades and floats. As a result of the debates, Lincoln became known nationally. Lincoln lost that election, but he was nominated for president in 1860.

LINCOLN'S "HOUSE DIVIDED" SPEECH (ACCEPTANCE OF THE WHIG NOMINATION FOR SENATOR), JUNE 16, 1858

"A house divided against itself cannot stand."

I believe this government cannot endure, permanently half *slave* and half *free*.

I do not expect the Union to be *dissolved* - do not expect the house to *fall* - but I *do* expect it will cease to be divided.

It will become *all* one thing, or *all* the other.

DECODED In this speech, Lincoln is comparing the nation—half of which allowed slavery and half of which did not—to a house divided. Violence had broken out in Kansas and things seemed to be getting worse, not better. Lincoln says here that the country couldn't continue to be split on the slavery issue—it would end up being all free territory or all slave territory.

Lincoln became the first Republican president. He was so unpopular in the South that some states didn't put his name on the ballot—but he still won in the electoral college, with 180 votes for Lincoln and 123 votes for his three opponents combined.

Mr. President

The two presidents before Lincoln, Franklin Pierce and James Buchanan, were two of the worst presidents in American history. The Union began splitting during Buchanan's term, and seven states had seceded by the time Lincoln took office. The nation was in crisis during Lincoln's entire presidency.

South Carolina was the first state to secede, in December 1860, followed by Mississippi, Florida, Alabama, Georgia, Louisiana, and Texas. Those states (with the later additions of Virginia, Arkansas, North Carolina, and Tennessee) formed the Confederate States of America (CSA). They elected Jefferson Davis to be their president, and Lincoln's friend Alexander Stephens to be vice president. The Confederates demanded that US troops leave Fort Sumter, located in the harbor of Charleston, South Carolina. When the fort ran low on necessities, Lincoln sent a supply ship. Davis ordered Confederate troops to fire on the fort; the attack began on April 12, 1861. It was the beginning of the Civil War.

President Lincoln responded forcefully, calling for troops to put down the insurrection. Attempts to limit slavery in the western territories had angered the South. Lincoln opposed slavery, but he didn't think the Constitution allowed him to end it. But once the South had left the Union—and then fired on American soldiers—Lincoln had to respond.

Letter from Abraham Lincoln to General George B. McClellan, October 13, 1862

You remember my speaking to you of what I called your over-cautiousness. Are you not over-cautious when you assume that you can not do what the enemy is constantly doing? Should you not claim to be at least his equal in prowess, and act upon the claim?

If he should . . . move towards Richmond, I would press closely to him, fight him if a favorable opportunity should present, and, at least, try to beat him to Richmond on the inside track. I say "try"; if we never try, we shall never succeed. . . .

DECODED General McClellan was Lincoln's general at the beginning of the Civil War—and he was a pro-slavery Democrat who wanted to end the rebellion without disrupting slavery in the South. McClellan moved against Confederate General Robert E. Lee very slowly and failed to pursue him time after time, which greatly upset the president. Lincoln once said pointedly that if McClellan wasn't going to use the army, he would like to borrow it. Lincoln fired him three weeks after writing this letter.

An armed minority couldn't be allowed to overthrow the will of the voters. The South left because it had lost a free and fair election. Stephen Douglas called it "the new system of resistance by the sword and bayonet to the results of the ballot-box."

The North got off to a slow start. The Army of the Potomac (North) and the Army of Northern Virginia (South) clashed in huge battles with horrifying casualty counts at Shiloh (April 1862), Antietam (September 1862), and Gettysburg (July 1863). At Gettysburg, Union forces stopped a Confederate army that was trying to invade the North. That November, President Lincoln dedicated a cemetery at the Gettysburg battlefield in one of the most eloquent and enduring speeches ever given on American soil.

Lincoln found the general he needed in the West: Ulysses S. Grant. Grant led Union troops against Fort Donelson and Fort Henry in Tennessee, capturing both and opening the upper South. That allowed Grant to capture Vicksburg, Mississippi, giving the Union control of the whole length of the Mississippi River and splitting the Confederacy. That made it much harder for the Confederate states to move soldiers and supplies. Lincoln promoted Grant, who took command of all Union armies.

After the Battle of Antietam in September 1862 improved the Union's chance of victory, Lincoln issued the Preliminary Emancipation Proclamation, which gave states in rebellion three months to return to the Union and be able to keep slavery.

GETTYSBURG ADDRESS, NOVEMBER 19, 1863

Fourscore and seven years ago our fathers brought forth on this continent, a new nation, conceived in Liberty, and dedicated to the proposition that all men are created equal.

Now we are engaged in a great civil war, testing whether that nation, or any nation so conceived and so dedicated, can long endure. We are met on a great battle-field of that war. We have come to dedicate a portion of that field, as a final resting place for those who here gave their lives that that nation might live. It is altogether fitting and proper that we should do this . . . .

It is rather for us to be here dedicated to the great task remaining before us—that from these honored dead we take increased devotion to that cause for which they gave the last full measure of devotion—that we here highly resolve that these dead shall not have died in vain—that this nation, under God, shall have a new birth of freedom—and that government of the people, by the people, for the people shall not perish from the earth.

DECODED A score is twenty years, so Lincoln's opening words, "four-score and seven years ago," are a fancy way of saying eighty-seven years. (Eighty-seven years before 1863 was 1776—the year the Declaration of Independence was signed.) While dedicating a cemetery on the Gettysburg battlefield, Lincoln asked Americans to rededicate themselves to the nation's founding principles of liberty and equality. His call to save democracy was stunning in its simplicity and eloquence.

When none returned, he issued the Emancipation Proclamation, which freed all enslaved people in rebel states as of January 1, 1863.

THE EMANCIPATION PROCLAMATION
JANUARY 1, 1863

. . . Now, therefore I, Abraham Lincoln, President of the United States . . . order and designate as the States and parts of States wherein the people thereof respectively, are this day in rebellion against the United States, . . . I do order and declare that all persons held as slaves within said designated States . . . are, and henceforward shall be free. . . .

DECODED Lincoln declared the enslaved people in those areas to be free, but it took the actions of General Ulysses S. Grant on the battlefield to turn the Emancipation Proclamation into reality.

The proclamation didn't change anything until the areas where slavery existed were occupied by Union armies. Grant's strategy to end the war was three pronged: he fought General Lee and pinned him down himself; Union general William Tecumseh Sherman marched through Georgia to the Atlantic coast, then turned up through South Carolina, which had been the first state to secede; and Union general Phil Sheridan's cavalry ripped up the Shenandoah Valley, the last breadbasket of the Confederacy.

The United States held a contested election during the Civil War—another test of the Constitution, which mandates elections be held every four years.

The twenty-five Union states included Kansas, West Virginia, and Nevada, all of which had become states since the last presidential election. (Nevada became a state eight days before the election.) Lincoln won easily, aided by General Sherman's capture of Atlanta two months before. Almost 80 percent of Union soldiers voted for their commander in chief, a strong show of support. Lincoln's opponent was George B. McClellan, who had been his general at the start of the war. He won only three states. (Confederate states didn't participate in this election.)

LINCOLN'S SECOND INAUGURAL ADDRESS, MARCH 4, 1865

With malice toward none with charity for all with firmness in the right as God gives us to see the right let us strive on to finish the work we are in to bind up the nation's wounds, to care for him who shall have borne the battle and for his widow and his orphan ~ to do all which may achieve and cherish a just and lasting peace among ourselves and with all nations.

DECODED Lincoln's second inaugural address was very short—just 701 words. The war was ending and Lincoln spoke about what would come next—taking care of veterans and their families and establishing a just peace.

Union troops took Richmond, Virginia, at the beginning of April 1865. Lincoln visited the city and sat quietly for a time at Jefferson Davis's desk. When General Lee surrendered to Grant at Appomattox Court House in Virginia on April 9, 1865, the war was effectively over.

After the war ended, Lincoln was unable to finish the work of reuniting the nation because he was assassinated in Ford's Theater on Good Friday, April 14, 1865, while watching the play *Our American Cousin* with his wife, Mary Todd Lincoln. They had invited Ulysses S. Grant and his wife to go with them, but the Grants had declined. John Wilkes Booth, a Confederate sympathizer, shot Lincoln in the head and then jumped to the stage shouting "Sic semper tyrannis," the Virginia state motto, which means "Thus always to tyrants." Lincoln was carried to a nearby boardinghouse and died the next morning without regaining consciousness.

Legacy

A train carried Lincoln's body across seven states and through 180 cities on its way back home for burial in Springfield, Illinois. The train also carried the casket of his son, Willie, who had died in the White House. When they got to Springfield, Lincoln's horse, Old Bob, walked draped in mourning cloth in the procession that took his casket for burial at its final destination.

Lincoln's legacy lies in the preservation of the Union and freeing enslaved people. The Thirteenth Amendment, which ended slavery, was passed during Lincoln's lifetime but was ratified and went into effect after his death. He occupies a place in the first rank of great Americans. No president faced greater challenges, defended democracy more vigorously, or led the nation with more courage, humor, and humility.

ANDREW
JOHNSON

BORN: 1808

DIED: 1875

IN OFFICE:
April 15, 1865–
March 4, 1869

FROM: born in Raleigh,
North Carolina; lived
in Tennessee

VICE PRESIDENT:
none

PARTY: Democratic
(National Union as
vice president and
president)

DID YOU KNOW?

- Andrew Johnson was the first president to be impeached.

- Johnson got married at the age of eighteen, the youngest of any president.

- Johnson is the only president to have served in the US Senate after his presidency.

Life Before the Presidency

Andrew Johnson was born into poverty in North Carolina. He became a tailor's apprentice at the age of fourteen and eventually ran away, and for some time there was a reward for his return. He moved to Tennessee and opened a tailor shop when he was seventeen.

Johnson served as mayor of tiny Greeneville, Tennessee, and held posts in the state government and US House of Representatives before he was elected to the US Senate. He served from 1857 until March 1862, when the Civil War was raging. Tennessee was a Confederate state, and Johnson became the only US senator to stay in the Senate after his state seceded.

When General Ulysses S. Grant captured Tennessee's forts and marched into the state, President Lincoln set up a new, temporary government in Tennessee and made Johnson its head.

Johnson had been poor all his life. He identified with hardscrabble farmers and despised rich plantation owners. But he wanted to help poor white people—not Black people—and he often used racist language. He approved of the Fugitive Slave Act of 1850 and he had supported a pro-slavery candidate in the 1860 election. He strongly opposed secession because he was pro-Union, not anti-slavery. Despite his pre-war support of slavery, Johnson thought that emancipation was necessary to win the war. He enslaved a small number of people and freed them in August 1863, hoping to set an example.

When Abraham Lincoln ran for reelection in 1864, he wanted to switch vice presidential candidates. Lincoln's reelection was very much in doubt until General William Tecumseh Sherman took Atlanta in September 1864—just two months before the election. Lincoln wanted to balance the ticket—that is, to run with a vice president who would appeal to a different group of voters. Andrew Johnson was the most famous of the War Democrats, who were pro-Union and wanted the North to win the Civil War. Other Republican leaders agreed with Lincoln, and they put Andrew Johnson on the ticket.

The Lincoln-Johnson ticket won on the strength of Union victories in the early autumn. Johnson was vice president for five weeks before Lincoln's assassination made him president.

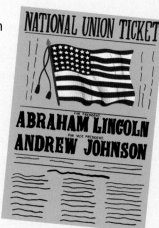

Mr. President

Andrew Johnson was the third vice president to take over the presidency upon the death of a president. Abraham Lincoln was shot on April 14, 1865, and died on April 15.

When Lincoln was assassinated, the Republican Congress was faced with a president who was a Southern Democrat, who was deeply racist, and who had never spoken forcefully against slavery. They also had a huge issue on their hands. The Civil War was ending and states that had been in rebellion had to be brought back into the Union somehow.

Reconstruction—the rebuilding of the Union—got under way. Johnson supported a plan Lincoln had drafted, the "10 percent plan," which required 10 percent of citizens from a state that had seceded to take an oath to uphold the US Constitution in order for the state to be readmitted to the Union. States also had to ratify the Thirteenth Amendment, which ended slavery. Then they could elect members to represent them in Congress again. These terms were generous, and Johnson made them more so by issuing a general pardon to Confederate soldiers. He followed that with pardons for individual

people. He gave out so many pardons that the forms were preprinted, with just a blank left in which to write the name of the person being pardoned.

Starting in 1865, Southern states enacted Black codes, which were laws that restricted the rights of freedmen. The codes were an attempt to continue slavery without calling it that, and they varied from state to state. Examples include prohibitions on Black people meeting at night, preaching, carrying guns, living in town, fishing, grazing livestock, and working for themselves or not working. In some places, Black codes required that Black people work for white people, and if they didn't have a work contract by a few days after the New Year, their labor would be sold to the highest bidder. The Black codes were explicitly designed to control Black Americans and subject them to extensive regulations that weren't imposed on white people.

In 1866, Congress passed legislation to continue the government's support of the Freedmen's Bureau, which had been established in early 1865, while Lincoln was still alive. The Freedmen's Bureau was the federal government's attempt to help people who had been freed, but without any money, land, or other support to survive. Johnson vetoed the extension. Congress was surprised at his opposition and passed the extension of the Freedmen's Bureau over his veto. Johnson also vetoed the

Civil Rights Act of 1866, which said that all people born in the United States are citizens and must all be treated equally. Congress passed the Civil Rights Act over that veto, too.

The Fourteenth Amendment was proposed the same year. It gave citizenship to Black Americans and it said that states couldn't violate a citizen's civil rights and that everyone would have "equal protection of the law." It was another attempt to protect freedmen. Johnson opposed the amendment, partly because it was written without former Confederate states being part of the process. Congress ratified the amendment anyway on July 9, 1868.

Johnson was uninterested in helping freedmen. Even when they were attacked, he was often silent or sided with local authorities. In 1866, a group of mostly Black delegates met at a convention in New Orleans to try to change the Louisiana state constitution. A mob of white people aided by the police slaughtered them, shooting and stabbing delegates and mutilating their bodies. The mayor of New Orleans had been a Confederate officer whom Andrew Johnson had pardoned. Across the South, freedmen had to deal with law enforcement and government officials who had been fighting to keep them enslaved only weeks before. The New Orleans Massacre was one of the worst outbreaks of violence in the Reconstruction period.

Message from Andrew Johnson to Major-General Phil Sheridan, August 4, 1866, on the New Orleans Massacre

Was not the assembling of this Convention and the gathering of the mob for its defense and protection a main cause of the riotous and unlawful proceedings of the civil authorities of New Orleans?

DECODED President Johnson here suggests that the reason for the riot was the convention; in other words, the delegates wouldn't have been murdered if they hadn't been there. This angered Radical Republicans in Congress, a group that wanted Reconstruction to have stricter requirements for Southern states reentering the Union. Johnson's indifference to the massacre prompted Congress to pass stronger legislation to help freedmen. And they began to think about impeaching the president.

As Congress and the president began to disagree more sharply over Reconstruction, Congress passed two acts. The Tenure of Office Act required the president to get congressional approval before making a change in his cabinet, a measure Congress passed because they suspected that Johnson wanted to remove his Secretary of War, Edwin M. Stanton.

The second measure was the Army Appropriations Act, which limited the commander in chief's control of the military. It required the president to issue orders through the General of the Army, who at the time was Ulysses S. Grant. No one doubted Grant's patriotism—but many people in Washington didn't trust Johnson's.

When President Johnson violated the Tenure of Office Act, which was probably unconstitutional, the House of Representatives wrote up impeachment charges against him. The main charge was firing Secretary of War Stanton, although there were eleven total charges, including insulting Congress with a "loud voice."

Andrew Johnson was the first president to be impeached. His trial was held in the Senate and presided over by the chief justice of the Supreme Court, Salmon Chase, as the Constitution requires. Johnson was found not guilty by one vote and was able to stay in office to the end of his term, but impeachment had damaged his effectiveness.

Johnson's term was dominated by Reconstruction and the fate of freedmen. He did have some successes in foreign policy, though. Secretary of State William Seward bought Alaska from Russia during Johnson's administration. Seward also purchased the Midway Islands in the Pacific, which would be important as military bases in World War II.

Legacy

After serving the rest of Abraham Lincoln's second term, Johnson tried to run for his own term as a Democrat, opposing political rights for Black people. He was too damaged after his impeachment, though, and the Democrats wouldn't nominate him. He was finally elected a US senator in 1874. He served with twelve senators who had voted to impeach him while he was president, and he died during his term.

Johnson wasn't especially educated, smart, or skillful as a politician. Pierce and Buchanan, the two presidents who served immediately before the Civil War, and Andrew Johnson, who served immediately after it, are usually ranked as three of the very worst presidents.

ULYSSES S. GRANT

BORN: 1822

DIED: 1885

IN OFFICE:
March 4, 1869–
March 4, 1877

FROM: Point Pleasant, Ohio

VICE PRESIDENT: Schuyler Colfax (first term), Henry Wilson (second term)

PARTY: Republican

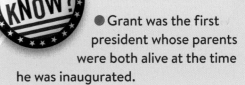

DID YOU KNOW?

- Grant was the first president whose parents were both alive at the time he was inaugurated.

- Grant was the youngest president up to that time. He was forty-six when he took office.

- In 1872, when Grant ran for reelection, the first female presidential candidate (Victoria Woodhull) and first Catholic presidential candidate (Charles O'Conor) were nominated. Neither was put forward by a major party and they had no chance of winning.

- Before the Mexican-American War, Grant had an offer to be a math teacher, and he was interested in taking it. Eventually, he decided he couldn't leave the army as it headed to war. He never became a math teacher.

- Grant loved fast horses. When he was president, a Washington, DC, police officer gave him a speeding ticket for going too fast in his carriage.

Life Before the Presidency

Grant was born in Ohio, the first of six children. His name was Hiram Ulysses Grant but he always went by his middle name. His father sent him to West Point, the military academy. He was an average student who got demerits for untied shoes, but West Point was where he made his name—literally. When he arrived he found the paperwork had his name wrong. Instead of H. Ulysses Grant he was listed as Ulysses S. Grant (probably because his mother's maiden name was Simpson). He had to accept the change or go home—so he became Ulysses S. Grant. The rest of the country enjoyed his initials, and he was nicknamed "United States Grant," "Uncle Sam Grant," and, during the Civil War, "Unconditional Surrender Grant."

Grant fought in the Mexican-American War and was decorated for bravery. He thought the war was wrong, writing later that he considered it "one of the most unjust ever waged by a stronger against a weaker nation."

Grant resigned from the army and struggled to make a living until the Civil War started and he reenlisted. After being given a command, Grant captured Fort Henry and Fort Donelson in northern Tennessee, opening the Tennessee Valley to the Union. The North hadn't been doing well in battles in the east. Grant's victories in the west were welcome news for President Lincoln and the country at large, and made him a national hero. On July 4, 1863, Grant took Vicksburg, a fort on the Mississippi River that was considered impossible to capture. The day before, the Union won at Gettysburg in the east. That was a turning point for the Union. Lincoln gave Grant overall command of the Union armies.

Order from Abraham Lincoln to Ulysses S. Grant, March 10, 1864

Under the authority of the act of Congress to revive the grade of Lieutenant General in the United States Army, approved February 29, 1864, Lieutenant General Ulysses S. Grant, U.S. Army, is assigned to the command of the armies of the United States. Abraham Lincoln

DECODED This order was written in calligraphy and signed by the president. It was worth having someone write it beautifully—Congress brought back a rank so high that no one since George Washington had had it, and they gave it to Grant. He was now in charge of all the armies of the United States. It was his war to win or lose. He won it.

On April 9, 1865, Grant forced Confederate General Robert E. Lee to surrender at Appomattox Court House, essentially ending the Civil War. Less than a week later, Lincoln was assassinated and Andrew Johnson took office. That made Grant's job much harder.

As the highest-ranking general of the army, Grant was responsible for sending home the soldiers and storing the equipment of the Union Army, which was the largest organization in the history of North America to that time. The Freedmen's Bureau was under the Department of the Army, so Grant was also responsible for the only organized federal help for freedmen. And his office was in Washington, DC, which meant he was accessible to any congressmen who didn't like the president and would rather deal with Grant. The general had a staggering workload. One thing he worked hard on was helping freedmen, something President Andrew Johnson had no interest in.

GENERAL ORDER NO. 3, ISSUED BY ULYSSES S. GRANT, JANUARY 1866

Southern states had to prevent prosecutions of Black people in which they were

"charged with offenses for which white persons are not prosecuted or punished in the same manner and degree."

DECODED After the Civil War, white people in many places wrote Black codes, which were laws that restricted the rights of Black Americans. The Black codes were an attempt to continue slavery in reality if not in name. In General Order No. 3 Grant strikes at the Black codes.

After Andrew Johnson was impeached, Grant ran for president in the election of 1868. It would seem impossible that the Union general who won the Civil War would win six Confederate states in the 1868 election—but Grant did.

Mr. President

The biggest issue of Grant's presidency was Reconstruction and the status of freedmen. Grant began his presidency by calling for ratification of the Fifteenth Amendment, which gave freedmen the right to vote. Andrew Johnson had done nothing to stop violence against Black people throughout the South—especially at the polls. Grant reversed that, signing the Civil Rights Act of 1870, which allowed federal troops to protect Black voters.

FIFTEENTH AMENDMENT, FEBRUARY 3, 1870

The right of citizens of the United States to vote shall not be denied or abridged by the United States or by any state on account of race, color, or previous condition of servitude.

DECODED The Fifteenth Amendment prevented anyone from denying the vote to a man based on his race or his having been enslaved. But it didn't work—states, especially in the South, put in poll taxes, which required a person to pay to vote, or they gave literacy or Constitution tests that were judged in whatever way the person grading the test wanted.

GRANT'S MESSAGE TO CONGRESS ON THE FIFTEENTH AMENDMENT, MARCH 30, 1870

> A measure which makes at once 4,000,000 people voters who were heretofore declared by the highest tribunal in the land not citizens of the United States, nor eligible to become so . . . is indeed a measure of grander importance than any other one act of the kind from the foundation of our free Government to the present day.

DECODED The "highest tribunal in the land" means the Supreme Court. Grant is taking a swipe at the court here for the *Dred Scott* decision in 1857, which said that Black Americans couldn't be citizens. (The Thirteenth and Fourteenth Amendments essentially overturned that decision.)

Grant was reelected in 1872. He was scrupulously honest, but some of the people around him were corrupt. In one scandal, people who made money by guessing whether the price of gold would go up or down caused problems for the economy. In another, the Union Pacific Railroad essentially bribed members of Congress with company stock. In 1873, a panic (or depression) brought hard times. For corrupt officials to profit from holding public office looked very bad, and Grant was deeply embarrassed even though he wasn't involved.

US policy toward Indigenous people shifted under Grant. George Washington had started the policy of treating Indigenous nations as sovereign, which meant that US treaties with Indigenous nations were ratified by the Senate just like a treaty with any other nation would be. The Indian Appropriations Act of 1871 changed that, saying that Indigenous people would no longer be considered members of sovereign nations. That meant the government couldn't make treaties with them—and made it harder for Indigenous people to act collectively to protect their land.

Grant appointed Ely S. Parker to be his Commissioner of Indian Affairs. Parker was a Seneca who'd been one of Grant's staff officers in the Civil War, and he was the first Indigenous person to hold the post. Grant followed what he called the Peace Policy, hoping

Ely S. Parker

that the years of war with Indigenous nations were over. He replaced corrupt government officials who were taking advantage of Indigenous people, tried to protect them from white encroachment, and encouraged them to become farmers. The intentions were good, but the discovery of gold in the Black Hills of South Dakota sent more white people into areas that were owned by Indigenous nations. In 1876, the Black Hills War broke out, with Lakota Sioux and Northern Cheyenne on one side and the United States on the other. In June of that year, Crazy Horse and his warriors wiped out

George Armstrong Custer's command at the Battle of the Little Bighorn. Grant tried to bring peace to the frontier—and failed.

Grant signed a law making Yellowstone the nation's first national park,

and he successfully negotiated reparations (which means payments to make up for damages you caused) from Great Britain for the destruction caused by the *Alabama*, a ship the British had built for the Confederacy in 1862. The *Alabama* was very successful at preying on US shipping—and it sailed with a mostly English crew. Many Americans considered the construction of the ship to have been a hostile action and wanted the United States to declare war against Great Britain. The settlement put a stop to those calls.

Grant worked to protect Black Americans and continued to use federal troops to do that, but in his second term the country was growing tired of Reconstruction. Southern states resented the presence of federal troops, who were charged with keeping order—and who tried to prevent attacks on Black people. They also disliked Northerners who came South to help with Reconstruction.

Reconstruction ended with the Grant era. After he left office, things got worse for Black Americans.

Legacy

The election of 1876 was disputed, and both Democrats and Republicans accused the other side of fraud. Grant remained in office until his successor's inauguration and provided calm, orderly leadership while the election results were in doubt. He helped ensure a peaceful transition of power, a critical characteristic of American democracy.

Grant had one of the most important post-presidential periods because he raised American visibility and popularity around the world. He went on a two-year tour of the world where he was received as a world leader. He gave a lot of speeches and furthered American interests with informal, personal diplomacy.

As a general, Grant kept the nation together; as a president, he tried to protect all Americans, regardless of their skin color. And he helped to mend the country after the Civil War.

RUTHERFORD B.
HAYES

PRESIDENT OF THE UNITED STATES

19

BORN: 1822

DIED: 1893

IN OFFICE:
March 4, 1877–
March 4, 1881

FROM: Ohio

VICE PRESIDENT:
William Almon Wheeler

PARTY: Republican

DID YOU KNOW?

- Hayes's wife, Lucy, was the first First Lady who had gone to college.

- During Hayes's term the White House got its first telephone—installed by Alexander Graham Bell.

Life Before the Presidency

Rutherford B. Hayes was born a few months after his father's death in 1822. His mother raised her children with the help of her bachelor brother, who provided Hayes with financial and emotional support throughout his life. Hayes went to Harvard Law School, and afterward he began to practice law in Ohio. He married Lucy Webb, who was an abolitionist. Hayes was already anti-slavery but Lucy nudged him even further in that direction. In court, Hayes defended people who had escaped from slavery.

When Confederate troops fired on Fort Sumter, Hayes led the members of his book club, the Literary Society of Cincinnati, in military drills. The governor made him a major in 1861, and by the end of the war he was a brevet major general. William McKinley, the future twenty-fifth president, was one of Hayes's men, the only time two presidents served in the same military unit.

Hayes was elected to the US House of Representatives in 1865 and then became governor of Ohio in 1868, a post he held when he became president.

The election of 1876 was the most disputed election in US history. The Republicans nominated Hayes, and the Democrats chose Samuel J. Tilden, the governor of New York.

The election ended with Tilden well ahead in the popular vote, but he was one vote shy of winning the electoral college. Four states had voting irregularities, though—Florida, South Carolina, Louisiana, and Oregon. Those states sent more than one set of electors to Congress because they didn't agree about who had won their state. Congress didn't know what to do. And the Constitution didn't provide any instructions.

Rutherford B. Hayes Diary Entry, November 11, 1876

From Wednesday afternoon the city and the whole country has been full of excitement and anxiety. People have been up and down several times a day with the varying rumors. ... [T]he news has fluctuated just enough to prolong the suspense and to enhance the interest. At this time the Republicans are claiming the election by one electoral vote. ...

All thoughtful people are brought to consider the imperfect machinery provided for electing the President. No doubt we shall, warned by this danger, provide, by amendments of the Constitution, or by proper legislation, against a recurrence of the danger.

DECODED Fair and free elections are the bedrock of American democracy. Hayes understood that a disputed election was a danger to the nation. Here he expressed hope that changes would be made so that the events of 1876 would never be repeated.

Congress passed the Electoral Commission Act on January 29, 1877, which created a commission of fifteen people that would decide who would be president. The Senate chose five senators; the House chose five representatives; and the Supreme Court chose five associate justices.

To decide which slate of electors it should recognize so they could count the votes for president, the commission had to look at the voting in each state. Democrats claimed that Republicans had committed fraud by throwing out Democratic ballots until they had enough votes to win. Republicans claimed that Democrats had committed fraud by keeping freedmen (who would have voted Republican) away from the polls, stealing the election in the first place.

The commission first decided that Florida's legitimate slate of electors was the pro-Hayes slate, and then they came to the same conclusion for Louisiana, Oregon, and South Carolina. On March 2, 1877, a joint session of Congress declared Rutherford B. Hayes to be the next president.

Historians believe that the price of getting Democrats to accept the commission's decision was a deal struck between Republicans and Democrats: Republicans agreed to Democrats' demands to locate a transcontinental railroad in the South, where it would help their supporters. And, more significantly, Republicans agreed to pull federal troops out of former Confederate states. That shifted power back into the hands of state officials—many of whom had fought to keep people enslaved only a decade before. White Southerners saw it as a restoration of their political rights; Black Southerners saw it as a catastrophe. This settlement came to be known as the Compromise of 1877—and it marked the end of Reconstruction.

RECONSTRUCTION ENDS

Mr. President

Once he was in office, Hayes tried to reform the civil service, which is the group of people working for the government who are hired, rather than being elected. Some people, like the powerful New York Senator Roscoe Conkling, gave out civil service jobs as a form of patronage. (*Patronage* means awarding jobs and contracts to your supporters.) Hayes thought these jobs should go to whoever would do them best.

During Hayes's first summer in office, railroad workers went on strike after the B&O Railroad announced the second pay cut in less than a year because of an economic downturn that had begun in 1873. This was the Great Railroad Strike of 1877. Workers in Martinsburg, West Virginia, went on strike first, and workers in other states quickly joined. The work stoppage had a major impact on rail traffic in the East and Midwest and lasted for several weeks. President Hayes sent in troops and crushed the strike, but it was a turning point in labor history as workers realized they had power when they worked together.

Hayes had wanted to become president in part to protect freedmen. But the deal that he made in order to take office required abandoning them. Hayes had agreed to withdraw federal troops from the South, ending Reconstruction and handing control back to state governments. This led to increased repression of freedmen, loss of voting rights for Black people, and the passage of local and state laws that made racial segregation and discrimination legal. The Fourteenth Amendment guaranteed equal protection for all citizens and the Fifteenth Amendment recognized Black voting rights, but both became unenforceable in the South. It would take another century—and the Civil Rights Movement—before Black Americans regained the rights they lost when Grant left office.

In 1877, a brief war over land with the Nimiipuu (Nez Perce) nation in the Pacific Northwest ended with the Nimiipuu being forced onto a reservation in Idaho.

But President Hayes thought that the reservation system was a failure: Indigenous people didn't stay on the reservations and white people didn't stay off the land. His answer was to move toward mainstreaming Indigenous people into American life as individuals, and he thought that land ownership and education would be key to that effort. The Carlisle Indian Industrial School in Pennsylvania became the most well-known boarding school for Indigenous children. It tried to strip them of their cultural identity and national affiliation. They weren't allowed to speak their native languages or practice their religions in an effort to mainstream them into white society. The boarding school program was traumatic for many Indigenous children and communities.

Hayes was a "sound money" man; he wanted paper currency to be backed by gold reserves so that banks had a dollar's worth of gold for each paper dollar in circulation. Congress wanted to allow unlimited coinage of silver, which would help people who were in debt, like farmers—and did so, over Hayes's veto. Hayes also vetoed a bill restricting Chinese immigration. Congress was unable to override that veto, and the bill died.

In 1879, Hayes signed the "Lockwood Bill," which allowed women to argue in front of the Supreme Court. Attorney Belva Lockwood had petitioned for the right. Her petition was dismissed, not because she didn't have the ability or education, but because she was a woman. Chief Justice Morrison Waite remarked that the Supreme Court wouldn't change its policy unless required by law to do so. Lockwood lobbied tirelessly for the government to take action. Congress passed the law and President Hayes signed it.

Belva Lockwood

Legacy

Hayes had said that he didn't want to run for a second term, and he didn't. When his term was over he retired to Spiegel Grove in Fremont, Ohio, and worked quietly for veterans' organizations and the education of underprivileged children. Hayes died at the age of seventy and is best remembered for the botched election that brought him to office. Hayes' election marked the end of Reconstruction. Although he was genuinely concerned about freedmen, withdrawal of federal troops from the South was a disaster for Black Americans. Hayes had been a courageous soldier and he was a decent and intelligent man. Most historians rank him in the lower half of presidents, however.

JAMES A. GARFIELD

BORN: 1831

DIED: 1881

IN OFFICE: March 4, 1881–September 19, 1881

FROM: Ohio

VICE PRESIDENT: Chester Alan Arthur

PARTY: Republican

DID YOU KNOW?

- Garfield was the first president whose mother came to his inauguration.

- Garfield was named for an older brother who had died as a toddler. Reusing names in that way was a common practice in the nineteenth century, when so many children died young.

- Garfield was the second president to be assassinated (and the fourth to die in office). Part of Garfield's spine, showing the passage of the bullet that killed him, is in the collection of the National Museum of Health and Medicine.

- Lucretia Garfield volunteered with the Red Cross during World War I. She was eighty-two when the war started. (Clara Barton had organized the Red Cross in May 1881, during James Garfield's brief time in office.)

Lucretia Garfield

Life Before the Presidency

James Garfield was the youngest of five children, and his father died when James was a year old. As a child, he attended school for a few months in the winters and spent the rest of his time working on the family's farm. He met his wife, Lucretia, at school and they had a long courtship before marrying in 1858. Both the Garfields were teachers for a time, with James teaching a number of subjects, especially languages. (He knew Latin, Greek, and German.) He became a lawyer and in 1859 was elected to the Ohio state senate on a strong anti-slavery platform. In 1860, he campaigned for Abraham Lincoln, and the next year, when the Civil War started, he joined the Ohio Volunteer Infantry as a colonel and fought in some of the bloodiest battles of the war.

Garfield was elected to the US House of Representatives in 1862, but didn't take his seat until the end of 1863 because of the Civil War. He was a member of the electoral commission that Congress created to straighten out the disputed Hayes-Tilden election of 1876. In 1880, he was elected to the US Senate and would have taken office in March 1881—but in the summer of 1880, the Republican Party nominated him for the presidency. Garfield won the presidency in November and turned down the Senate seat. He had never lost an election. He took the presidential oath of office on the same day that he would have become a senator. It might have been a poor choice; he was assassinated later that year.

Letter from James Garfield to John Sherman, November 16, 1880

My Dear Sir:

The letter of Mr Hudson of Detroit, with your endorsement came duly to hand. I do not think there is any serious danger in the direction to which he refers—Though I am receiving, what I suppose to be the usual number of threatening letters on that subject. Assassination can no more be guarded against than death by lightning; and it is not best to worry about either. I expect to go to Washington before long to close up some household affairs—and I shall hope to see you.

DECODED John Sherman was a powerful senator from Ohio. He had forwarded a letter to Garfield from a Mr. Hudson of Detroit, who was afraid that Garfield was in danger of assassination. Garfield wasn't concerned. He took few measures to ensure his own safety, and here he replies, dismissing the concerns. He was shot ten months later.

Mr. President

Garfield was the second of the three presidents in 1881. He took office after Rutherford B. Hayes, and his vice president, Chester Arthur, succeeded him. He was in office for four months before he was shot, and he lived for another ten weeks after that. He didn't have time to do much.

Still, a scandal came to light early in his term, called the Star Route case. The US Post Office had set up Star Routes, which were contracts with private companies (stagecoaches, for example) to deliver mail in areas that were remote or hard to get to. The contracts to deliver mail on these routes were being awarded corruptly, and some of the companies that got Star Route contracts were being paid far more than was reasonable. Garfield ordered the case to be prosecuted even though it looked like his campaign manager was involved.

He also tried to get legislation passed to reform the civil service. The civil service of his time was ruled by patronage. The Republican Party divided into two factions on the issue of patronage: the Stalwarts, who supported the patronage system, and the Half-Breed Republicans, who opposed it. The Half-Breed Republicans wanted to reform the civil service so that jobs were awarded based on merit and experience.

Garfield was a Half-Breed Republican, and his vice president, Chester A. Arthur, was a Stalwart.

On July 2, 1881, just after Garfield arrived at the Washington, DC, train station, a man named Charles Guiteau shot him twice. Guiteau then shouted that he was a Stalwart and "Arthur is president now!" Guiteau had previously tried to get an ambassadorship under Garfield, although he had no qualifications or experience.

Letter from Charles Guiteau to James Garfield

I hereby make a formal application for the Austrian Mission. I feel I have a right to do it on account of my services during the canvass; also, on account of having called Gen. Garfield's attention to it just after the October elections; and in January, and also recently. I ask this as a personal tribute. . . . So long as Mr. Kasson wished to remain at Vienna I had no disposition to disturb him; but now, that he has resigned I feel I have a right to press my claim.

DECODED Charles Guiteau didn't have much education and certainly had no experience in foreign affairs or governmental service, but he felt that he had a right to be the ambassador to Austria. That's what the "Austrian Mission" means. His reference to the "canvass" means the campaign, but he didn't do much to help with that. When he didn't get the post he wanted—which he was wildly unqualified for—he murdered the president. Guiteau was hanged on June 30, 1882.

Garfield did not die immediately. The first bullet had grazed his shoulder but the second was lodged near his pancreas, resting against an artery. Garfield was moved to the White House and then by train to the seaside resort in New Jersey where his wife was recuperating from malaria. Attempts to find the bullet in his body failed, although doctors called in Alexander Graham Bell, who brought an early metal detector that he passed over the president's body. (The metal detector failed because there were metal coils under the mattress.)

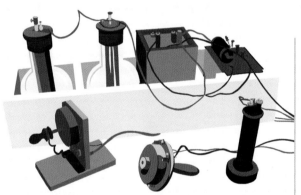

Garfield lingered in pain for weeks before dying. Medical historians disagree on whether he died from the attempts to extract the bullet, medications he was given, or an aneurysm caused by the pressure of the bullet on his artery, but most agree that his medical treatment made his condition worse.

Memoir of Thomas Donaldson

As to the Doctors, there are too many of them— and there should have been a corps of trained nurses. If he dies it will be by reason of fear on the part of the Doctors. If it had been myself or an ordinary man we would have been out long ago.

DECODED Medical historians agree with Garfield's friend Thomas Donaldson: If the doctors had left Garfield alone, he probably would have lived.

Legacy

James Garfield opposed slavery and fought against it on the battlefield as a soldier. He also wanted government to be more honest and was known as a reformer. He tried to make sure that people with government jobs were competent, and that's what got him killed. He was an honest and intelligent person, but today we remember him most for his lingering death. Garfield survived the Civil War—but not the presidency.

BORN: 1829

DIED: 1886

IN OFFICE:
September 20, 1881–
March 4, 1885

FROM: Vermont

VICE PRESIDENT:
none

PARTY: Republican

CHESTER A. ARTHUR

DID YOU KNOW?

● Arthur was the child of an immigrant. His father came to the United States from Ireland.

● Arthur was sworn in as president at his New York home in the middle of the night after James Garfield died.

● Arthur's wife died at the age of forty-two after a very brief illness and never saw him become vice president or president. In her memory, he purchased a stained glass window showing the Resurrection for St. John's Church, located near the White House. He asked the church to put the window on the south side so that he could see it in the evenings from the White House.

Life Before the Presidency

Chester Arthur was one of eight children. His father was a minister and strong abolitionist. Arthur was a decent but not exceptional student, and he became a schoolteacher and lawyer in New York. He worked on a case trying to free seven enslaved people whose enslaver had moved them through New York, which was free territory. His firm won that case and another that resulted in New York City railroad companies letting Black people sit in any seat on a streetcar instead of having to sit in a designated area.

During the Civil War, Arthur was in charge of housing and supplies for New York troops, a job he did well. In 1871, President Grant made him the collector of the Port of New York. Arthur supervised thousands of employees and controlled the customs money coming in at America's biggest East Coast port. It was a powerful position. He collected customs money honestly but gave jobs to more people than were needed as a way of getting support for Roscoe Conkling, a political boss with enormous power in New York.

Conkling didn't get the Republican presidential candidate he wanted in 1880. To make it up to him, the party nominated Arthur, who was one of Conkling's men, as vice president on James Garfield's ticket. As vice president, Arthur continued to agree with Roscoe Conkling and to oppose reform of the partronage system. Since Garfield was pro-reform, the president and vice president disagreed on a major issue of the day.

Roscoe Conkling

ARTHUR'S ADDRESS UPON TAKING OFFICE, SEPTEMBER 22, 1881

Men may die, but the fabrics of our free institutions remain unshaken. No higher or more assuring proof could exist of the strength and permanence of popular government than the fact that though the chosen of the people be struck down his constitutional successor is peacefully installed without shock or strain except the sorrow which mourns the bereavement.

DECODED The peaceful transfer of power is one of the most important aspects of the American political system. Although James Garfield and Chester Arthur were both Republicans, Garfield was a Half-Breed Republican, meaning that he was pro-reform, and Chester Arthur was a Stalwart. So when Arthur suddenly became president, power shifted to a different group even though it stayed within the same party. Arthur here comments on the importance of government elected by the people.

Mr. President

Chester Arthur was an accidental president; he reached office because of Garfield's assassination. When Arthur took over as president, many people didn't expect much from him. But he surprised everyone by switching positions and becoming pro-reform.

During this time, Reformers, known as Half-Breed Republicans, wanted to change the civil service system so that the most qualified candidates got the jobs; they thought that would be best for the country. Reformers were stunned when Arthur, who had been close to Conkling, suddenly agreed with them.

One possible explanation for the surprising shift is Arthur's diagnosis with kidney disease around the time he became president. The illness was expected to kill him within a few years, and he was sick most of the time he was in office. Maybe he decided to do what he thought was right since there was no point storing up future favors by putting incompetent people in office. He wasn't going to have a future.

Arthur used the national grief over Garfield's death to get legislation passed. In 1883, Congress passed the Pendleton Act, which established a bipartisan Civil Service Commission. (*Bipartisan* means both parties working together.) It also made it illegal to force someone who held a government job to contribute to a political group. (Sometimes people were required to give a small part of their salary back to the political party that had given them the job.) The act also called for competitive exams for some government jobs and protected people from losing their jobs for political reasons.

PENDLETON ACT, 1883

First, for open, competitive examinations for testing the fitness of applicants for the public service now classified or to be classified here under. Such examinations shall be practical in their character, and so far as may be shall relate to those matters which will fairly test the relative capacity and fitness of the persons examined to discharge the duties of the service into which they seek to be appointed.

NEWS TIMES

CIVIL SERVICE REFORM PASSED

DECODED The Pendleton Act required some government positions to be filled by the most qualified person who wanted the job, as judged by a test. And the test should relate to the job in question.

Congress also passed the first general federal law on immigration during Arthur's presidency. It prevented poor people, criminals, and the mentally ill from immigrating to the United States. And in 1882, they put in place the Chinese Exclusion Act, which kept Chinese people from immigrating. Chinese immigration had begun in the 1850s, and some American workers were afraid that they would lose their jobs to Chinese immigrants. The exclusion was supposed to last for ten years, but Congress later made it permanent. (It was ended in 1943 during World War II.)

CHINESE EXCLUSION ACT, 1882

(SEC. 1) . . . [T]he coming of Chinese laborers to the United States be, and the same is hereby, suspended; and during such suspension it shall not be lawful for any Chinese laborer to come, or having so come after the expiration of said ninety days to remain within the United States.

SEC. 14. That hereafter no State court or court of the United States shall admit Chinese to citizenship; and all laws in conflict with this act are hereby repealed.

DECODED Tensions between American workers and Chinese immigrants and racial prejudice led to the Chinese Exclusion Act. The act was an effort that had been under way for years—President Hayes had vetoed an earlier attempt to ban Chinese immigration. In 2011, the Senate unanimously passed a resolution apologizing for the Act.

Legacy

Chester Arthur was the unlikeliest champion of reform, but he helped clean up corruption and make the government more competent and efficient. He did better than most people expected, but historians still rank him in the lower half of presidents. Arthur didn't do much after he left office in 1885—he died in 1886.

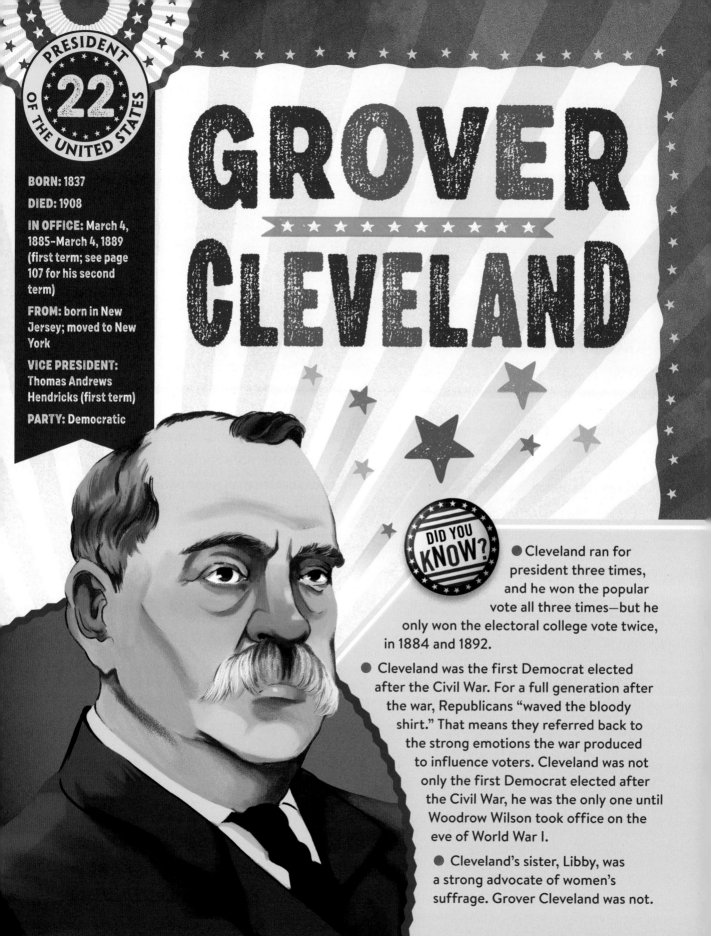

GROVER CLEVELAND

BORN: 1837

DIED: 1908

IN OFFICE: March 4, 1885–March 4, 1889 (first term; see page 107 for his second term)

FROM: born in New Jersey; moved to New York

VICE PRESIDENT: Thomas Andrews Hendricks (first term)

PARTY: Democratic

DID YOU KNOW?

● Cleveland ran for president three times, and he won the popular vote all three times—but he only won the electoral college vote twice, in 1884 and 1892.

● Cleveland was the first Democrat elected after the Civil War. For a full generation after the war, Republicans "waved the bloody shirt." That means they referred back to the strong emotions the war produced to influence voters. Cleveland was not only the first Democrat elected after the Civil War, he was the only one until Woodrow Wilson took office on the eve of World War I.

● Cleveland's sister, Libby, was a strong advocate of women's suffrage. Grover Cleveland was not.

Life Before the Presidency

Grover Cleveland was the fifth of nine children born to a Presbyterian minister and his wife. His father died when he was sixteen, and Cleveland had to work to help support his family. He eventually became a bookkeeper for his uncle, which gave him enough time to study, and he became a lawyer. He opposed Abraham Lincoln's candidacy and in 1863 was drafted by the Union Army—but he didn't go. The Conscription Act, which drafted men to be soldiers for the war, allowed a person to pay the government $300 to get out of going to war, or to pay someone else to go in their place. Cleveland paid $150 to a Polish immigrant to take his spot.

Cleveland continued with his career in law and politics. He earned a reputation for resisting patronage in New York, a state that was dominated by Roscoe Conkling and his political machine.

Cleveland ran for president in 1884. His opponent, James G. Blaine, was expected to win. But a few days before the election a Protestant minister made a speech in which he called Cleveland's party, the Democrats, the party of "rum, Romanism, rebellion." *Rum* meant alcohol; the idea was that Democrats didn't support temperance, an anti-alcohol campaign. *Romanism* meant Roman Catholicism. The mid-nineteenth century had seen a huge influx of Catholic immigrants who were met by an anti-immigrant and anti-Catholic backlash. *Rebellion* meant the Civil War. Democrats had split over slavery and secession, but some Northern Democrats became Republicans when that party was formed in the late 1850s, and many others voted with the Republicans because they opposed secession. The anti-Cleveland speech pointed to Democrats as having favored the Confederacy. The comment irritated many immigrants, and they responded by registering to vote. Blaine lost New York State as a result—and that gave the presidential election to Cleveland.

Mr. President

When he came into office, Cleveland had support from some immigrants because he was anti-temperance. For many immigrants the local pub was a place to socialize and get news from home. While advocates of temperance saw pubs as immoral places, most immigrants saw them as an important part of their social life. Cleveland lost the support of many Civil War veterans, however. In 1887, when Congress passed a bill giving pensions to Civil War veterans for disabilities that weren't caused by army service, Cleveland vetoed it. (In fact, he vetoed 584 of the bills Congress sent him; of all the bills ever vetoed, more than 20 percent were vetoed by Grover Cleveland. He rejected almost as many bills as Franklin Roosevelt—and Roosevelt was elected four times.)

Cleveland also vetoed a bill that would have provided drought relief for western farmers. He didn't think that was the federal government's role.

While Cleveland didn't put forward many new initiatives, he did support the Dawes Severalty Act of 1887. This act continued the effort to strip Indigenous people of their identities and cultures and integrate them into American life as individuals. The act allowed land that was held collectively by nations to be broken up and sold to Indigenous people as individual allotments—

SENATE DEBATE, FEBRUARY 23, 1887, ON A BILL FOR THE RELIEF OF THOMAS S. HOPKINS

The PRESIDENT *pro tempore*. Two-thirds of the Senate having voted in favor of the passage of the bill, it is passed, the objections of the President of the United States to the contrary notwithstanding.

DECODED In 1887, the Senate debated a bill to help Thomas S. Hopkins. He suffered from a severe case of "nervous exhaustion" that began during the Civil War and worsened until he was fully disabled. Senator Henry W. Blair of New Hampshire introduced a bill that would give a pension to any veteran disabled during or after the war. That would greatly expand the number of pensions the government was paying, and Cleveland vetoed the bill. It didn't matter, though—when Benjamin Harrison became president in 1889, he signed the Blair bill.

SENATE DEBATE ON THE DAWES ACT, FEBRUARY 23, 1887

Senator John Tyler Morgan (AL): The abuses under the judicial power of the United States in Indian country are simply horrible. They violate every instinct of Christian civilization. . . . There is no bill that may concern those Indians that is so material to their welfare as this bill. . . . They deserve the consideration of this country. . . . [I]n their constitution, in their laws, in their civil polity, in their courts, and in every other institution that they have established there they have shown remarkable wisdom and remarkable excellence of judgment in the control of their government. So I hope the Senate will not adopt a system that is contrary to the one which is recommended by the Judiciary Committee. . . .

DECODED The Dawes Act is generally considered today to have been harmful to Indigenous people. Cleveland thought Indigenous people needed government oversight, in part to protect them from people trying to get their land. He favored the Dawes Act, which was intended to integrate Indigenous people into society in general—with the loss of their traditional cultures. Here Senator Morgan of Alabama, who had been a Confederate general and enslaved people, speaks in favor of the Dawes Act. Morgan noted the abuses of Indigenous people, said they were not at fault, and urged passage of the Dawes Act. He felt the Act would be beneficial to them, although it is widely criticized today.

and the leftover could be sold to white people. The result was that Indigenous people lost more land.

Cleveland appointed former Confederates to federal positions and returned captured Confederate battle flags, rousing fierce opposition. He opposed the protections of Black Americans' rights, including voting rights, and considered the freedmen's status to be a social problem that legislation couldn't solve. He also opposed integrating schools. The period after Reconstruction saw many instances of violence against Black people and the constant threat of lynching. Cleveland was not sympathetic to Black Americans' calls for justice and took a hands-off approach throughout his terms in office.

Cleveland also remained silent on the women's suffrage movement as it gained momentum, with advocates calling for voting rights for women at the state and national level.

Cleveland signed the Interstate Commerce Act of 1887, which regulated the railroad industry. Railroads had been charging different rates for different customers. It was the first industry to come under federal regulation. The act also established the Interstate Commerce Commission to provide oversight.

One more significant thing happened during Cleveland's first term: He got married. It was one of the most popular things he did

as president. Frances Folsom was the twenty-one-year-old daughter of his former law partner. They married on June 2, 1886, in the Blue Room at the White House. Frances became the youngest First Lady in US history. She was also the first First Lady to remarry. (Cleveland died in 1908, and she remarried in 1913.)

Legacy

Cleveland usually gets low marks for his treatment of Civil War veterans, especially since he avoided service himself, and lower marks for his policies toward Black and Indigenous Americans. His marriage, however, delighted people and they were fascinated by his young bride. Cleveland ran in the 1888 election against Benjamin Harrison. Harrison won because he had more electoral college votes, although Cleveland won the popular vote. When Cleveland ran again in 1892, the outcome was different—and he made his way back to the presidency—the only president to serve two nonconsecutive terms.

BENJAMIN ★ HARRISON

BORN: 1833

DIED: 1901

IN OFFICE: March 4, 1889–March 4, 1893

FROM: born in Ohio; moved to Indiana

VICE PRESIDENT: Levi P. Morton

PARTY: Republican

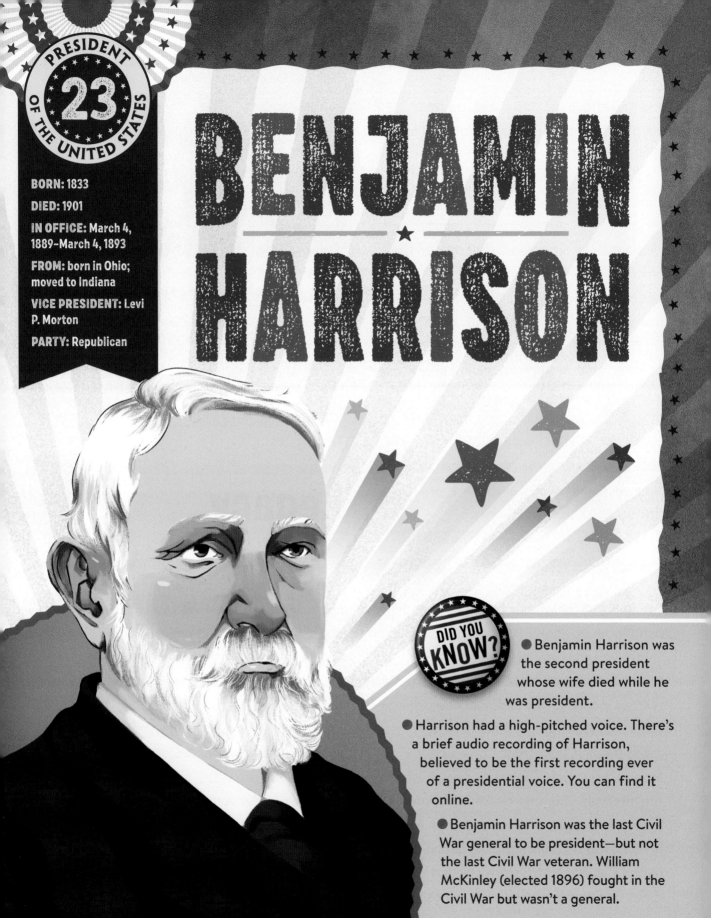

DID YOU KNOW?

● Benjamin Harrison was the second president whose wife died while he was president.

● Harrison had a high-pitched voice. There's a brief audio recording of Harrison, believed to be the first recording ever of a presidential voice. You can find it online.

● Benjamin Harrison was the last Civil War general to be president—but not the last Civil War veteran. William McKinley (elected 1896) fought in the Civil War but wasn't a general.

Life Before the Presidency

Benjamin Harrison's great-grandfather signed the Declaration of Independence. His grandfather, William Henry Harrison, had been president forty-eight years before. And his father was a congressional representative. Perhaps this impressive family history gave Harrison his characteristic self-confidence. Whatever the reason, he sometimes came off as aloof or arrogant. Harrison studied law and practiced in Indianapolis, Indiana; he prosecuted the first woman convicted of murder in Indiana. He campaigned for Abraham Lincoln, and during the Civil War he fought for the Union. He served under General William Tecumseh Sherman in his Atlanta campaign and was one of the first troops to enter Atlanta after it surrendered.

Harrison ran for Indiana governor in 1876. His chances were hurt by the Republicans' temperance platform, which drove drinkers away, and he lost.

Harrison rebounded to serve in the US Senate from 1881 to 1887. He opposed the Chinese Exclusion Act of 1882, which ended Chinese immigration. And he disagreed with Grover Cleveland on the issue of Civil War pensions; perhaps because he had served, Harrison supported the pensions. In the 1888 presidential election he beat Grover Cleveland in the electoral college, although Harrison had one hundred thousand fewer popular votes.

Mr. President

During Benjamin Harrison's presidency things got bigger. More new states were admitted into the Union than in any other presidency: North Dakota, South Dakota, Montana, Washington, Idaho, and Wyoming.

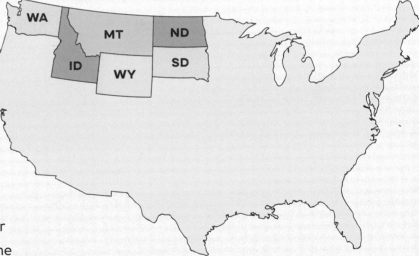

Some businesses were becoming so large that Congress passed the Sherman Antitrust Act in 1890 to keep them from forming monopolies. (If a company has a monopoly, it controls an area of production, like making cars. A monopoly reduces competition and gives consumers fewer choices.) The Sherman

Antitrust Act made companies compete freely. The Act was weak, but it was an important first step. And the nation's budget passed a billion dollars for the first time in peacetime.

Harrison signed two major pieces of legislation. The first was the McKinley Tariff Act, which established the highest tariff in US history. It raised rates on goods being imported into the United States by an average of almost 50 percent. (For example, if the tariff on imported toys had been $2, it could now be almost $3. Businesses paying those higher costs would raise the price of their products, passing the expense on to the people buying them.) Some people in Congress opposed the McKinley Tariff because it would hurt consumers. Since those people also wanted to back paper dollars with silver, Congress passed the Sherman Silver Purchase Act, which allowed banks to back paper dollars with silver as well as gold. That way both sides got something they wanted.

Harrison also signed the Forest Reserve Act, which gave the president the authority to set aside forest land for conservation. The act addressed concerns about how much logging was taking place. Harrison used the act seventeen times, the first time to create a forest reserve in Wyoming.

THE FOREST RESERVE ACT OF 1891, MARCH 3, 1891

The President of the United States may, from time to time, set apart and reserve, in any state or territory having public land bearing forests, in any part of the public lands, wholly or in part covered with timber or undergrowth, whether of commercial value or not, as public reservations; and the President shall, by public proclamation, declare the establishment of such reservations and the limits thereof.

DECODED The Forest Reserve Act was a rider (that is, a small addition to a different bill) that gave the president power to set up forest reserves from public land.

Harrison supported the Federal Elections Bill in 1890, which would have given the federal government oversight of elections. After the Civil War, Black Americans' rights were guaranteed at the federal level and violated at the state level, so favoring federal control generally meant helping Black people, and favoring states' rights meant allowing Black people's rights to be violated. The Federal Elections Bill didn't get through Congress, in part because few people saw it as a high priority. Harrison was a strong supporter of Black voting rights and was disappointed by the failure. He was able to appoint the great abolitionist speaker Frederick Douglass to be ambassador to Haiti, representing the United States at a time when Black people were seldom given positions of leadership and visibility.

Significant events in the West occurred during Harrison's term. Throughout its history America had had a frontier, a line where white and Black settlement ended. By 1890, the frontier had closed. That meant that the average number of people living per square mile was high enough that no part of the country could be considered unsettled. It was a shock. For white and Black people, it felt like the end of something important. For Indigenous people, it was a stark indication of how much they had lost.

In foreign policy, Harrison was in favor of American expansion. When a group of American planters overthrew the Hawaiian queen and replaced her with a government that did not represent, and was not supported by, the people of Hawaii, Harrison sent 150 marines to protect the new government. When the new Hawaiian government requested that the United States annex Hawaii, Harrison agreed. (When Grover Cleveland won the 1892 election, though, he withdrew the proposal.)

HARRISON'S INAUGURAL ADDRESS
MARCH 4, 1889

Shall the prejudices and paralysis of slavery continue to hang upon the skirts of progress? . . .

Is it not quite possible that the farmers and the promoters of the great mining and manufacturing enterprises which have recently been established in the South may yet find that the free ballot of the workingman, without distinction of race, is needed for their defense as well as for his own? I do not doubt that if those men in the South . . . would courageously avow and defend their real convictions they would not find it difficult, by friendly instruction and cooperation, to make the black man their efficient and safe ally, not only in establishing correct principles in our national administration, but in preserving for their local communities the benefits of social order and economical and honest government. At least until the good offices of kindness and education have been fairly tried the contrary conclusion can not be plausibly urged.

DECODED Harrison tried, unsuccessfully, to protect Black voting rights. Here he points out that the economic interests of Black Southerners were the same as those of white Southerners, and restricting the Black vote didn't make much sense. He felt that Black people and white people could work together—and that white people couldn't say they weren't able to live peacefully together until they'd actually tried it.

Harrison had a difficult situation with Italy in 1891. A popular New Orleans police chief was murdered, and Italian immigrants were arrested for the crime. Several of them were found not guilty at trial, a verdict many people thought the jury had reached because it had been threatened. A mob pulled eleven people who had been charged with the murder out of jail and lynched them. Italy threatened war on the United States in response to the lynchings. Harrison smoothed things over with a payment to Italy and by establishing Columbus Day to honor the Italian explorer.

Harrison also expanded the navy. At the end of the Civil War, the United States had the strongest navy in the world. But it didn't maintain it and by the time Harrison came to office, the US Navy didn't have any battleships. Harrison called for a two-coast navy, capable of dealing with threats in the Atlantic and the Pacific. Nineteen ships were built during Harrison's term in office, and eighteen more began construction. It was a remarkable increase in naval power in a short period of time, and the first time the United States stationed a sizable fleet in the Pacific.

Harrison also dealt with a crisis with Chile in 1891 after two American sailors were killed in a brawl there. The two nations almost went to war over the event, but Harrison was able to get an apology and payments for damages from Chile. And the first Pan-American Congress was held in Washington in 1889, designed to improve relations with Southern and Central American nations.

Benjamin Harrison ran against Grover Cleveland again in 1892. And while Harrison had beaten Cleveland in 1888, this time Cleveland won.

South America

Chile

BENJAMIN HARRISON'S THIRD ANNUAL MESSAGE TO CONGRESS, DECEMBER 9, 1891

I strongly recommend that provision be made for improving the harbor of Pearl River and equipping it as a naval station.

DECODED Harrison is suggesting a naval base at Pearl Harbor. It wouldn't be built until 1908 during Theodore Roosevelt's presidency. In December 1941, Japan would bomb the base, and the United States would enter World War II.

Legacy

Harrison isn't remembered much today. His lack of personal warmth hurt his popularity, but he did an average job during an ordinary time. Harrison makes for a common trivia question: Who was the only president to serve between someone else's terms?

GROVER ★★★★★★★★★ CLEVELAND

BORN: 1837

DIED: 1908

IN OFFICE: March 4, 1893–March 4, 1897 (second term; see page 98 for his first term)

FROM: born in New Jersey; moved to New York

VICE PRESIDET: Adlai Stevenson (second term)

PARTY: Democratic

DID YOU KNOW?

- Cleveland's second and third children were born in the White House. His first, Ruth, was born between his terms as president. The fourth and fifth children were born after he left office for good.

- The Baby Ruth candy bar was named after President Cleveland's daughter.

Life Between Presidencies

Grover Cleveland is the only president to have had a life *between* being president. During this time he lived in New York City, where he enjoyed playing cribbage and attending plays.

Cleveland had lost to Benjamin Harrison in 1888, but the two competed again in 1892 and this time Cleveland won. The 1892 election was unusual because a third-party candidate gained some real attention. The Populist Party, sometimes called the People's Party, tried to represent farmers and workers with the Omaha Platform. It was a broad pro-reform agenda that included shorter work days and regulation of the railroads. The Populists lost, but many of the reforms they wanted would become law over the next few decades.

Mr. President

In 1893, right after he took office for the second time, Cleveland was diagnosed with cancer in his mouth. He had to have part of his upper jaw removed. A serious health threat to the president can cause the stock market to go down and people to panic, so Cleveland wanted to keep it secret. On July 1, 1893, he sailed off on the *Oneida*, a friend's yacht, allegedly for a vacation. Dr. Joseph D. Bryant performed surgery on the president on a moving ship. A second secret operation on July 17 removed the rest of the growth. Cleveland was fitted with a rubber jaw and returned to work.

A severe economic depression, called the Panic of 1893, began when several large businesses failed. Cleveland didn't think the federal government should aid impoverished Americans, and he didn't try to help struggling farmers or unemployed workers. The Panic affected all areas of the economy and was the worst depression in US history to that point. It caused industrial unrest, protests, and tremendous suffering among people who lost their jobs.

In 1894, the labor movement flexed its muscle when Pullman railway car workers went on strike. The American Railway Union went on strike, too, in support. It was a major strike that interfered with transportation and shipping in large parts of the country. It also interfered with delivery of the mail, and Cleveland used that issue as a pretext to send in federal troops to break up the strike.

Letter from Grover Cleveland to Illinois Governor John P. Altgeld, July 5, 1894, Regarding the Railroad Strike

Federal troops were sent to Chicago in strict accordance with the Constitution and laws of the United States upon the demand of the Post Office department that obstruction of the mails should be removed. . . .

DECODED Illinois Governor John P. Altgeld didn't want federal troops to come to his state to put down the railroad strike. Cleveland sent them anyway—and he didn't bother to tell the governor. Altgeld, a Democrat, had campaigned for Cleveland but now became convinced that the president was anti-labor.

Cleveland believed in the gold standard, the idea that paper money should be backed by an equal value of gold. He pushed back against the coinage of silver, and when the gold deposits became dangerously low he arranged for the rich industrialist J. P. Morgan to lend gold to the United States. That helped stabilize the supply, but many people were upset at the unequal distribution of wealth that made it possible for one person to lend $65 million in gold to the United States.

Cleveland opposed American expansion and imperialism. The Hawaiian queen, Lili'uokalani, had been overthrown in a coup led by American planters who wanted the United States to take over the islands because it would help their business interests. But Cleveland refused to annex the islands. He did, however, recognize the new Hawaiian government that they put in place.

The Panic of 1893 caused widespread suffering, and Cleveland's popularity sank. The Democratic Party didn't back him for president again in 1896.

Legacy

After he left office, Grover and Frances Cleveland moved to New Jersey. He vetoed a large number of bills in his second term, but not at the same level as he had before. The Panic of 1893 dominated his return to office, and most Americans were dissatisfied with how he handled it. Cleveland was a member of the Anti-Imperialist League, which opposed United States expansion. Some people felt that taking over other parts of the world, as European nations had done, would make the United States stronger and be an important step to international power and prestige. Cleveland wasn't one of them. Imperialism would become a major issue during William McKinley's presidency.

GROVER CLEVELAND'S STATEMENT ON THE OVERTHROW OF HAWAIIAN QUEEN LILI'UOKALANI, DECEMBER 18, 1893

By an act of war, committed with the participation of a diplomatic representative of the United States and without authority of Congress, the Government of a feeble but friendly and confiding people has been overthrown. A substantial wrong has thus been done which a due regard for our national character as well as the rights of the injured people requires we should endeavor to repair. The Provisional Government has not assumed a republican or other constitutional form, but has remained a mere executive council or oligarchy, set up without the assent of the people. It has not sought to find a permanent basis of popular support and has given no evidence of an intention to do so.

DECODED Cleveland here recognizes that the American planters who overthrew the Hawaiian queen did not have the support, or "the assent of the people", and had made no effort to set up a democratic government. He calls it a "substantial wrong." The annexation of Hawaii wouldn't occur until 1898, in William McKinley's presidency.

Hawaiian Queen Lili'uokalani

WILLIAM McKINLEY

BORN: 1843

DIED: 1901

IN OFFICE: March 4, 1897–September 14, 1901

FROM: Ohio

VICE PRESIDENT: Garret Augustus Hobart (first term), Theodore Roosevelt (second term)

PARTY: Republican

DID YOU KNOW?

● William McKinley was the last Civil War veteran to be president.

● McKinley had a pet parrot named Washington Post that could whistle "Yankee Doodle."

● Robert Todd Lincoln, Abraham Lincoln's eldest son, had close ties to three presidential assassinations. He was in Washington, DC, when his father was shot. He was at the Washington, DC, railroad station when James Garfield was shot. And he traveled to Buffalo the day that William McKinley was assassinated there.

Life Before the Presidency

William McKinley was the seventh of nine children. He had to drop out of college when he ran out of money, and he taught briefly. Then the Civil War started. McKinley served on the staff of future president Rutherford B. Hayes. He was promoted for bravery after the bloody Battle of Antietam and promoted again for gallant and meritorious service at the battles of Opequan, Fisher's Hill, and Cedar Creek. Friends called him "Major McKinley" for the rest of his life.

After the war, McKinley worked as a lawyer and was elected to the US House of Representatives in 1876. His tariff bill, the McKinley Tariff Act, was passed by Congress and set tariffs at an extremely high level. Raising tariffs helps a country's own industries because it makes foreign goods more expensive, so that consumers are less likely to buy the imported goods. The McKinley Tariff did result in higher prices on imported goods, which helped protect American industries—but it angered consumers because of the higher prices they had to pay. McKinley was voted out of office. He bounced back, though, winning a race for governor of Ohio in 1892.

A serious depression struck in 1893, and farmers in particular were hit hard. The Populist Party, or People's Party, formed, backed by people in the West and South who wanted aid for farmers and the coinage of silver. McKinley, the Republican candidate, favored business interests; his opponent, William Jennings Bryan, was pro-silver. Bryan was nominated by both the Democratic and Populist Parties. McKinley came out in favor of the gold standard and high tariffs, both positions that would aid big businesses but hurt farmers. He won the presidency in a close race.

Letter from a Former Civil War Comrade to William McKinley After His Election

I knew you as a soldier, as a congressman, as a governor, and now as president-elect. How shall I address you?

McKinley's Answer

Call me Major. I earned that. I am not so sure of the rest.

DECODED McKinley's old friends did continue to call him "Major" for decades after the Civil War. You can find examples in the Library of Congress.

Mr. President

William McKinley generally favored business interests and didn't support much government regulation of business. Many business monopolies were forming during this period, like Standard Oil, which had a monopoly in the oil industry.

One of the most shocking episodes in American electoral history happened while McKinley was president. On November 10, 1898, a mob of white people in Wilmington, North Carolina, murdered at least sixty people, overthrew the elected city government and replaced it with white supremacists, and destroyed a newspaper office. It was led by a former congressmen, Alfred Moore Waddell, and is the only coup d'état in US history. (The Wilmington Massacre didn't appear in textbooks for decades.)

McKinley's time in office was dominated by foreign policy, and it's what we remember most about him. Cuba was a Spanish colony. It tried to throw off Spanish rule, and American newspapers covered Cuban affairs closely—but not necessarily accurately. Newspapers of the time engaged in "yellow journalism"—reporting sensational stories to sell more papers while making misleading claims and not verifying facts with multiple sources. William Randolph Hearst and Joseph Pulitzer were prominent newspaper publishers locked in a bitter rivalry. They both published information about Spanish abuses of Cubans, like forcing Cubans into camps where thousands of them died.

Letter **from an Anonymous Woman of Wilmington, North Carolina, to William McKinley, November 13, 1898**

Can we call on any other Nation for help? Why do you forsake the Negro? Who is not to blame for being here. This Grand and Noble Nation who flies to the help of suffering humanity of another Nation? And leave the Secessionists and born Rioters to slay us. . . . When our parents belonged to them, why, the Negro was all right. Now, when they work and accumalate [sic] property they are all wrong. . . .

DECODED The United States had aided Cubans trying to gain independence from Spain—but wouldn't help its own citizens. Her reference to "Secessionists" means Confederates. Across the South, former Confederates took positions in local and state governments and police forces and used them to control—and terrorize—Black citizens. William McKinley did not provide federal protection or force Wilmington to reinstate the biracial elected government that Waddell's mob overthrew.

MAINE

The abuses were real, but they were presented in a scandalous and inflammatory way. And newspapers at this time were moving from headlines that covered only one column of type to headlines that ran across several columns or even the whole page. It gave people the impression that the news was more urgent, and it created a pro-war feeling among many Americans about Spain.

In February 1898, the US battleship *Maine* blew up in the harbor of Havana, Cuba. McKinley wanted to wait for the results of an inquiry into the cause of the mysterious explosion, but American sentiment was pro-war, especially since most people assumed that Spain had put mines in the harbor. Two hundred and sixty-six sailors were killed, including the US Navy's best baseball team.

In April 1898, President McKinley asked Congress to declare war on Spain. The Spanish-American War lasted only a few months and ended in a US victory—and new landholdings. Spain gave Guam and Puerto Rico to the United States and let it buy the Philippines. Cuba became a US protectorate, and the Platt Amendment gave the United States the right to intervene in Cuban domestic affairs in order to preserve Cuban independence until 1934. Three thousand Americans died in the war, the great majority of them from disease.

THE CALL, SAN FRANCISCO, FEBRUARY 18, 1898

A FLOATING TORPEDO DESTROYED THE MAINE

Seen by a Sailor on Board

Came From the Shore and Struck the Warship.

Then Was Perpetrated the Atrocious Crime for Which Spain Will Be Held by America to a Strict Accounting.

KEY WEST, FEB. 18 (3 a.m.)—Gradually the details connected with the disaster to the Maine are coming out, and as the facts become known they point more positively to the deliberate destruction of the vessel and the murder of her crew.

DECODED This San Francisco newspaper is reporting on the "atrocious crime" of the sinking of the *Maine*. President McKinley had fought in the Civil War and didn't want to go to war again, but the destruction of a battleship was an offense that couldn't be ignored. Later inquiries, however, didn't support the idea that Spain had mined Havana harbor. Today, historians think that ammunition in the ship's hold caught fire and exploded and that Spain had nothing to do with it.

PLATT AMENDMENT, MARCH 2, 1901

III. That the government of Cuba consents that the United States may exercise the right to intervene for the preservation of Cuban independence.

DECODED The Platt Amendment said that Cuba couldn't make any treaty that impaired its independence, let the US intervene to preserve Cuba's independence, and allowed the US to lease a naval base on Cuba. It contained seven provisions, and an eighth one saying that Cuba had to agree to it. Franklin Roosevelt canceled it in 1934, but the US still has a naval base at Guantánamo Bay.

McKinley favored expansion and empire. In 1898, the United States annexed Hawaii. And when Filipinos led by Emilio Aguinaldo revolted in 1899, wanting Philippine independence, McKinley sent in US troops to suppress the revolt. The United States was now a colonial power, and the war against Filipino independence killed more than five thousand Americans—and two hundred thousand Filipinos.

McKinley pushed for an "open door" policy with China. European nations had been trying to secure areas of China in which they could dominate trade.

United States, Territories, and Possessions

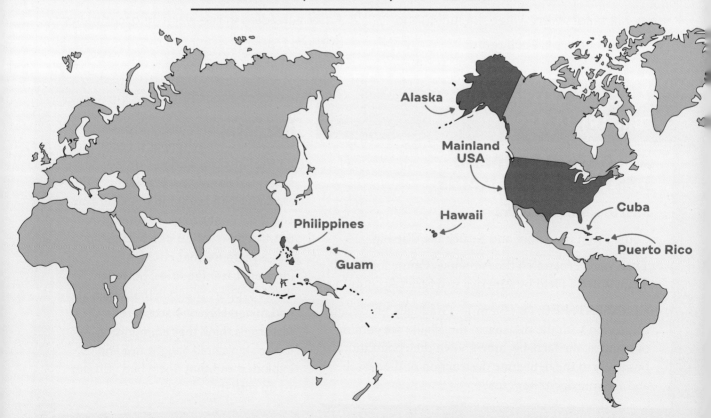

McKinley countered that nations should have equal trade opportunities in China and that the country should remain independent and not be colonized. In 1900, the Boxer Rebellion broke out in China. McKinley sent 2,500 American troops to China to rescue the diplomats, and he didn't consult Congress before he did it.

By 1900, the economy had recovered and the United States had become a major power on the world stage. When it came time for a reelection campaign, McKinley needed a new running mate because his first-term vice president, Garret Hobart, had died in office. Republican allies in New York wanted to move Theodore Roosevelt, their energetic, pro-reform governor, out of office, so McKinley took him on. The vice presidency seemed a good place to park Roosevelt because vice presidents seldom do much and don't have much power. Roosevelt was a strong candidate because he was a war hero and a pro-reform governor (which most people liked, even if certain New York Republicans did not). McKinley won in a landslide reelection victory.

In September 1901, McKinley gave a speech at the Pan-American Exposition in Buffalo, New York, a fair celebrating the nations of the Western Hemisphere. It would be his last. The next day, while McKinley was shaking hands with people at the exposition, a man named Leon Czolgosz came up and shot him with a gun hidden under a handkerchief. McKinley died of gangrene a week after the shooting.

Legacy

William McKinley is best remembered for his impact on foreign policy and the growth of American imperialism. He signed the bill annexing Hawaii. And he used the armed forces of the United States, a nation that itself had begun as a group of colonies fighting for independence, to put down an independence movement in the Philippines.

McKinley's reputation has changed in the more than twelve decades since his death. His legacy is American expansionism. How a person evaluates McKinley depends largely on whether they view that expansion as imperialistic overstep or a strategic approach to international security.

THEODORE ROOSEVELT

BORN: 1858

DIED: 1919

IN OFFICE:
September 14, 1901–
March 4, 1909

FROM: New York

VICE PRESIDENT:
Charles Warren
Fairbanks

PARTY: Republican

DID YOU KNOW?

- Roosevelt watched Lincoln's funeral procession as a young boy. There's a photograph that shows the procession near the Roosevelt house at the corner of Broadway and Union Square in New York. Roosevelt and his brother Elliott are in the window.

- Roosevelt was the first president to travel out of the country while he was in office. He went to Panama in 1906.

- The teddy bear is named for Roosevelt.

- Roosevelt was the youngest man to *serve* as president—he was forty-two when he took office after McKinley's assassination. (John F. Kennedy was the youngest person to be *elected* president—he was forty-three at the time of his inauguration.)

- Roosevelt was the first president to ride in an airplane.

Life Before the Presidency

Theodore Roosevelt was born to a wealthy family in New York. He was often ill as a child, was very smart, and loved to read. In his free time he learned French, German, and Latin, hunting, swimming, riding horses, taxidermy, plant identification, and more.

Roosevelt went to Harvard, where he joined several clubs, rowed, and boxed. He met and married Alice Hathaway Lee and wrote *The Naval War of 1812*. Roosevelt won a seat in the New York state legislature in 1881 and became known as a courageous reformer.

And then tragedy struck. His wife and mother died on the same day—Valentine's Day, 1884. A distraught Roosevelt ran back and forth between their rooms, trying to be with each as she died.

A grieving Roosevelt went west and worked on a ranch in Dakota territory, throwing himself into physical labor with the energy he brought to every job. At one point he tangled with a nine-foot grizzly bear.

In 1886, he married an old childhood friend, Edith Kermit Carow. They would have five children in addition to Alice, his daughter by his first wife. Roosevelt served on the Civil Service Commission that had been created under President Arthur. That got him appointed as the police commissioner of New York (1895–1897), where he continued to root out corruption, such as police officers blackmailing civilians. In 1897, President McKinley appointed him assistant secretary of the navy, and Roosevelt lobbied for a strong fleet that could support a more active US foreign policy. He successfully modernized and expanded the navy.

Theodore Roosevelt Diary Entry, February 16–17, 1884

. . . [W]e spent three years of happiness greater and more unalloyed than I have ever known fall to the lot of others; on Feb. 12th 1884 her baby was born and on Feb. 14th she died in my arms. . . . For joy or for sorrow my life has now been lived out.

DECODED Roosevelt wrote a brief biography of his wife that covered two pages.

Letter from Assistant Secretary of the Navy Theodore Roosevelt to Secretary of the Navy John D. Long, March 25, 1898

[I have seen] some interesting photographs of Professor Langley's flying machine. The machine has worked. It seems to me worth while for this government to try whether it will not work on a large enough scale to be of use in the event of war.

DECODED Orville and Wilbur Wright would make the first flight in 1903, beating Professor Samuel Langley, whose work Roosevelt talks about here. Roosevelt was right: Air power would become critical in the coming world wars.

When the Spanish-American War started, Roosevelt served as second-in-command of the First US Volunteer Cavalry—the Rough Riders—and he became a hero. In 2001, President Clinton awarded the Medal of Honor to Roosevelt posthumously—that is, after death—for his bravery in battle.

When he returned from the war, Roosevelt ran for governor of New York, and he won. He continued to fight corruption and improve working conditions. For example, he wanted employers to make payments when a worker was killed on the job so the worker's family didn't fall into poverty. He became tremendously popular with the people. But what made the people trust him, made him a problem for the corrupt officials and political bosses in New York. The Republicans nominated him as William McKinley's running mate in 1900 as a way to get him out of their way.

McKinley and Roosevelt won the election, but that September McKinley was shot. He seemed to be recovering, so Roosevelt went hiking in the Adirondacks. He was on his way down from the highest peak when a ranger ran up to him with a telegram saying that McKinley had died. Roosevelt hurried out of the mountains and took the oath of office while he was still in New York.

THEODORE ROOSEVELT'S SPEECH AT THE MINNESOTA STATE FAIR, SEPTEMBER 2, 1901

Right here let me make as vigorous a plea as I know how in favor of saying nothing that we do not mean, and of acting without hesitation up to whatever we say. A good many of you are probably acquainted with the old proverb: "Speak softly and carry a big stick—you will go far." . . . So it is with the nation.

DECODED Roosevelt was pro-expansion. He explained his foreign policy ideas with the proverb—speak softly and carry a big stick—and cartoons of the era often showed him with a giant bat over his shoulder. At the time he gave this speech he was the vice president; four days later McKinley was shot. McKinley would be dead in less than two weeks, and Roosevelt's foreign policy ideas suddenly became much more important.

Mr. President

Roosevelt had made a name for himself fighting corruption and supporting workers' rights in New York, and he carried those interests with him to the White House. He became a leader of the Progressive movement, which wanted a broad range of reforms related to worker rights and limiting abuses by big businesses and corrupt politicians. Wasting no time, Roosevelt announced in 1902 that the federal government would sue Northern Securities, a company created by two rival railroad companies working together in the northwestern United States. Northern Securities prevented competition and limited the choices available to the public and the rail workers. This violated the Sherman Antitrust Act. When a federal court ordered the company dissolved, the Supreme Court upheld the decision. This was called "trust-busting"—forcing huge companies that held virtual monopolies to break up into multiple smaller companies so they didn't have so much control over the economy and workers. Roosevelt earned a reputation as a trustbuster. He believed that the federal government should regulate businesses to protect the public welfare, especially as more people moved to cities and worked in factories.

Roosevelt secured passage of the Elkins Act (1903), which stopped railroads from giving lower rates to large companies that shipped bigger loads. That practice made small companies unable to compete. When railroad companies found ways to work around the Elkins Act, Roosevelt pushed for passage of the Hepburn Act, which would allow the Interstate Commerce Commission to regulate railroad rates. When Congress balked, Roosevelt took his case directly to the people, a tactic he'd used effectively in the New York state legislature. Roosevelt's political savvy got him what he wanted, and the Hepburn Act passed.

In 1902, nearly 150,000 Pennsylvania coal miners walked off the job, demanding higher wages, an eight-hour workday, and recognition of their union. Roosevelt threatened to send in federal troops to take over the mines from their owners. The owners, who had refused to talk to workers about their demands, now backed down and agreed to find a solution to the dispute. Roosevelt announced that the resulting compromise was a "square deal," or fair for everybody—and that came to be the nickname for his domestic program in general.

Roosevelt won a term of his own in a landslide victory in 1904. It was the largest margin of victory since James Monroe had run essentially unopposed in 1820, and he was the first vice president who was elevated on the death of a president to win the office himself.

In his second term, Roosevelt secured passage of the Pure Food and Drug Act of 1906. The act required accurate labels on products, and it prohibited the manufacture, sale, or interstate transportation of adulterated food, medicine, and liquor. Before this act was passed, food, beverages, and medicine could be full of things that would make people sick and the labels didn't have to show the ingredients accurately. He also signed the Meat Inspection Act to regulate the meatpacking industry. Many people had learned about meatpacking practices from Upton Sinclair's novel *The Jungle*, published in 1906. The book included a scene where raw meat is piled on a meatpacking factory floor, rats run through it, and workers sprinkle rat poison on the meat to kill them. Then they toss the whole thing in the sausage grinders—meat, rats, and poison. Americans were disgusted; their president did something about it.

Letter from Theodore Roosevelt to Upton Sinclair, March 15, 1906

I have now read, if not all, yet a good deal of your book, and if you can come down here during the first week in April I shall be particularly glad to see you. . . .

But all this has nothing to do with the fact that the specific evils you point out shall, if their existence be proved, and if I have power, be eradicated.

DECODED The book to which Roosevelt refers is *The Jungle*, in which Sinclair writes about the Chicago meatpacking industry in horrifying, stomach-churning detail. The book, and Roosevelt's response, led to the Meat Inspection Act of 1906.

Roosevelt's record on racial issues is mixed. While governor of New York he had ended school segregation in the state, and as president he appointed some Black people to patronage positions in the South. Those patronage jobs were much sought after, and they had generally gone to white people in the past. In 1901, Roosevelt invited Booker T. Washington to dinner at the White House. Washington was an important educator and Black leader, and Roosevelt wanted his advice. Southern newspapers erupted in fury, but Roosevelt refused to apologize.

Booker T. Washington

His legacy is tarnished by the Brownsville Incident, however. In 1906, some Black soldiers stationed in Brownsville, Texas, were accused of shooting two white men, killing one of them. The army assumed they were guilty despite the lack of physical evidence, and the president discharged three full companies of Black soldiers without a trial.

Roosevelt was a conservationist. He believed that natural resources should be used intelligently and in sustainable ways, and he preserved some areas from exploitation by private companies so that the land would remain untouched. When a speculator wanted to build businesses along the rim of the Grand Canyon, Roosevelt

★ ★

declared the site to be a national monument. Altogether Roosevelt created 150 new national forests and protected 230 million acres of land. He set up five national parks, fifty-one wildlife refuges, and eighteen national monuments.

Roosevelt's foreign policy was just as decisive. Under McKinley the United States had become an empire, with holdings in other parts of the world. Roosevelt was an expansionist and wanted to see the United States become a great power. Congress authorized him to negotiate with Colombia for land to create a canal in its Panama territory. This would allow ships to move between the Atlantic and Pacific oceans without going around South America. When the Colombian legislature demanded significantly more money from the United States in return for ratifying the treaty, Panama revolted, encouraged by Roosevelt, who sent a US warship to float off the coast and prevent Colombian troops from restoring order. Panama separated from Colombia and became an independent country, and Roosevelt got his treaty. The Panama Canal was finished in 1914.

In 1904, Roosevelt issued the Roosevelt Corollary to the Monroe Doctrine. The Dominican Republic wasn't able to pay debts to several European countries and defaulted, which means it wasn't going to try to repay what it owed. Britain, Germany, and Italy threatened to send their navies to take the money. Roosevelt worried that financial problems in general could lead to European intervention in the Americas. With the Monroe Doctrine, the United States had rejected European involvement in affairs in the Americas. The Roosevelt Corollary added to that, saying that the United States would intervene in any Latin American country that had serious economic problems in order to keep European countries out.

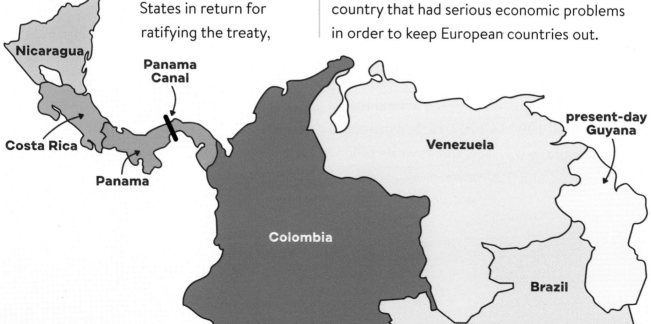

Nicaragua

Costa Rica

Panama

Panama Canal

Colombia

Venezuela

present-day Guyana

Brazil

Roosevelt wanted nations in the Americas to be independent, democratic, and prosperous, but the Roosevelt Corollary led to resentment in Latin America over the United States acting as the region's "policeman."

The United States had acquired the Philippines in the Spanish-American War (1898). Suppression of the Filipino resistance to US control caused suffering among civilians as well as soldiers on both sides. On July 4, 1902, Roosevelt issued an amnesty, which means a pardon, and declared the war to be over, although it occasionally flared up afterward. The United States recognized the Philippines' independence in 1946.

Roosevelt's foreign policy victories included his successful negotiation of an end to the Russo-Japanese War in 1905, for which he won a Nobel Peace Prize. Those countries had gone to war in 1904, and Roosevelt, worried about the balance of power being upset in the Pacific, pressured them to make peace. He also sent the "Great White Fleet"—a group of US Navy battleships—on a voyage around the world from 1907 to 1909. He had increased the size of the US Navy, and its world tour showcased American power.

Legacy

After finishing William McKinley's term and serving a term of his own, Roosevelt endorsed William Howard Taft as his successor and left on an African safari. Taft was duly elected, but he proved more conservative than Roosevelt and the two men split. Roosevelt tried to get the Republican nomination for president in 1912, but the Republicans backed Taft again. Roosevelt formed his own party, the Bull Moose Party, and ran against Republican Taft and Democrat Woodrow Wilson. His candidacy split the Republican vote, and Wilson won the presidency.

Theodore Roosevelt gets high marks from most historians. He was a leader in Progressive reforms, which helped ensure Americans' safety and welfare, and in the conservation movement. He moved to prevent large businesses from gaining too much power over the economy and their workers. And Roosevelt pursued an active role for the United States on the world stage.

WILLIAM H. TAFT

PRESIDENT 27 OF THE UNITED STATES

BORN: 1857

DIED: 1930

IN OFFICE: March 4, 1909–March 4, 1913

FROM: Ohio

VICE PRESIDENT: James S. Sherman

PARTY: Republican

DID YOU KNOW?

- Taft was a heavyweight wrestling champion in college.

- When he was secretary of war, Taft held the same cabinet position his father, Alphonso Taft, had once held.

- Helen Taft's memoirs were the first memoirs ever to be published by a First Lady.

- Helen Taft brought cherry trees to Washington, DC. Tourists still visit to see them blossom each spring.

- Taft is the only person to have been both president and chief justice of the Supreme Court.

Life Before the Presidency

Taft was a good student and hard worker. His father, Alphonso Taft, served in President Grant's cabinet and was an ambassador. William Howard Taft attended Yale University, became a lawyer, held several positions as a judge, and was a law school dean.

In 1900, President McKinley appointed Taft to be president of the Philippines Commission, which governed the Philippines, a territory the United States had gotten as a result of the Spanish-American War. In 1901, he became governor of the Philippines. McKinley told him to bring Filipinos into the government, but Taft brought in very few. He returned to the United States to serve as Theodore Roosevelt's secretary of war (1904–1908).

Mr. President

Theodore Roosevelt was such a popular president that whoever he picked to succeed him was likely to win. He chose Taft. Most people expected Taft to continue Roosevelt's policies—Roosevelt certainly did. Taft was more conservative than Roosevelt, though. When Congress passed the Payne-Aldrich Tariff Act in 1909, Taft signed the bill. The tariff act lowered the tariff on many goods but raised it on others and left the rate for most items unchanged. The Progressives, the core of the Republican Party under Roosevelt, had wanted to lower tariffs and were angry that the Payne-Aldrich Tariff Act didn't do what they wanted.

PAYNE-ALDRICH TARIFF ACT, 1909

. . . All paints, colors, pigments, stains, lakes, crayons, including charcoal crayons or fusains, smalts and frostings, whether crude or dry or mixed, or ground with water or oil or with solutions other than oil, not otherwise specially provided for in this section, thirty per centum ad valorem; all glazes, fluxes, enamels, and colors used in the manufacture of ceramic, enameled, and glass articles, thirty per centum ad valorem; . . .

DECODED Tariff bills are very specific. They have to be exact about the product being taxed as well as the amount of the tax, because if they aren't, people will try to get out of paying. Taft promised to lower tariffs while campaigning, but as president he signed the Payne-Aldrich Tariff Act, which didn't lower tariffs very much and actually raised rates on some goods.

Taft did continue some of Roosevelt's Progressive policies. When manufacturers tried to get around the Pure Food and Drug Act of 1906, which required accurate labeling of food products, President Taft had to request a report about whether bleached flour violated the Act.

The Sixteenth and Seventeenth Amendments were passed while Taft was in office. The Sixteenth Amendment allowed Congress to tax people's incomes. It was Taft's successor, Woodrow Wilson, who signed the Revenue Act of 1913, which established an income tax. The Seventeenth Amendment allowed people in each state to vote for their senators. Originally the state legislatures chose the senators.

Report from the Secretary of Agriculture, May 4, 1909, on whether Flour Bleached with Nitrogen Peroxide Is "Adulterated" under the Pure Food and Drug Act of 1906

Dear Mr. President:

In response to your request I submit the following report. . . . The bleaching of flour is accomplished by mechanically treating flour, after the milling process is complete, with various agents. . . . During the early part of 1908, flour bleached with nitrogen peroxid [sic] was made the subject of a thorough investigation by the Bureau of Chemistry of the Department of Agriculture. . . . The conclusions reached in the different investigations were uniform in every important particular. It was demonstrated that the bleaching process—. . . improves the color of clear or second quality flour, macaroni flour, allowing millers to mix flour of an inferior grade with flour of higher and more expensive grades. . . . Changes the constitution of the fat in the flour so as to injure the flavor when baked into bread. The injury to the flavor is not always apparent in bread made from moderately bleached flour, but bread made from overbleached flour is usually nauseating. . . . (It) is apparent that flour bleached with nitrogen peroxid [sic] is adulterated within the Food and Drugs Act of June 30, 1906.

DECODED Millers bleached flour with nitrogen peroxide, which left a residue in the bread and made the bread taste "nauseating"—but this process allowed bakers to mix cheap flour with better-quality flour without anyone knowing the difference. Reports like this were part of the Progressive emphasis on consumer protection in the early 1900s.

SEVENTEENTH AMENDMENT

The Senate of the United States shall be composed of two Senators from each state, elected by the people thereof, for six years; and each Senator shall have one vote.

DECODED As originally written, the Constitution (Article I, Section 3) gave state legislatures the power to elect each state's senators. In 1912, Congress passed the Seventeenth Amendment. (It was ratified and went into effect in 1913.) The amendment transferred the power to choose senators to the people, who would vote directly. Progressives thought that this would help reduce corruption in the election of senators.

Taft's handling of the Ballinger-Pinchot Affair, a land conservation issue, upset many people. A federal law stopped new land sales in Alaska in order to preserve some of the land. Anyone who had already made a land claim, however, would still have it processed. *Collier's* magazine ran an article saying that some friends of Richard Ballinger, the secretary of the interior, seemed to be trying to trick the government into okaying illegitimate claims, which Ballinger approved so that they got the land. The head of the US Forest Service, Gifford Pinchot, criticized Ballinger and then President Taft fired Pinchot. Theodore Roosevelt was outraged, as were most Progressives, who thought Taft had fired the wrong man. By the end of his term, Taft had protected almost as much public land as Roosevelt had, but the Ballinger-Pinchot Affair made people think Taft wasn't a good conservationist.

Roosevelt was upset about the Ballinger-Pinchot Affair and ran against Taft in 1912. Since the Republican vote was split between them, the Democratic candidate, Woodrow Wilson, won.

Legacy

After leaving office, Taft was a law professor at Yale University until President Warren G. Harding made him chief justice of the Supreme Court, a post he held from 1921 to 1930. He liked being a Supreme Court justice much more than being president. Taft had the temperament of a judge, not a president: He tried to see all sides of an issue, but he didn't act decisively, and he was a poor leader. Expected to follow Theodore Roosevelt's policies, Taft instead veered right; the Republican party developed a moderate branch, which was heir to Roosevelt, and a conservative branch, which was heir to Taft.

WOODROW ★★★★★★ WILSON

BORN: 1856

DIED: 1924

IN OFFICE: March 4, 1913–March 4, 1921

FROM: born in Virginia; grew up in Georgia

VP: Thomas Riley Marshall

PARTY: Democratic

DID YOU KNOW?

- Wilson was the first president who earned a doctoral (PhD) degree. His dissertation was about Congress.

- Wilson appointed the first Jewish Supreme Court justice, Louis Brandeis.

- Wilson won the 1919 Nobel Peace Prize for his efforts in setting up the League of Nations—even though the United States rejected the treaty that established it.

Life Before the Presidency

Woodrow Wilson lived in the South as a little boy and saw the destruction of the Civil War. His parents supported the Confederacy and his first memory was of hearing that Abraham Lincoln had been elected president. Wilson had to drop out of college with health problems, but eventually he went to law school and earned a doctoral degree. He began a promising academic career teaching political science at Bryn Mawr College, Wesleyan University, and then Princeton University. When he was named president of Princeton, he raised expectations for students so much that 25 percent of the class of 1902 quit. While he was there, he wrote a five-volume history of the United States in which he romanticized the Confederacy and praised the Ku Klux Klan.

New Jersey's political bosses, who controlled the state's Democratic party, persuaded Wilson to run for governor with the promise that if he won, they would try to get him to the White House. He didn't require much persuading, as he'd always wanted to hold office. He won the race for governor in 1910 but proved independent of the political bosses who had hoped to control him. As governor, Wilson enacted progressive reforms, such as increasing regulation on utility companies.

When Wilson got the Democratic nomination for president in 1912, he had an excellent chance of being elected. Former president Theodore Roosevelt was running as a third-party candidate against the incumbent, William Howard Taft, splitting the Republican vote, and Wilson won easily. He is the only president who defeated two other presidents in one election.

Mr. President

A month after he took the oath of office, Woodrow Wilson went to Congress to ask for a lower tariff. Congress responded with the Underwood Tariff Act. Lower rates help consumers but they bring in less money, so Congress made up for the shortfall by putting an income tax in place. The Sixteenth Amendment, which was ratified in February 1913, authorized income taxes. Wilson also asked Congress to prohibit board members of one company from also being on the board of another company. Congress gave him the Clayton Antitrust Act, but it was watered down before passage.

Wilson was a progressive on business issues but not on race. Several federal departments segregated their workers during his administration. The postmaster general segregated his department and fired or downgraded Black postal workers in the South. William Monroe Trotter, a newspaper editor and civil rights leader, led a delegation that visited Wilson—and Wilson threw him out. Trotter complained, "For the first time in history, a President . . . pronounced his administration's policy as one of racial discrimination." And Wilson—who supported women's suffrage—opposed Black voting rights, although the Fifteenth Amendment had given Black men the right to vote in 1870.

Part of the reason that Wilson supported suffrage was because of the unrelenting pressure of women's suffrage advocates. Alice Paul organized a march from the Capitol building to the White House on the day before Wilson's inauguration. She helped organize the Silent Sentinels, women who stood outside the White House with signs demanding the right to vote. They didn't talk even when bystanders insulted them and they were arrested and mistreated in jail. The president announced that he supported voting rights for women and what became the Nineteenth Amendment, which was passed in 1919 and ratified in 1920.

Letter from Woodrow Wilson to Carrie Chapman Catt, President, International Woman Suffrage Alliance, June 7, 1918

The services of women during this supreme crisis of the world's history have been of the most significant usefulness and distinction. The war could not have been fought without them, or its sacrifices endured. It is high time that some part of our debt of gratitude to them should be acknowledged and paid, and the only acknowledgment they ask is their admission to the suffrage. Can we justly refuse it? As for America, it is my earnest hope that the Senate of the United States will give an unmistakable answer to this question by passing the suffrage amendment to our federal constitution before the end of this session.

DECODED Wilson wrote this after the United States had entered World War I. He's acknowledging that women made huge contributions to the war effort and that they deserve the right to vote.

Wilson's presidency was dominated by World War I. Wilson declared American neutrality, which meant that the United States wouldn't take sides, and that was a popular position in the country.

As World War I began, Wilson's wife Ellen died. In 1915, the president met widow Edith Galt. He proposed to her that May, and they got married in December.

World War I, called the Great War until World War II, had shockingly high casualty counts. Horrified Americans read the reports from Europe and wanted

MR. PRESIDENT HOW LONG MUST WOMEN WAIT FOR LIBERTY

Edith Galt

to stay out of the conflict, and there was no strong reason for them to get involved. Wilson faced reelection in 1916, two years after the war in Europe had started. When Americans went to the polls, two of the largest battles in world history were raging: Verdun and the Somme. Casualties for the war already numbered in the millions, and casualties at the Battle of the Somme alone topped a million. Wilson's campaign emphasized that he had kept the United States out of a dangerous foreign war.

Wilson wasn't confident that he would win reelection against his opponent, Charles Evan Hughes. He worried about the four months after he might be defeated and Hughes hadn't yet taken office. He had an astonishing plan in case he lost, which would make Hughes president immediately.

Wilson won the 1916 election on a platform of staying out of the war, but American neutrality didn't hold. Americans traded more with Britain than with Germany, and they lent Britain more money. Meanwhile, Germany relied on U-boats, which were submarines, to stop British shipping. In May 1915, the British passenger liner *Lusitania* sank, killing 1,197 people, including 128 Americans. More Americans died in other U-boat attacks and Wilson protested sharply. Germany began unrestricted submarine warfare in early 1917, sinking commercial ships without warning. That made American entry inevitable.

Letter from Woodrow Wilson to Secretary of State Robert Lansing, November 5, 1916

What would it be my duty to do were Mr. Hughes to be elected? Four months would elapse before he could take charge of the affairs of the government. . . . The direction of the foreign policy of the government would in effect have been taken out of my hands and yet its new definition would be impossible until March. I feel that it would be my duty to relieve the country of the perils of such a situation at once. . . . I would ask your permission to invite Mr. Hughes to become Secretary of State and would then join the Vice President in resigning, and thus open to Mr. Hughes the immediate succession to the presidency.

[DECODED] Wilson's plan is ingenious—the secretary of state was at that time next in line to be president after the vice president. Wilson is writing to his secretary of state to explain that, if he loses, he plans to make his opponent his secretary of state—and then both he and the vice president will resign, making the man who won the election president immediately. It turned out that the man who won was Wilson, but he proves here that he was willing to give up office for the good of the country.

The decision was made easier by a revolution in Russia in the winter of 1917. The tsar abdicated, which means he stepped down. The Russian government, which up until then had been the most conservative in Europe, abruptly became the most liberal. Americans entered World War I with the idea that they were fighting to make the world safe for democracy. It would have been difficult to explain fighting on the same side as tsarist Russia, which wasn't remotely democratic. But with Russia's new government (which lasted only until the fall of 1917), American entry seemed more reasonable. Wilson asked Congress for a declaration of war—and led the United States into World War I in April 1917, a month after he took the oath for the second time.

The American presence proved decisive, especially its naval convoys that brought food and munitions to US allies. In January 1918, Wilson issued his Fourteen Points, an idealistic basis for America's aims for the postwar world. Wilson's plan was ambitious; French prime minister Georges Clemenceau commented that even God only had ten points (the Ten Commandments).

At home, civil liberties were under attack. The Espionage Act of 1917 and Sedition Act of 1918 made it illegal to criticize the government or to speak publicly against the war. Wilson worried that in a nation of immigrants, Americans might split along ethnic lines, with people of German ancestry favoring the other side, for example. Appearing unified in the war effort was a high priority.

In addition to the wartime crackdown on speech critical of the government and the war effort, there was an anti-immigrant backlash.

From November 1919 to January 1920, Attorney General A. Mitchell Palmer raided suspected radical organizations and immigrant groups, sometimes arresting people who had committed no crime and frequently violating constitutional safeguards that guarantee the rights of the accused.

WOODROW WILSON'S WAR MESSAGE TO CONGRESS, APRIL 2, 1917

It is a fearful thing to lead this great peaceful people into war, into the most terrible and disastrous of all wars, civilization itself seeming to be in the balance. But the right is more precious than peace, and we shall fight for the things which we have always carried nearest our hearts—for democracy, for the right of those who submit to authority to have a voice in their own governments, for the rights and liberties of small nations, for a universal dominion of right by such a concert of free peoples as shall bring peace and safety to all nations and make the world itself at last free.

DECODED The last paragraph of Wilson's war message is very idealistic. He was already thinking about the peace treaty that would come, but when the time came he couldn't get the Senate to ratify the treaty.

Many people were deported. The United States had a poor record on civil liberties during World War I.

ESPIONAGE ACT, JUNE 15, 1917

Whoever . . . shall willfully cause or attempt to cause insubordination, disloyalty, mutiny, or refusal of duty, in the military or naval forces of the United States, or shall willfully obstruct the recruiting or enlistment service of the United States, to the injury of the service or of the United States, shall be punished by a fine of not more than $10,000 or imprisonment for not more than twenty years, or both.

DECODED Criticizing the war was thought to hurt recruitment efforts and efforts to raise war bonds to help pay for the war.

In domestic affairs, the temperance movement scored a major victory late in Wilson's second term when the Eighteenth Amendment was ratified. This was the Prohibition amendment. It was the result of temperance advocates' efforts to reduce alcohol consumption, which they blamed for a wide range of social ills, including workplace accidents and domestic violence.

As part of his campaign against leftist thought and under pressure from Britain and France, Wilson sent troops to Russia in July 1918 to fight its new communist government, put in place after the October Revolution in 1917—the second Russian revolution in a year. The communist Bolsheviks under Vladimir Lenin had come to power, overthrowing an ineffective but vaguely American-style government that had been in place during the summer of 1917. Americans were disappointed to see that government fall and alarmed that a nation as large as Russia had become communist. American military intervention had little effect except to sour relations with Russia.

On November 11, 1918, Germany agreed to an armistice, which wasn't a surrender but meant that the fighting would stop. Wilson sailed to Europe in person to attend the postwar peace conference. He was the first sitting president to go to Europe.

The Treaty of Versailles (1919), which ended World War I on the Western Front, didn't follow Wilson's Fourteen Points. After four years of bitter fighting, the French and British were not inclined to be generous to Germany and Austria.

The provision that mattered most to Wilson, however, was the one establishing the League of Nations, which he hoped would prevent future wars by negotiating conflicts before wars could start. Some members of Congress objected to the League of Nations, fearing that it would force the United States to fight foreign wars in which it had no interest.

incapacitated that his wife, Edith, prevented visitors from seeing him and chose what documents he saw. Edith Wilson—who had only been his wife for four years—didn't set policy and she let the cabinet officers take over many duties of the presidency. But in many ways Edith Wilson ran the country for the rest of Wilson's term, although she didn't yet have the right to vote.

Legacy

The Senate holds the power to ratify or reject treaties, but instead of compromising, the stubborn Wilson began a tour around the country speaking in favor of ratifying the Treaty of Versailles and its provision to set up the League of Nations.

While on his speaking tour in support of ratification of the Treaty of Versailles, Wilson suffered a small stroke and returned to Washington, DC, where he had a major stroke a week later. The next month the Senate rejected the Treaty of Versailles—and with it, the League of Nations. Wilson was so

Woodrow Wilson was incapacitated by his stroke and never regained full health. He died less than three years after leaving office.

Wilson is most remembered for his leadership during World War I and the effort to establish the League of Nations, an international organization to keep the peace. At the same time, he was deeply racist and set Black Americans back. Where President Grant had shut down the Ku Klux Klan in the years after the Civil War, Wilson inspired its resurrection in the early twentieth century.

BORN: 1865

DIED: 1923

IN OFFICE: March 4, 1921–August 2, 1923

FROM: Ohio

VICE PRESIDENT: Calvin Coolidge

PARTY: Republican

WARREN G.
★
HARDING

DID YOU KNOW?

- Harding was the first president to visit Alaska.

- Harding was the first president to own a radio and the first president to give a speech over the radio.

- Harding popularized (and possibly invented) the word *bloviate*—which means to talk for a long time without really saying anything.

- Harding played more musical instruments than any other president.

Life Before the Presidency

Warren Harding was a poor student who wasn't interested in his studies. He became a teacher but lasted for only one year. After that he struggled to find something he could do. He studied law and sold insurance for a little while, but he didn't like either occupation. Eventually he bought the *Marion Star*, a newspaper in Marion, Ohio. Harding ran for county auditor (the person who keeps track of the county's money), but he lost. He was handsome and a good public speaker, though, and when he ran for the Ohio state senate in 1899 he won. Harry M. Daugherty, a political boss who controlled the Republican Party in the area, pushed Harding to run for lieutenant governor. Harding won that office in 1904 but lost a run for governor. He ran for a seat in the US Senate in 1914 and won. He spent much of his time as a senator playing poker and golf and going to the horse races. He missed 40 percent of roll call votes, where members' names are recorded so it's possible to tell if they were present or not.

Harding was the Republican candidate for president in 1920. That was the first presidential election in which women could vote. Fewer women than men voted in 1920, but it was a significant milestone in democracy.

Mr. President

The Treaty of Versailles, which ended World War I, was an issue in the 1920 election. It included a provision setting up a League of Nations, an international organization that was meant to help keep the peace in the future. Most Democrats, like President Woodrow Wilson who was leaving office, wanted the League of Nations, hoping to prevent another disaster like World War I. Many Republicans opposed it and were worried that an international organization could ask Americans to fight for things that they didn't care about. Harding agreed. As president, Harding signed the Knox-Porter Resolution, which simply declared the United States to be at peace with its World War I enemies.

KNOX-PORTER RESOLUTION

Joint resolution (S. J. Res. 16) terminating the state of war between the Imperial German Government and the United States of America and between the Imperial and Royal Austro-Hungarian Government and the United States of America. Resolved, etc., That the state of war declared to exist between the Imperial German Government and the United States of America by the joint resolution of Congress approved April 6, 1917, is hereby declared at an end.

DECODED The Treaty of Versailles ended World War I for most of the nations that had fought in it, but the US Senate rejected the treaty. Instead, Congress passed the Knox-Porter Resolution, which simply declared the United States to be at peace with Germany and its allies. President Harding signed it on July 2, 1921, ending American involvement in World War I.

The country wanted a return to "normalcy" after World War I. People lost interest in international affairs; they chased popular fads, danced, and watched sports. Harding followed an isolationist policy, making the US less active in foreign affairs. Internally, he wanted a small government that provided minimal regulation for businesses and less US involvement in foreign affairs. He opposed a measure that would have given World War I soldiers a bonus to make up for the wages they lost by being in the army instead of working civilian jobs. The legislation was popular, but Harding vetoed it.

"Normalcy" was harder for Black Americans. Lynchings still occurred and the threat was frightening. In addition, instead of being honored for their service, Black soldiers returning from World War I were often treated badly. Harding addressed this situation explicitly in his nomination speech, saying that Black Americans should be safe and have their rights. His statement didn't make much difference.

Harding is remembered best for the corruption in his administration. There were several scandals involving Harding's officials taking bribes in exchange for favorable treatment, but the worst was the Teapot Dome Scandal. In April 1915, President Woodrow Wilson had created Naval Petroleum Reserve No. 3, nicknamed "Teapot Dome" after a nearby rock formation shaped like a teapot. The oil there was meant for US Navy ships, which were starting to run on oil instead of coal. In November 1921, Harding's secretary of the interior, Albert Fall, took approximately $400,000 from oil companies and then illegally leased oil deposits to them, allowing them to drill the Teapot Dome for the reserved oil. Fall resigned in 1923, and was convicted of bribery and conspiracy to defraud the government. The problems with the oil deal went beyond bribery, though. The oil had been set aside for emergency use by the navy. Fall let private companies take it and sell it for their own profit, which hurt national security.

The scandal was splashed across newspaper headlines as President and Mrs. Harding left Washington on a speaking tour across the country. On the way back from Alaska, the president got sick. Harding died in San Francisco on August 2, 1923. He probably died of a heart attack or stroke, but rumors swirled that he might have been poisoned because his physician wouldn't let any other doctors look at him, and his wife refused to allow an autopsy.

Legacy

Harding was the sixth president to die in office. Although he was popular during his term, Harding is remembered today primarily for the scandals of his administration, especially Teapot Dome, and for a hands-off, pro-business approach to the economy that many economists think helped lead to the Great Depression.

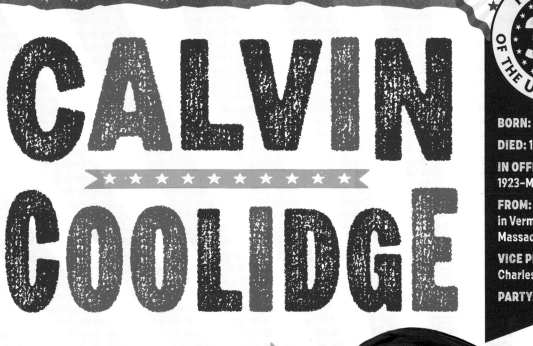

CALVIN
★ ★ ★ ★ ★ ★ ★ ★ ★ ★
COOLIDGE

BORN: 1872

DIED: 1933

IN OFFICE: August 3, 1923–March 4, 1929

FROM: born and raised in Vermont; moved to Massachusetts

VICE PRESIDENT: Charles Gates Dawes

PARTY: Republican

DID YOU KNOW?

- Calvin Coolidge was born on the Fourth of July.

- The only election Coolidge ever lost was for the school board in Northampton, Massachusetts.

- Coolidge was at his father's house when he learned of Harding's death. He found a copy of the Constitution in a book, typed out the oath, and was sworn in by his father, a notary public, by the light of a kerosene lamp.

- Coolidge became the first president to travel to Cuba. He gave a speech there in 1928.

Life Before the Presidency

Calvin Coolidge was born in Vermont. He was a quiet child who was uncomfortable with people he didn't know and he stayed that way as an adult. Coolidge went to college, became a lawyer, and moved to Northampton, Massachusetts, where he was elected to several positions in the city and state governments.

At the end of World War I, a wave of strikes swept across the country. One of the most important was a police strike in Boston, where police had low pay and bad working conditions so they joined a union. The police commissioner resisted unionization—and Governor Coolidge agreed with him on the grounds of public safety. The commissioner fired the striking police officers and broke the union. Coolidge became nationally known as a law-and-order candidate. The next year he was nominated for vice president on Warren G. Harding's ticket.

Vice President Coolidge was visiting his father when Harding died. His father woke him up in the middle of the night—and called him "Mr. President."

Mr. President

Coolidge was the only president ever sworn in by his father. His second inauguration was unique, too. William Howard Taft, by then the chief justice of the Supreme Court, administered the oath, making Coolidge the only president ever sworn in by another president.

The postwar economy was booming when Coolidge came to office. The GNP, or gross national product, which is one of the best indicators of economic growth, rose rapidly through the 1920s. Consumers benefited as electric appliances like vacuum cleaners became popular and made life easier. Coolidge wanted high tariffs to protect industry, lower taxes, and fewer regulations on businesses. Under Coolidge, businesses began to take control over the agencies meant to regulate them. Coolidge believed in frugality and small government—that is, government doing as little as possible. His philosophy was to stay out of the way. As a president he was known for delegating responsibilities to others—while he took a nap.

His famous lack of energy may have resulted in part from tragedy: A year into office, the Coolidges' younger son died. The grief-stricken president had a reputation for napping every afternoon and probably slept more hours per day than any other president.

Coolidge worked to lower the national

debt and cut taxes, especially for the wealthy and for corporations. He vetoed a farm relief bill, feeling that it wasn't the place of government to help struggling people. Prices of agricultural products fell through the 1920s and the prosperity of that decade didn't reach farm families.

Coolidge didn't have an active foreign policy, either. The United States did sign on to the Kellogg-Briand Pact of 1928, which outlawed war in the wake of World War I. There was no provision for enforcing it, though, so it didn't mean much.

The Fourteenth Amendment, ratified in 1868, had appeared to grant citizenship to Indigenous people, but it was interpreted in ways that denied them citizenship. In 1924, Coolidge signed the Indian Citizenship Act, which specifically gave citizenship to all Indigenous people who were born in the United States.

KELLOGG-BRIAND PACT, 1928

The President of the German Reich, His Majesty the King of the Belgians, the President of the French Republic, His Majesty the King of Great Britain, Ireland and the British Dominions beyond the Seas, Emperor of India, His Majesty the King of Italy, His Majesty the Emperor of Japan, the President of the Republic of Poland, and the President of the Czechoslovak Republic,

Deeply sensible of their solemn duty to promote the welfare of mankind;

Persuaded that the time has, come when a frank renunciation of war as an instrument of national policy should be made to the end that the peaceful and friendly relations now existing between their peoples may be perpetuated. . . .

DECODED The Kellogg-Briand Pact outlawed war. It was signed eleven years before World War II began.

INDIAN CITIZENSHIP ACT, 1924

Be it enacted by the Senate and House of Representatives of the United States of America in Congress assembled, That all non-citizen Indians born within the territorial limits of the United States be, and they are hereby, declared to be citizens of the United States. . . .

DECODED The Fourteenth Amendment says that all people born in the United States are citizens. But in 1884, the Supreme Court ruled that the amendment didn't apply to Indigenous people because it included the words "subject to the jurisdiction thereof" (meaning "living under the rules of"), and that excluded the great majority of Indigenous people. The Indian Citizenship Act finally settled the issue. But some states still tried to avoid giving Indigenous people voting rights, and it took the Voting Rights Act of 1965 to clarify that they also had the right to vote.

There was a surge in racism in the 1920s, especially with the revival of the Ku Klux Klan. Former Confederate officers had founded the Klan during Reconstruction as a way of terrorizing and controlling Black Americans. It had died out during the years when Ulysses S. Grant was president, in part because of the hard line he took against the intimidation of freedmen. But in 1915, the Klan revived as an anti-Black, anti-Catholic, anti-Jewish, and anti-immigrant domestic terrorist organization. It had several million followers in the 1920s, when it was at its most powerful.

Legacy

The prosperity of the Coolidge years wasn't evenly distributed—and didn't last. The booming economy of the 1920s didn't help farm families. There were a few very wealthy people, but most Americans didn't have much money. This unbalanced distribution of wealth resulted in a weak economy because so many people didn't have enough money to purchase goods to keep the economy moving.

In addition, stocks in companies had become worth more than the companies themselves. People would buy one stock and use its value to cover the purchase of stock in a different company, but underneath it all they didn't have money to back their purchases. When Secretary of Commerce Herbert Hoover asked for more regulation of banking, Coolidge turned him down. The stock market crashed during Hoover's term, but the roots of that crash grew in Coolidge's.

Letter from Pastor Shelton Bissell to Calvin Coolidge, July 3, 1925

Dear President Coolidge:—Allow me to add one more to the stream of protests coming to you, against recognition of the Klan in connection with their contemplated parade in Washington Aug. 8. It will publish America's shame to the four corners of the world to have an organization, founded on exclusiveness, fostered by secrecy, grown fat on hate, and promoting as un-American a spirit as can be conceived, flaunt its banners in the capitol city of our land.

DECODED A minister writes here to President Coolidge asking him to prevent the Ku Klux Klan from parading through the streets of the nation's capital in 1925. The march proceeded as planned, with about thirty thousand Klansmen in their traditional white robes. Although Klan members often wore pointed hoods to hide their identities, they were powerful enough in the 1920s that most of the marchers in Washington, DC, didn't bother to hide their faces.

HERBERT
HOOVER

PRESIDENT
31
OF THE UNITED STATES

BORN: 1874

DIED: 1964

IN OFFICE: March 4, 1929–March 4, 1933

FROM: Iowa

VICE PRESIDENT: Charles Curtis

PARTY: Republican

DID YOU KNOW?

- Hoover was the first president born west of the Mississippi River.

- During the Great Depression, Hoover's name was used for the shantytowns of newly homeless people that grew up at the edge of cities—they were called "Hoovervilles." An empty, outturned pocket was called a "Hoover flag."

- Hoover's vice president, Charles Curtis, was the first vice president of color. He was from the Kaw nation and learned the Kaw language before English.

- The national anthem was adopted in 1931 during Hoover's presidency.

Life Before the Presidency

Herbert Hoover grew up in West Branch, Iowa. His father died when he was six and his mother when he was nine. He and his siblings were farmed out among relatives. He was shy and had poor grades in school, but he managed to get into the first class of the newly built Stanford University in Stanford, California. He met a fellow geology major there, Lou Henry, and they married in 1899. She was one of the first female geologists. They each won a gold medal from the Mining and Metallurgical Society of America for translating a work on mineralogy. Lou was the first woman to receive the medal.

Hoover traveled to Australia for work as a mining engineer, and the Hoovers went together to China. Lou learned Mandarin—she is the only First Lady who could speak an Asian language—and Hoover spoke a little; in their White House years they would speak in Mandarin when they wanted privacy.

Hoover was in London when World War I broke out in the summer of 1914, and American diplomats there asked him to help the 120,000 Americans caught overseas get home. He did, and he also helped organize the Commission for Relief in Belgium after Germany invaded Belgium. Hoover and his friends got the job done without government help by raising private funds. It was an impressive achievement, but it may have made him overly confident in what private relief efforts could do.

When the United States entered the war, President Wilson made Hoover head of the US Food Administration, which helped to conserve food and make sure there was enough for the war effort. It was an important job, and he did it well. His name became a common word during the war when Americans referred to stretching their food supply as "Hooverizing." He was secretary of commerce under Presidents Harding and Coolidge, and he pushed businesses to standardize parts and tools so they were all made in the same size or shape and could be used interchangeably. That increased efficiency.

When Calvin Coolidge decided not to run for reelection in 1928, Hoover got the Republican nomination for president. He had an international reputation for helping people in crisis and for competent administration. He seemed like an excellent candidate.

HERBERT HOOVER'S SPEECH ACCEPTING THE REPUBLICAN NOMINATION, AUGUST 11, 1928

Unemployment in the sense of distress is widely disappearing. . . . We in America today are nearer to the final triumph over poverty than ever before in the history of any land. The poor-house is vanishing from among us.

DECODED Hoover said that the booming economy was ending poverty. But the stock market would crash in late 1929, bringing in a worldwide depression that lasted for a decade.

Mr. President

Hoover's administration had a promising start. He opened the Grand Teton and Carlsbad Caverns national parks, although the decision to preserve the areas was made before he was elected, and he increased funds for national parks.

The 1920s had been a mixed decade for Black Americans. During World War I, a large population shift started to occur as many Southern Black Americans moved north in what is called the Great Migration. Some Black Americans were able to get better jobs, and the Negro Leagues were established in baseball, giving visibility to Black athletes. There was a thriving Black artistic community. But Black soldiers returning from the war were often the targets of harassment. There were also large-scale attacks on Black communities, like the Tulsa Race Massacre of 1921, in which white residents destroyed a prosperous Black neighborhood and killed a number of people in Tulsa, Oklahoma, after a Black man was accused of hurting a white woman.

The Ku Klux Klan was very active in the 1920s. And lynching continued to be a constant threat. There were almost 4,500 lynchings between the end of Reconstruction and 1968.

Letter from Horace Robinson to Herbert Hoover, November 20, 1929

Dear Sir: I, a Negro of twenty years, have just learned of another lynching of a member of my Race, which took place in Florida a few days ago. Although I dislike to bother you Sir, I am compelled to appeal to you to stop lynching in the United States of any man, regardless of race or color. I feel that you, as President of this nation, are better able to stop this outrage than any other person.

Are the members of my Race and I, to be murdered and hacked by other Americans whose faces are white, but whose souls are of the blackest? Are we, who after having suffered numerous insults at the hands of the white race, who have, nevertheless fought and died for the Red, White and Blue to be continually restricted [in] natural rights? . . . Sir, I appeal to you, I beg of you to protect my Race, who after all, are citizens of America as well as the white Race.

Respectfully yours

Horace Robinson

 DECODED The United States didn't have a federal anti-lynching law until 2022.

Hoover pushed passage of the Agricultural Marketing Act of 1929, which helped farmers who worked together to sell and store their produce and tried to stabilize farm prices. The 1920s were a prosperous time, but farmers hadn't shared in the boom.

On October 24, 1929, and again on October 29, the stock market plunged, in part because stocks were overpriced and people were able to buy them with credit rather than being able to pay for the whole price of the stock. The stock market crash sent the United States into a severe economic depression whose effects were felt around the globe. The Smoot-Hawley Tariff, passed in June 1930, made things worse. It raised tariffs on agricultural raw materials, such as mangoes, pineapples, plums, walnuts, potatoes, ginger ale, and lemonade. The tariff reduced trade with Europe because other nations retaliated—and that sent European economies spiraling downward, too. When trade declined, European countries were unable to pay off their World War I debts to the United States. Hoover gave them a months-long break before they had to start paying again.

By 1933, almost 25 percent of American workers were unemployed. Industrial production had fallen by almost half. As suffering increased, so did pressure on Hoover to start relief efforts to individuals. He didn't want to do that, though, because he thought helping individual Americans would hurt their work ethic. He was also unwilling to start programs that would require deficit spending, which means spending money the government didn't already have.

HOOVER'S INAUGURAL ADDRESS, MARCH 4, 1929

Self-government does not and should not imply the use of political agencies alone. Progress is born of cooperation in the community—not from governmental restraints. The Government should assist and encourage these movements of collective self-help by itself cooperating with them.

DECODED When the Depression hit, Hoover continued to believe in collective self-help and in relief by the private sector. Most people wanted more active government intervention—and in the next election they turned to Franklin Roosevelt for help.

Hoover made voters angrier when he vetoed the Norris Dam project in 1931. The project would have provided jobs for workers and electric power for people in the Tennessee Valley, but Hoover thought it sounded like "the dole"—that is, a handout. In 1932, President Hoover set up the Reconstruction Finance Corporation to help businesses and banks by giving them loans. Some voters were angry that the president was willing to provide direct aid to businesses but not to the people.

Hoover acknowledged that the Depression was caused in part by the unequal distribution of wealth—the majority of people couldn't afford to buy consumer goods. Indigenous people and Mexican Americans in particular hadn't shared in the decade's prosperity. The wealthiest people got richer through the 1920s, but they had different spending patterns than poorer people, buying more luxury items and saving more money. That meant that the money in their hands didn't fuel the economy in the same way that it would have in the hands of the middle or working classes. Hoover wanted to raise the tax rate on the rich and add extra taxes to luxury items. He got part of what he wanted when the Revenue Act of 1932 increased taxes on the wealthy. It also raised estate taxes, which are taxes on the money left by very wealthy people when they die.

In the summer of 1932, hungry World War I veterans marched on Washington, DC, with their families while Congress was deciding whether to pay them a promised bonus earlier than scheduled; they needed the money then. The veterans called themselves a "Bonus Army" and camped out in the capital. Hoover didn't want to pay the bonus early and Congress rejected the bill, but the Bonus Marchers refused to leave. Hoover ordered General Douglas MacArthur to clear them out. MacArthur attacked with

tear gas, bayonets, and tanks. Two Bonus Marchers were killed. Future president Dwight Eisenhower was present with the troops and was appalled, but Hoover refused to say that MacArthur shouldn't have

General Douglas MacArthur

attacked in that manner. If the economy hadn't ensured that Hoover would lose the 1932 election, the attack on the Bonus Marchers would have. Franklin Delano Roosevelt won in a landslide.

Legacy

Hoover was an honest and decent man with a record of effective administration before he became president. He was an excellent candidate for the presidency, and it would have been reasonable to think he would do well in the role. If times had been different, he might have. The economic catastrophe of the Great Depression required a stronger response than Hoover was willing to give. To many Americans, he seemed out of touch with their suffering, and he is remembered for a late and inadequate reaction to the Depression.

BORN: 1882

DIED: 1945

IN OFFICE: March 4, 1933–April 12, 1945

FROM: New York

VICE PRESIDENT: John Nance Garner (first and second terms), Henry A. Wallace (third term), Harry S Truman (fourth term)

PARTY: Democratic

FRANKLIN DELANO ROOSEVELT

DID YOU KNOW?

● Franklin Roosevelt was related to eleven other presidents: John Adams, James Madison, John Quincy Adams, Martin Van Buren, William Henry Harrison, Zachary Taylor, Andrew Johnson, Ulysses S. Grant, Benjamin Harrison, William Howard Taft, and Theodore Roosevelt.

● Roosevelt was first elected in November 1932 but not inaugurated until March 1933. The country was in acute crisis and wanted new leadership. The frustration over the length of that period led to ratification of the Twentieth Amendment (1933), which set the presidential inauguration date on January 20.

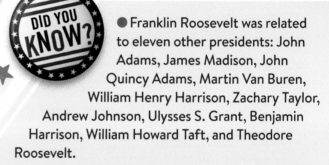

● In 2021, an Eleanor Roosevelt Barbie doll was released. Roosevelt is the only First Lady to have a Barbie doll made in her likeness.

● FDR appointed the first female cabinet secretary, Secretary of Labor Frances Perkins.

Life Before the Presidency

Franklin Delano Roosevelt was born into a wealthy family who made their home in Hyde Park, New York. He was an only child, although he had an older half brother. Roosevelt's mother, Sara, doted on him. When he was a freshman at Harvard his father died. His mother rented an apartment by campus, and young Roosevelt frequently escorted her to social events. He fell in love with a distant cousin, Eleanor, while he was in college, and they married in 1905. Roosevelt became a lawyer and won a seat in the New York senate (1911–1913), where he supported women's suffrage and regulation of business.

In 1912, FDR supported Woodrow Wilson for president, even though his fifth cousin, Theodore Roosevelt, was running on the Bull Moose ticket. Wilson won and made FDR the assistant secretary of the navy, a post he held until 1920.

The next year, Roosevelt got polio and lost the use of his legs for the rest of his life. He made trips to Warm Springs, Georgia, hoping that swimming in the natural warm water there would help him regain the use of his legs, but he was never able to walk again. He kept the extent of his disability private, and news photographers generally didn't take photographs while he was being transferred to a car—or show his wheelchair at all.

Roosevelt won the New York governor race in 1928 and implemented progressive policies, trying to use the government to help ordinary people. He also began informal radio addresses, made directly to the public, to explain the issues and the government's response. It was a technique he would use successfully as president.

When the Great Depression hit in 1929, Herbert Hoover lost popularity. The Democrats nominated Roosevelt in 1932, and he showed up to the convention in person to accept the nomination—he was the first presidential nominee to do so.

FRANKLIN ROOSEVELT'S SPEECH ACCEPTING THE DEMOCRATIC NOMINATION FOR PRESIDENT, JULY 2, 1932

I pledge you, I pledge myself to a new deal for the American people. Let us all here assembled constitute ourselves prophets of a new order of competence and courage. This is more than a political campaign. It is a call to arms.

DECODED Roosevelt's phrase of a "new deal" came to be applied to his domestic program. The New Deal is among the most famous of presidential programs and helped lift the country out of the Great Depression.

Roosevelt campaigned hard, promising to improve the economy and provide relief to the unemployed; he won 472 electoral college votes to Hoover's 59.

Mr. President

Franklin Delano Roosevelt was president through two of the largest crises in American history—the Great Depression and World War II—and he is the only person to have been elected more than twice. And with Franklin Roosevelt, the Democratic Party took on its modern shape.

DEMOCRAT

REPUBLICAN

The Depression dominated his first two terms. Roosevelt focused on the economy and the goals of relief, recovery, and reform. That meant helping with people's immediate needs, fixing what had gone wrong with the economy, and putting in regulations to make sure a depression didn't happen again. With Congress controlled by the Democrats, Roosevelt was able to take immediate action. He declared a bank holiday that went into effect two days after his inauguration, which temporarily shut down the banks in order to keep people from pulling out their money and causing the banks to crash. He also communicated immediately with people, holding a press conference after just four days in office and starting fireside chats eight days into his term. He eventually gave around thirty fireside chats—which were informal radio addresses to the American people, explaining in straightforward language what was going on and how they could help.

Letter from Anonymous Writer in Chicago to Franklin Roosevelt, February 1936

Dear Mr. President,

I'm a boy of 12 years. I want to tell you about my family. My father hasn't worked for 5 months. He went plenty times to relief, he filled out application. They won't give us anything. I don't know why. Please you do something. We haven't paid 4 months rent, Everyday the landlord rings the bell, we don't open the door for him. We are afraid that will be put out, been put out before, and don't want to happen again. We haven't paid the gas bill, and the electric bill, haven't paid grocery bill for 3 months. . . . Were American citizens and were born in Chicago, Ill. and I don't know why they don't help us Please answer right away because we need it. will starve Thank you.

God bless you.

DECODED Roosevelt got thousands of letters like this from desperate citizens who needed help. He used the powers of the government to provide relief.

Roosevelt was practical more than ideological; he would try something, and if it didn't work, he'd try something else. Roosevelt's first hundred days in office were an astonishing flurry of activity—some of his officials worked in hallways until their offices were set up so they wouldn't lose any time. Roosevelt's domestic program was called the New Deal, and to make it happen, he pushed an enormous amount of legislation through Congress. New Deal programs included the Civilian Conservation Corps (CCC), which gave young men jobs planting trees and building roads, and the Federal Emergency Relief Administration (FERA), which provided unemployment relief, or direct payments to people for emergency needs like food. The Agricultural Adjustment Act (AAA) paid farmers to produce less in an effort to increase prices for farm products. And the Tennessee Valley Authority (TVA) brought electric power and flood control to an impoverished area, allowing it to develop economically. In general, New Deal programs provided more help to white people than to Black people and to men than to women.

In 1935, Roosevelt called Congress into a special session to debate reform proposals. Big businesses had opposed many of his New Deal programs, and he was fighting back. FDR pushed through the National Labor Relations Act, also known as the Wagner Act, which helped workers unionize. He also established the Works Progress Administration (WPA), a program designed to give jobs to the unemployed; its workers built more than 650,000 miles of highways, created 17,744 sculptures for public buildings, and built or improved tens of thousands of buildings. The WPA employed both skilled and unskilled workers and included artists and writers.

Other major legislation included the creation of the Federal Deposit Insurance Corporation (FDIC), which safeguarded bank deposits. Knowing their money was safe in a bank should help prevent people from withdrawing their money at the same time, which could cause a bank to fail. The FDIC was part of the effort to reform the US financial system to prevent future depressions. Congress also passed the Revenue Act of 1935, which increased estate and gift taxes and the taxes on the richest Americans. It angered wealthy Americans, but FDR saw it as a way to save capitalism, the American economic system. Roosevelt thought that getting the economy to work for everyone would help preserve it and prevent radical change. And in 1935, the Social Security Act passed, providing monthly payments to the elderly so they would have some income. Republicans fought hard against it. Roosevelt had to remove a proposal to provide health insurance in order to get the rest of the bill approved.

In 1936, Roosevelt won in an electoral college blowout of 523–8. But the Supreme Court ruled some of his New Deal programs unconstitutional.

Roosevelt had new legislation drafted, wording it more carefully, and was able to get it through. He also tried to expand the number of Supreme Court justices with the hope that the new justices would rule in favor of New Deal programs, but the public didn't support his plan.

Eleanor Roosevelt was a much-admired First Lady. The Roosevelts' marriage wasn't good, but they respected each other politically, and she helped Franklin achieve his policy goals—and pushed him to include more women in New Deal programs. For example, while young men were given jobs with the CCC, Eleanor Roosevelt established camps for young women, called She-She-She. She tried to get jobs for female reporters and tried to help Black and Asian Americans. When the Daughters of the American Revolution (DAR) refused to let Black opera singer Marian Anderson use Constitution Hall for a concert because they booked only white performers, Eleanor resigned from the organization. She arranged for Anderson to perform at the Lincoln Memorial on Easter Sunday, and a crowd of 75,000 people showed up. Another time Eleanor attended a meeting in the South and found that the seating was segregated—Black people on one side and white people on the other. She moved her chair between the sections and sat down, bridging the gap between them. In an era when segregation was enforced, her move was widely reported and influential.

In the 1930s, Adolf Hitler took power in Germany, and on September 1, 1939, Germany invaded Poland, beginning World War II. The United States tried to remain neutral in what was initially seen as a European tragedy, while helping the British as much as they could. In 1940, FDR won a third term, the only person ever to do so, and in 1941, he persuaded Congress to pass the Lend-Lease Act in which the United States lent weapons to the British when they could no longer afford to buy them.

When Japan bombed the US Naval base at Pearl Harbor, Hawaii, on December 7, 1941, Roosevelt asked Congress for a declaration of war against Japan. Fascist Germany under Hitler and fascist Italy under Benito Mussolini promptly declared war on the United States.

The nation had a much better record on civil liberties during World War II than it had during World War I. But the exception was Japanese internment. During World War II, about 120,000 Japanese Americans, most of whom had been born in the United States, were sent to "relocation centers"—camps where they were forced to stay— out of fear that they would side

Marian Anderson

with Japan in the war. German Americans were not sent to camps, even though the United States was also at war with Germany.

During the war, Roosevelt met in person several times with British prime minister Winston Churchill and Soviet (Russian) premier Joseph Stalin. The countries the United States fought with were not natural allies—Stalin was communist and Churchill strongly anticommunist, and they all knew their postwar goals would be different.

Winston Churchill   Roosevelt   Joseph Stalin

FRANKLIN ROOSEVELT'S WAR MESSAGE TO CONGRESS, DECEMBER 8, 1941

Mr. Vice President, and Mr. Speaker, and Members of the Senate and House of Representatives:

YESTERDAY, December 7, 1941—a date which will live in infamy—the United States of America was suddenly and deliberately attacked by naval and air forces of the Empire of Japan.

The United States was at peace with that Nation and, at the solicitation of Japan, was still in conversation with its Government and its Emperor looking toward the maintenance of peace in the Pacific. Indeed, one hour after Japanese air squadrons had commenced bombing in the American Island of Oahu, the Japanese Ambassador to the United States and his colleague delivered to our Secretary of State a formal reply to a recent American message. And while this reply stated that it seemed useless to continue the existing diplomatic negotiations, it contained no threat or hint of war or of armed attack.

It will be recorded that the distance of Hawaii from Japan makes it obvious that the attack was deliberately planned many days or even weeks ago. During the intervening time the Japanese Government has deliberately sought to deceive the United States by false statements and expressions of hope for continued peace.

. . . As Commander in Chief of the Army and Navy I have directed that all measures be taken for our defense.

I ask that the Congress declare that since the unprovoked and dastardly attack by Japan on Sunday, December 7, 1941, a state of war has existed between the United States and the Japanese Empire.

DECODED Roosevelt asks Congress to declare war and calls December 7, 1941, the date of the bombing of Pearl Harbor, "a date which will live in infamy." *Infamy* means being famous in a bad way. His first draft said "a date which will live in world history"—the change made the line much stronger.

EXECUTIVE ORDER 9066 AUTHORIZING THE SECRETARY OF WAR TO PRESCRIBE MILITARY AREAS, APRIL 22, 1828

I hereby authorize and direct the Secretary of War . . . whenever he or any designated Commander deems such action necessary or desirable, to prescribe military areas in such places and of such extent as he or the appropriate Military Commander may determine, from which any or all persons may be excluded, and with respect to which, the right of any person to enter, remain in, or leave shall be subject to whatever restrictions the Secretary of War or the appropriate Military Commander may impose in his discretion.

DECODED Roosevelt issued this order—which never specifically mentions Japanese Americans, though it resulted in their being forced into relocation centers. They had very little time to prepare to move and often lost their homes, cars, and businesses as they were imprisoned, without charge or recourse, for an undetermined period of time. In 1988, the United States apologized and paid reparations.

The Russians, bearing the brunt of the German forces after France fell early in the war, desperately needed the Allies to open a second front. Stalin wanted a second front in western Europe in order to split German forces. Churchill delayed in order to preserve British colonial interests. Britain had colonies around the world and Churchill wanted to make sure it still held them at the end of the war. Roosevelt finally sided with Stalin and ordered the Normandy invasion (D-Day), which opened a second front in France in June 1944. Normandy was history's largest amphibious invasion, which means bringing land troops in by water. Troops from the United States, Great Britain, and Canada, along with some troops from other nations, crossed the English Channel and landed on the coast of France under heavy fire from the German army. General Dwight D. Eisenhower was in command at D-Day, which helped make him a war hero—and eventually a president.

General Dwight D. Eisenhower

Roosevelt died of a massive stroke on April 12, 1945. Germany was all but defeated by this point, but the war against Japan in the Pacific theater was left to his successor, Harry Truman.

Letter **from William Hogan to Eleanor Roosevelt, April 15, 1945**

Dear Mrs. Roosevelt: I am terribly grieved by the death of my pal and President, Mr. Roosevelt. I am a shipyard welder here in Wilmington [California] and when I first heard the news I was dazed and refused to believe it. Mr. Roosevelt was like a member of my family. . . .

DECODED Roosevelt was a wealthy man from a privileged background, but he had the common touch. Many people felt as if they knew him because of the fireside chats, in which he spoke by radio to them in their living rooms, and because he was in office so long. Here a shipyard welder refers to him as "my pal and President."

Legacy

Roosevelt was elected president four times and served twelve years (1933–1945), by far the longest of any president. Roosevelt guided the United States through two of its worst crises, the Great Depression and World War II. He transformed the presidency and the government, marshalling for the first time the full powers of the federal government to relieve the suffering of private citizens.

And his wartime meetings with other world leaders, especially Britain's Churchill and Russia's Stalin, helped guide strategy. Roosevelt's confidence helped comfort and inspire a generation of Americans shaken by world events.

HARRY S TRUMAN

BORN: 1884

DIED: 1972

IN OFFICE: April 12, 1945–January 20, 1953

FROM: Missouri

VICE PRESIDENT: Alben William Barkley

PARTY: Democratic

DID YOU KNOW?

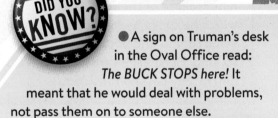

- A sign on Truman's desk in the Oval Office read: *The BUCK STOPS here!* It meant that he would deal with problems, not pass them on to someone else.

- Truman's 1949 inauguration was the first to be shown on television. It was also the first in which a rabbi participated; the rabbi, a friend of Truman's, gave a prayer.

- The US Army's Battery D served as honor guards at Truman's 1949 inauguration. That was the unit Truman had served with in World War I.

- Truman's parents thought he should have a middle initial—an "S" because both of his grandfathers had names that began with "S." They didn't specify what the "S" stood for so they wouldn't hurt anyone's feelings, and it doesn't have a period after it.

Life Before the Presidency

Harry Truman was born in Lamar, Missouri, and grew up in Independence, Missouri. He was a serious kid and liked to read and play the piano. He wanted to go to college, but his father went bankrupt in the summer after Truman finished high school, so Truman went to work for a newspaper, then as a contractor for a railroad company, and then for a bank. He studied for a semester at a business college but never earned a college degree and went back to work on the family farm. Truman would be one of the least wealthy presidents.

Truman had been in the National Guard and joined the army when World War I began. He was the only president to fight in World War I.

Truman returned from war in 1919 and opened a men's clothing store in Kansas City with a partner, but by 1922, Truman & Jacobson had failed after an economic downturn. At that point, local Democratic political boss Mike Pendergast asked him to run for a county judgeship. He won that election, and then he won the position of presiding, or head, judge, a post he held until 1935.

In 1934, Pendergast asked Truman to run for US Senate. He won that race, too. Truman supported FDR's New Deal programs. He strongly favored civil rights legislation, including ending the poll tax that restricted Black voting rights. He wasn't expected to win reelection in 1940 but squeaked out a victory.

Truman got the Senate to create the Special Committee to Investigate the National Defense Program, usually called the Truman Committee, which checked on the billions of dollars being spent on the military buildup as World War II was beginning. It saved the country money by making sure contractors did the work they had agreed to do, but it also discovered things like airplane engines that didn't work properly. It was an important discovery right before the United States entered World War II.

In 1944, Franklin Roosevelt needed a new vice president who would appeal to the South. The political parties were morphing into their modern identities, and the loyalty of Southern and rural voters wasn't guaranteed. (After the Civil War, the Democratic Party had been popular in the South and the Republican Party in the North. When the Democratic Party began to defend Black people's rights, that support switched, and Republicans got more support among white Southerners.)

Truman was reluctant to accept the nomination for vice president, however. It took an angry phone call from Roosevelt to get Truman to cave and agree to run. Truman wasn't well known in Washington before he was nominated to be FDR's vice president in 1944. He was a senator but had little influence. When Roosevelt died in April 1945, Truman became president of the United States.

Mr. President

When Truman came to office after Franklin Roosevelt's death, World War II was winding down, but it wasn't over yet, and it was Truman who had to make the decision whether to use atomic bombs in Japan. Horrified by the tremendous numbers of casualties in the Pacific theater, Truman ordered an atomic bomb dropped on Hiroshima, Japan, on August 6, and another on Nagasaki on August 9. Japan surrendered on August 15.

Truman wanted to extend the government activism of the New Deal. His domestic agenda included a higher minimum wage, national health insurance, and guaranteed full employment, which means that everyone who wanted a job could find one. He also wanted to continue the Fair Employment Practices Committee (FEPC) that had tried to protect Black Americans in government and defense industries from employment discrimination during the war. He got little of what he wanted. In 1945 and 1946, a wave of strikes hit the country as soldiers returned home from World War II and reentered the workforce. Their wages weren't keeping up with inflation. Coal miners and railroad workers both went on strike, and Truman seized the mines to force

TRUMAN'S ADDRESS TO THE NATION ON THE BOMBING OF JAPAN, AUGUST 6, 1945

Sixteen hours ago an American airplane dropped one bomb on Hiroshima, an important Japanese Army base. That bomb had more power than 20,000 tons of T.N.T. It had more than two thousand times the blast power of the British "Grand Slam" which is the largest bomb ever yet used in the history of warfare. . . .

It is an atomic bomb. It is a harnessing of the basic power of the universe. The force from which the sun draws its power has been loosed against those who brought war to the Far East.

DECODED President Truman reports here on the bombing of Hiroshima—and the opening of the atomic age. Truman had not been briefed on the atomic bomb project as vice president and had to make a quick decision on whether to use the new weapon. The United States had only two atomic bombs, and they weren't identical. No one was entirely sure that they would work, but when the *Enola Gay* bomber dropped an atomic bomb on Hiroshima, Japan, it killed about 66,000 people and injured another 69,000, although it's very difficult to estimate the casualties because the destruction was so complete.

TRUMAN'S SPECIAL MESSAGE TO CONGRESS, NOVEMBER 19, 1945

In my message to the Congress of September 6, 1945, there were enumerated in a proposed Economic Bill of Rights certain rights which ought to be assured to every American citizen.

One of them was: "The right to adequate medical care and the opportunity to achieve and enjoy good health." Another was the "right to adequate protection from the economic fears of . . . sickness. . . ."

Millions of our citizens do not now have a full measure of opportunity to achieve and enjoy good health. Millions do not now a settlement and then threatened to draft railroad workers into the military to end that strike.

During the war, US factories had produced things needed by the military instead of consumer goods. It took time for industries to switch back from wartime production. The readjustment was bumpy and people were angry that they couldn't immediately buy things that hadn't been available during the war.

Truman, a Democrat, was working with a Republican-controlled Congress, and they didn't always agree with each other. In 1947, Congress passed the Taft-Hartley Act, which sharply curtailed the power of labor unions, making it harder

to strike. Truman vetoed the act, but Congress passed it over his veto.

In 1947, Jackie Robinson became the first Black major league baseball player and Harry Truman became the first president to speak to the National Association for the Advancement of Colored People (NAACP).

Jackie Robinson

have protection or security against the economic effects of sickness. The time has arrived for action to help them attain that opportunity and that protection.

DECODED Truman worked hard to get a national health insurance bill passed, but he wasn't able to do so. It was one of the biggest disappointments of his presidency. When legislation creating Medicare (health insurance for the elderly) and Medicaid (health insurance for the poor) passed under President Lyndon Johnson in 1965, Johnson invited Harry and Bess Truman to the signing of the bill. The Trumans were the first to sign up for the plan. Harry Truman received the first Medicare card, and Bess got the second.

TRUMAN'S ADDRESS TO THE NAACP, JUNE 29, 1947

I should like to talk to you briefly about civil rights and human freedom. It is my deep conviction that we have reached a turning point in the long history of our country's efforts to guarantee freedom and equality to all our citizens. Recent events in the United States and abroad have made us realize that it is more important today than ever before to insure that all Americans enjoy these rights.

When I say all Americans I mean all Americans. . . .

We must keep moving forward, with new concepts of civil rights to safeguard our heritage. The extension of civil rights today means, not protection of the people against the Government, but protection of the people by the Government.

We must make the Federal Government a friendly, vigilant defender of the rights and equalities of all Americans. And again I mean all Americans.

DECODED Truman spoke to the NAACP, the major organization pushing for civil rights for Black Americans, from the steps of the Lincoln Memorial. His broadcast was carried live on radio.

The next year Truman sent civil rights proposals to Congress and called for civil rights laws in his State of the Union address. Truman wanted a federal law against lynching, protection of the right to vote, and protection from discrimination in employment. His proposals were stiffly opposed in Congress. Truman used an executive order, which doesn't require congressional consent, to desegregate the military.

At the Democratic convention in 1948, Truman got the nomination but was expected to lose in November to Republican candidate Thomas Dewey. The *Chicago Tribune* was so confident Dewey would win that on election night its staff went ahead and printed the next day's paper with a giant headline: DEWEY DEFEATS TRUMAN. But the world woke the next morning to a Truman victory, and a few days later Truman was photographed holding that very same newspaper. It's the most famous photograph from his presidency.

Truman announced his "Fair Deal" programs after the election. They included a higher minimum wage, expanded Social Security, national health insurance, repeal of the Taft-Hartley Act, and more. Congress didn't give him most of what he wanted, although he got an increase in the minimum wage, which went from forty to seventy-five cents an hour, as well as a public housing bill meant to provide decent housing for low-income families and an increase in Social Security.

Foreign affairs dominated Truman's terms. The Cold War, or hostile relations with the Soviet Union, had an impact on domestic affairs, too. After World War II a Red Scare—that is, a fear of communists, who were nicknamed "Reds"—gripped Americans. A couple of prominent spy cases shook Americans, especially the cases of Alger Hiss, who had worked in the State Department and was accused of spying for the Soviet Union, and Julius and Ethel Rosenberg, who were executed for passing atomic secrets to the Soviet Union.

Wisconsin Republican senator Joseph McCarthy claimed that the State Department was full of communists. He spent the last years of Truman's administration, and the first years of Eisenhower's, pushing McCarthyism, which meant making charges based on untrue and misleading allegations that people in the US government were communists. He made outrageous claims without evidence—he just plain lied—but many people believed him. They thought that a US senator would know what he was talking about and that he would be honest. People were genuinely afraid of the spread of communism, thinking that it would hurt US interests. Despite Truman's efforts to stop him, McCarthyism continued past Truman's term in office.

In 1947, Truman's secretary of state, George C. Marshall, started the Marshall Plan, which provided economic aid to European countries devastated by the war. It was a success and helped Europe recover economically.

The postwar settlement of Germany divided that nation into four zones, each controlled by a wartime ally: the Soviet Union, Britain, France, and the United States. The capital, Berlin, was entirely inside the Soviet zone, but because it was an important city it was divided in half. The Western allies controlled the western half of the city. The Soviets controlled the eastern half. Soviet leader Joseph Stalin pinched off access to West Berlin in June 1948—which was easy, because the road to the capital lay inside the Soviet zone, and he could simply close the road. Truman responded with the Berlin Airlift. Planes took off every three minutes around the clock, bringing food and necessities to the people of West Berlin. It continued for almost a year, and finally Stalin called off the blockade.

WEST BERLIN
(American, British & French)

EAST BERLIN
(Soviet-controlled)

British Zone

Soviet Zone

Allied-Occupied Germany, 1948

American Zone

French Zone

In 1945, in the wake of World War II, the United Nations (UN) was created to try to prevent future wars and foster international cooperation and communication. President Truman signed the charter that created the UN. The UN had an early test when in June 1950, North Korea invaded South Korea. The UN voted to send an international force to Korea, with more than a dozen nations contributing troops, but the United States did most of the fighting. General Douglas MacArthur was in command. When MacArthur pushed too close to the border between North Korea and China, Chinese troops entered the war, and Truman fired MacArthur.

The Korean War ended with an armistice, which means that the fighting stopped, but a peace has never been concluded.

Legacy

After leaving office the Trumans returned to Independence, Missouri. Truman remained an interested observer in politics, and once his presidential library was built in Independence, he spent a lot of time there writing his memoirs and answering letters. He even gave tours of the library himself. Truman is buried in its courtyard.

Truman is remembered for his tough stance on foreign policy issues, bringing World War II to a close, authorizing the use of the atomic bomb, and fighting to protect South Korea. He also advanced civil rights for Black Americans.

PRESIDENT

34

OF THE UNITED STATES

BORN: 1890

DIED: 1969

IN OFFICE:
January 20, 1953–
January 20, 1961

FROM: born in Texas;
grew up in Kansas

VICE PRESIDENT:
Richard Nixon

PARTY: Republican

DWIGHT
D ★ A ★ V ★ I ★ D
EISENHOWER

DID YOU KNOW?

● Dwight Eisenhower didn't have a birth certificate until he ran for president. His 1890 birth was officially recorded in 1952, two weeks ahead of his sixty-second birthday.

● Eisenhower renamed the presidential retreat that was built in the 1930s after his grandson. It's now Camp David.

● Eisenhower was the only president who fought in the army during World War II. (Ronald Reagan was in the army but didn't fight.)

Life Before the Presidency

Dwight David Eisenhower grew up in Abilene, Kansas. He went to West Point, the US military academy. He wanted to try for a spot in the naval academy, but he was too old. The army would still let him take their competitive exam for a spot, so he did. He finished second. When the person who had won couldn't pass the physical, Eisenhower got the spot at West Point. He played football there. He loved it but he was a mediocre player. After seriously injuring a knee, he had to quit football and became the head cheerleader, one of four presidents to be a cheerleader (Franklin Roosevelt, Ronald Reagan, and George W. Bush were the others). He was an average student and got in trouble for playing pranks.

Eisenhower almost didn't get a job with the army after he graduated. His knee was bad enough that West Point's medical board voted unanimously against giving him a commission. West Point's chief medical officer disagreed and appealed Eisenhower's case to the War Department, which decided to take a chance on him. The bad knee kept him out of World War I, although he wanted to fight. But after the war, the army had him write a guide to World War I battle sites, and he served as an aide to General Douglas MacArthur in the Philippines.

In 1941, Eisenhower was planning to retire from the army. But on December 7, Japan bombed Pearl Harbor.

Eisenhower stayed in the army and rose quickly in rank; by the time he did retire in 1948, he was a five-star general, the army's highest rank. He helped President Franklin Roosevelt and British Prime Minister Winston Churchill figure out strategy for the war. He impressed them so much that they put him in charge of the Allied war effort. He was the Supreme Allied Commander of D-Day, the invasion of Normandy, France, on June 6, 1944, when Allied forces opened a western front against Germany. It was the largest amphibious operation (meaning troops were landed from the water) in history—and Eisenhower was in charge.

Eisenhower became president of Columbia University in 1948. In 1950, President Truman asked him to head NATO, the United States' military alliance, a job for which he was better suited. Eisenhower ran for president in 1952. He was a victorious general and well-liked—and he won in a landslide.

Mr. President

Once in office, Eisenhower quickly negotiated an armistice ending the Korean War, as he had promised during his campaign. The Cold War competition with the Soviet Union continued, and Senator Joseph McCarthy claimed that communists were active inside the US government, even though he had no evidence, at a time when many Americans were deeply worried that communism would spread. Eisenhower tried to stay above it all.

The Indian Termination Act of 1953 tried to end the Indigenous nations' reservation and tribal system and move Indigenous people into the mainstream of American life as individuals, stripped of their traditional culture. Some nations were forced to divide their lands up among individuals and end their own governments. Federal benefits for Indigenous nations ended, too. Eisenhower signed the bill, which is widely criticized today.

The president had a major heart attack in 1955, on the birthday of his son who'd died as a little boy. His wife, Mamie, thought the grief he still felt for little "Ikky" was the reason he had the heart attack. But in 1956, Eisenhower ran for reelection and won in another landslide, despite concerns about his health.

While Senator McCarthy whipped up fear, Eisenhower took action against the spread of communism, announcing the Eisenhower Doctrine in 1957, after brief fighting around the Suez Canal in Egypt the previous year. The Eisenhower Doctrine said that the United States would aid any Middle Eastern country that asked for help in staying independent.

The Civil Rights Movement was given a major boost in 1954 when the Supreme

TELEGRAM FROM DWIGHT EISENHOWER TO GOVERNOR ORVAL FAUBUS, SEPTEMBER 5, 1957

Your telegram received requesting my assurance of understanding of and cooperation in the course of action you have taken on school integration recommended by the Little Rock School Board and ordered by the United States District Court pursuant to the mandate of the United States Supreme Court.

When I became President, I took an oath to protect and defend the Constitution of the United States. The only assurance I can give you is that the Federal Constitution will be upheld by me by every legal means at my command.

DECODED The president not only sent this terse telegram to Governor Faubus in Arkansas, he also released it to the press. Eisenhower reminded the governor that Supreme Court decisions also applied in Arkansas.

Court ruled in *Brown v. Board of Education of Topeka* that schools had to be desegregated, so that kids of different races would be in school together. When nine Black students enrolled in Little Rock Central High School in 1957 as part of a gradual desegregation plan, Arkansas Governor Orval Faubus called in the National Guard to surround the school and keep the Black students from entering, while a mob of white protesters threatened violence. Eisenhower called in the army to ensure that the students got in.

LITTLE ROCK NINE

STATEMENT OF GOVERNOR ORVAL FAUBUS,
SEPTEMBER 14, 1957

The President and I had a friendly and constructive discussion of the problem of compliance with Court orders respecting the high schools of Little Rock. . . . The people of Little Rock are law-abiding and I know that they expect to obey valid court orders. In this they shall have my support. In so doing it is my responsibility to protect the people from violence in any form. As I interpret the President's public statements, the national Administration has no thought of challenging this fact. In meeting this obligation, it is essential that, in proceeding to implement the orders of the Court, the complexities of integration be patiently understood by all those in Federal authority. When I assured the President, as I have already done, that I expect to accept the decision of the Courts, I entertained the hope that the Department of Justice and the Federal Judiciary will act with understanding and patience in discharging their duties.

DECODED Governor Faubus admits that Supreme Court decisions must be obeyed, even in Arkansas. The phrase "valid court orders" is a throwback to nullification, the idea that a state could reject a federal law or action if it didn't feel it was legitimate. Governor Faubus's statements that federal authorities need patience were part of segregationists' attempts to slow integration.

Letter from Jackie Robinson to Dwight Eisenhower, May 13, 1958

My dear Mr. President:

I was sitting in the audience at the Summit Meeting of Negro Leaders yesterday when you said we must have patience. On hearing you say this, I felt like standing up and saying, "Oh, no! Not again." . . . 17 million Negroes cannot do as you suggest and wait for the hearts of men to change. We want to enjoy now the rights that we feel we are entitled to as Americans. This we cannot do unless we pursue aggressively goals which all other Americans achieved over 150 years ago.

DECODED White supremacists repeatedly asked for patience in the face of calls for Black civil rights. Jackie Robinson's letter to President Eisenhower urges the president to make change immediately, pointing out that Black Americans were being denied what others had for over 150 years.

The Cold War continued in Eisenhower's second term. He signed the Federal-Aid Highway Act in 1956, which led to the construction of interstate highways. Ike thought roads were a national security issue—he wanted soldiers and weapons to be able to move around the country quickly if necessary. The Soviet Union launched the first man-made satellite, *Sputnik 1* (pronounced *spoot-neek*), in 1957, and the United States established the National Aeronautics and Space Administration (NASA) in 1958—the Cold War was moving into space. Achievements in space were a splashy way to enhance a nation's prestige.

On May 1, 1960, near the end of Eisenhower's presidency, the Soviet Union shot down a US U-2 high-altitude spy plane over Soviet airspace. The Eisenhower administration scrambled to come up with a cover story, including starting a search for the spy plane, knowing it wasn't in the area they were searching. The US assumed that the pilot was dead—his plane had been hit by a missile and then fell as far as seventy thousand feet. When the Russians produced him—quite alive—the United States had to admit it had been flying spy planes over the Soviet Union.

Legacy

Dwight Eisenhower is better remembered for being the general who oversaw D-Day in World War II than for his presidency. When he was in the White House, many people thought of him as a "caretaker" president: one who doesn't do much, but preserves the office to hand off to the next person. But Eisenhower did negotiate an end to fighting in the Korean War and helped guide the United States through difficult years of the Cold War with the Soviet Union. During the Eisenhower presidency, the United States was mostly peaceful and prosperous.

JOHN FITZGERALD KENNEDY

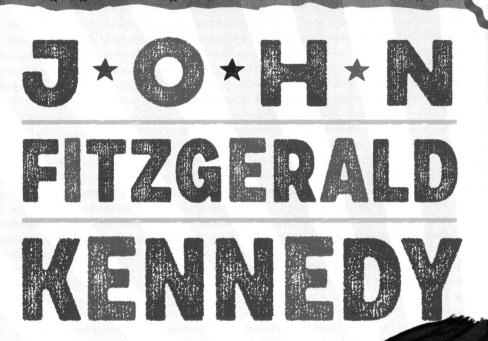

PRESIDENT 35 OF THE UNITED STATES

BORN: 1917

DIED: 1963

IN OFFICE:
January 20, 1961–
November 22, 1963

FROM: Massachusetts

VICE PRESIDENT:
Lyndon Baines
Johnson

PARTY: Democratic

DID YOU KNOW?

- Kennedy was the first president to be born in the twentieth century.

- Kennedy won the 1960 election with the smallest popular vote margin of any presidential election in the twentieth century.

- Kennedy wrote *Profiles in Courage* while hospitalized after one of the four surgeries to help his back after an injury while at Harvard. It won a Pulitzer Prize.

Life Before the Presidency

John F. Kennedy, known as Jack, was born to a wealthy Irish-Catholic Boston family, the second of nine children. Kennedy had a privileged childhood, but he suffered a series of serious illnesses, including measles and whooping cough. The most dangerous was a monthlong bout of scarlet fever, a potentially fatal illness, when he was two years old. He played football at Harvard and ruptured a disk in his spine, which would cause him lifelong problems. When World War II broke out Kennedy tried to join the navy but he couldn't pass the physical. His father used his political clout to get Kennedy in. He was sent to the South Pacific in command of *PT-109*. (PTs were small patrol torpedo boats with motors.)

In August 1943, a Japanese ship rammed *PT-109*, causing it to explode. The eleven survivors hung on to debris from the ship for hours. Eventually they swam toward a nearby island; Kennedy, who had been on the swim team at Harvard, towed a badly injured crewmate three miles through the ocean, the man's life-jacket straps clamped in his teeth.

Kennedy received a US Navy and Marine Corps Medal for Valor and a Purple Heart.

After the war, Kennedy worked briefly as a journalist, an experience that helped him later when dealing with White House reporters. As president, Kennedy acknowledged that the press could be irritating but said that it was essential to a free society.

Kennedy's older brother, Joe, was killed in World War II, and Kennedy's father transferred his ambitions onto Jack, persuading him to run for political office. In 1946, he won a seat in the US House of Representatives. He was twenty-nine. In 1952, he won a US Senate seat from Massachusetts. In 1956, he failed to get the Democratic vice presidential nomination, but he got the nod for president in 1960. He ran against Republican candidate Richard Nixon, who had been Eisenhower's vice president. Kennedy proposed a televised debate, the first in the nation's history. Kennedy gave the impression of youth and vigor while Nixon, who was unshaven, looked sweaty and nervous. People who saw the debate on television thought that Kennedy won, and he went on to win the 1960 election.

JOHN F. KENNEDY'S ACCEPTANCE SPEECH AT THE DEMOCRATIC CONVENTION, JULY 15, 1960

I am fully aware of the fact that the Democratic Party, by nominating someone of my faith, has taken on what many regard as a new and hazardous risk. . . . And you have, at the same time, placed your confidence in me . . . to uphold the Constitution and my oath of office—and to reject any kind of religious pressure or obligation that might directly or indirectly interfere with my conduct of the Presidency in the national interest. . . .

DECODED Kennedy was the first Roman Catholic President. Some Protestants worried that a Catholic president would do whatever the Pope told him. Kennedy addresses this concern directly, saying that he would put the nation first.

Today some would say that those struggles are all over—that all the horizons have been explored— that all the battles have been won—that there is no longer an American frontier.

But I trust that no one in this vast assemblage will agree with those sentiments. For the problems are not all solved and the battles are not all won—and we stand today on the edge of a New Frontier. . . .

Beyond that frontier are the uncharted areas of science and space, unsolved problems of peace and war, unconquered pockets of ignorance and prejudice, unanswered questions of poverty and surplus. It would be easier to shrink back from that frontier, to look to the safe mediocrity of the past, to be lulled by good intentions and high rhetoric— and those who prefer that course should not cast their votes for me, regardless of party.

DECODED This speech was later called the "New Frontier" speech. It showcases Kennedy's optimism and idealism.

Mr. President

Once Kennedy was in office he gave televised press conferences in order to reach more people. An average of eighteen million people watched.

PIERRE SALINGER, IN AN ORAL INTERVIEW ABOUT THE FIRST LIVE TELEVISED PRESS CONFERENCE, JANUARY 25, 1961

The fact of the matter is that the time when President Kennedy started televised press conferences there were only three or four newspapers in the entire United States that carried a full transcript of a presidential press conference. Therefore, what people read was a distillation. . . . We thought that they should have the opportunity to see it in full.

DECODED Pierre Salinger was President Kennedy's press secretary. Kennedy read several newspapers every day, but he understood that he could reach the public better through television.

Kennedy promoted new social programs, including proposals to allow retirement at the age of sixty-two, improve insurance programs for the elderly, and safeguard children of unmarried parents, but Congress rejected many of them. He raised the minimum wage to $1.25 an hour by January 1, 1963. He set up the President's Appalachian Regional Commission to address poverty in

Appalachia, where incomes were consistently lower than the national average. In 1961, he issued an executive order establishing the Peace Corps, which sent young Americans to aid other countries and tried to promote peace and help people of different nations understand each other.

He also promoted the space program. The National Aeronautics and Space Administration (NASA) had been established in 1958 and made its first launch that year. It also sent a spacecraft out of Earth's orbit, launched a satellite to observe Earth's weather, and put a chimpanzee named Ham into suborbital flight for sixteen minutes and then recovered him safely. But in May 1961, President Kennedy announced that the United States would try to land astronauts on the moon before the decade ended. It was an incredibly bold statement—NASA wasn't anyplace close to being able to do that.

Kennedy thought education was extremely important and he worked to lower dropout rates, improve teacher training, and provide more services for deaf students. He knew that tackling civil rights issues would provoke great hostility and wanted to delay dealing with civil rights until he could get the rest of his program passed. In particular, Kennedy thought that Southern Democrats were likely to leave the Democratic Party as it continued to advocate for the rights of Black Americans, an issue that didn't appeal to them. But events pushed Kennedy into earlier action.

In 1960, before Kennedy's election, four college students held a "sit-in" at a lunch counter in Greensboro, North Carolina, that wouldn't serve Black customers. When they were refused service, they stayed seated. Their protest succeeded in getting the lunch counter to integrate and sparked similar sit-ins in other cities. Then in 1961, groups of Black and white people rode buses together on "freedom rides" through the South to fight segregation.

Letter from Jackie Robinson to John F. Kennedy, February 9, 1961

My dear Mr. President:

. . . I thank you for what you have done so far, but it is not how much has been done but how much more there is to do. I would like to be patient Mr. President, but patience has caused us years in our struggle for human dignity. I will continue to hope and pray for your aggressive leadership but will not refuse to criticise [sic] if the feeling persist [sic] that Civil Rights is not on the agenda for months to come.

DECODED Jackie Robinson was the first Black major league baseball player of the modern era. He used his fame to help prod Kennedy toward a more active stance on civil rights.

In September 1962, a young Black man named James Meredith enrolled at the University of Mississippi. Up to this point, the university had been all-white. A federal court ruled that the university had to let Meredith in, but Governor Ross Barnett tried to stop him anyway. A riot erupted when Meredith went to campus, and it took fifteen hours for National Guardsmen and soldiers to restore order. Hundreds of people were injured and two killed. Meredith attended classes under guard by federal troops and graduated in 1963.

In June 1963, Kennedy submitted a civil rights bill to Congress. It proposed protecting Black voting rights by prohibiting discriminatory tests (like Constitution tests), outlawing discrimination in hotels, restaurants, theaters, and public accommodations, enforcing school desegregation, not giving federal funds to any organization that practiced discrimination, and outlawing discrimination by businesses that employed twenty-five or more people. It would also set up the Equal Employment Opportunity Commission to handle discrimination complaints.

His proposal didn't end the unrest. The next day NAACP official Medgar Evers, a WWII veteran who organized voter registration drives and wanted schools to integrate, was shot to death in his driveway.

And in August 1963, a quarter of a million people came to the nation's capital for the March on Washington, which continued to pressure the Kennedy administration to protect civil rights.

Kennedy didn't live to see his civil rights proposals become law, but Lyndon Johnson would use the national grief over his assassination to get the legislation passed in 1964 and 1965.

KENNEDY'S TELEVISED ADDRESS TO THE NATION ON CIVIL RIGHTS, JUNE 11, 1963

. . . Today we are committed to a worldwide struggle to promote and protect the rights of all who wish to be free. And when Americans are sent to Viet-Nam or West Berlin, we do not ask for whites only. It ought to be possible, therefore, for American students of any color to attend any public institution they select without having to be backed up by troops.

. . . This is not a sectional issue. Difficulties over segregation and discrimination exist in every city, in every State of the Union, producing in many cities a rising tide of discontent that threatens the public safety. Nor is this a partisan issue. In a time of domestic crisis men of good will and generosity should be able to unite regardless of party or politics. This is not even a legal or legislative issue alone. It is better to settle these matters in the courts than on the streets, and new laws are needed at every level, but law alone cannot make men see right.

We are confronted primarily with a moral issue. It is as old as the scriptures and is as clear as the American Constitution. . . .

DECODED It was important for the president to acknowledge that discrimination wasn't just a legal or constitutional issue, but that it was simply wrong. He asked Congress for legislation so that Black people could finally, fully, be free. It energized the Civil Rights Movement.

Kennedy had an ambitious domestic program—most of which Congress blocked—but foreign affairs dominated his term. Eisenhower had left a plan for invading Cuba with the hope of driving out Cuban leader Fidel Castro, who had ties to the Soviet Union. Kennedy signed off on the plan. The CIA helped train Cubans living in the United States who wanted to overthrow Castro, and in April 1961 they invaded, landing at the Bay of Pigs on Cuba's coast. The mission quickly failed. The invaders had thought Cubans would rise up to help them, but that didn't happen. It was a major foreign policy failure and Kennedy was embarrassed.

The Cold War with the Soviet Union continued to influence foreign affairs. In Berlin, divided into an East and West after World War II, the Soviet-backed East Germans built a wall through the middle of the city, physically dividing it. This was the Berlin Wall, built to prevent East Germans from moving to the West, and it lasted until 1989.

The Cold War was played out closer to home, too. In October 1962, the United States discovered that the Soviet Union was planning to put nuclear missiles in Cuba that could reach the US mainland, which was only ninety miles away.

Kennedy consulted with advisors for several tense days and ultimately stationed US naval ships around Cuba to prevent the Soviets from getting further missiles into the country. The world was on the verge of nuclear war.

Finally Soviet leader Nikita Khrushchev backed down. Many Americans considered it Kennedy's finest hour. In the wake of the Cuban missile crisis, the Russian and American governments began arms reduction talks. Both sides worried that continuing to increase their nuclear arsenals would eventually result in a nuclear war or simply an accident. They thought that reducing their quantities of nuclear arms might make the world safer.

In Vietnam, communist nationalists fought to push out France after World War II. France had colonized Vietnam a hundred years before. The United States sent advisors to help France because of the Cold War idea that any communist movement was a threat, but the Vietnamese nationalists won, ending French colonial rule. The country was then divided into two parts, North and South Vietnam, and the United States set up a pro-American government in the south. Kennedy sent more advisors to Vietnam, but near the end of his presidency he announced that he was going to reduce the American presence there. Whether American involvement in the Vietnam War could have been avoided if he had lived is an unanswerable question.

Kennedy made a trip to Texas in November 1963 in preparation for a reelection run in 1964. On November 22, he rode beside his

CUBA

wife, Jackie, in an open motorcade through Dallas. Lee Harvey Oswald, a former marine, shot Kennedy from a building as his car passed by. Kennedy died immediately.

Lady Bird Johnson Audio Diary Entry, November 22, 1963

It all began so beautifully. . . .

Then almost at the edge of town, on our way to the Trade Mart where we were going to have the luncheon, we were rounding a curve, going down a hill and suddenly there was a sharp loud report - a shot. It seemed to me to come from the right above my shoulder from a building. Then a moment and then two more shots in rapid succession. There had been such a gala air that I thought it must be firecrackers or some sort of celebration. Then in the lead car the Secret Service men were suddenly down. I heard over the radio system, "Let's get out of here," and our ss (Secret Service) man who was with us, Ruf Youngblood, I believe it was, vaulted over the front seat on top of Lyndon, threw him to the floor, and said, "Get down."

As we ground to a halt - we were still the third car — Secret Service men began to pull, lead, guide and hustle us out. I cast one last look over my shoulder and saw in the President's car a bundle of pink, just like a drift of blossoms, lying on the back seat. I think it was Mrs. Kennedy lying over the President's body.

DECODED Vice President Lyndon Johnson's wife, Lady Bird Johnson, recorded this account of Kennedy's assassination. First-person accounts can help you understand how events unfolded in real time.

Legacy

John F. Kennedy is remembered as a young president taken too soon. Historians give him high marks for his handling of the Cuban missile crisis and the Cold War in general. Domestically, he helped the Civil Rights Movement and funded education. And he inspired a generation of young people to strive to improve society and to believe that government could help make things better. Kennedy didn't survive to see his civil rights legislation passed or men land on the moon, although he set those things in motion and they're an important part of his legacy.

Robert Caro, Oral Interview, May 16, 2012

He touched something in me. I still remember, actually, his inaugural address; I think it touched something in my whole generation. Someone once said to me at Harvard, one minute everybody was going to law school or business school, and the next minute they were all in the Peace Corps or going to join the Justice Department. I think that's the way I felt about him.

DECODED Journalist and biographer Robert Caro talks here about how Kennedy inspired many young people.

BORN: 1908

DIED: 1973

IN OFFICE:
November 22, 1963–
January 20, 1969

FROM: Texas

VICE PRESIDENT:
Hubert Horatio
Humphrey

PARTY: Democratic

LYNDON
B·A·I·N·E·S
JOHNSON

DID YOU KNOW?

● Johnson appointed the first Black cabinet member, Robert Weaver, who headed the Department of Housing and Urban Development.

● Lyndon Johnson asked for Judge Sarah Hughes to come to the airport in Dallas on November 22, 1963, to administer the oath of office. Kennedy had appointed her as the third woman ever to be a federal judge (1961). That appointment is what gave her the authority to give Johnson the oath of office.

● LBJ is the only president to have been sworn in by a woman.

● Johnson had a car that also worked as a boat. He liked to pretend he'd lost control of the car and drive into a lake to terrify passengers who didn't know the car would float.

Life Before the Presidency

Lyndon Baines Johnson was born in Texas. His father was a member of the Texas state legislature and a struggling farmer. Johnson didn't do well enough in school to make it to college. He worked on a road crew, fought, drank—and got arrested. Eventually he became a teacher and was a good one. He did his student teaching at an elementary school in Cotulla, Texas, teaching the children of Mexican American farmers. He didn't speak Spanish and many of them didn't speak English, but that didn't stop him. In 1937, at the age of twenty-eight, Johnson was elected to the US House of Representatives. Johnson was the first member of Congress to enlist after the United States entered World War II. He was a congressional inspector in the Pacific and flew in only one bombing mission against Japanese troops.

In 1948, Johnson won a US Senate seat by eighty-seven votes, picking up the ironic nickname "Landslide Lyndon." He became majority leader in 1955. Johnson had a tremendous work ethic and was politically smart—the combination turned him into one of the most powerful Senate majority leaders in history. Members of Congress joked about getting the "Johnson treatment," in which Johnson persuaded people any way

necessary—begging, threatening, or prodding. Johnson could be very effective at lining up the votes he needed to pass a bill. He tried to get the Democratic nomination for president in 1960, but John F. Kennedy got the nod instead. Kennedy asked Johnson to run as his vice presidential candidate.

When Kennedy was assassinated in a motorcade on November 22, 1963, Johnson was two cars behind him. He took the oath of office on *Air Force One* the same day.

Mr. President

Lyndon Johnson came to office after John Kennedy's assassination in November 1963. He called his domestic agenda the "Great Society." Johnson saw an active role for the government and pursued a significant list of legislation. He set up the Department of Housing and Urban Development to oversee national policies on housing and to enforce fair housing laws, and he increased funding to education, from elementary schools to colleges. He won passage of Medicare, which helps older adults with health care expenses. Lady Bird Johnson pushed for a highway beautification act that limited billboards along highways so that motorists could see the countryside.

Johnson also established the Head Start program to give poor children access to early education and another program to provide legal help to the poor. The War on Poverty worked; the poverty rate fell significantly.

In one decade, from 1964 to 1973, it fell from 19 percent to 11.1 percent, or by a little less than half. It was a remarkable achievement.

JFK had asked for a civil rights bill, and Johnson pushed it through. The Civil Rights Act of 1964 ended segregation in public facilities. Then he won an even bigger battle, the Voting Rights Act of 1965. Black people had been denied voting rights through poll taxes, which required people to pay in order to vote, and hurt all poor people. They also faced literacy or Constitution tests, which were given in such a way that they ensured failure. The Voting Rights Act allowed federal officials to register Black voters and in effect ended literacy tests in the South. Black voter registration exploded, with most Black voters joining the Democratic Party—while white conservatives who were upset with Johnson's civil rights bills left the Democratic Party. As Johnson used the national grief over Kennedy's death to secure passage of the Civil Rights Act, he used the shock over the assassination of civil rights leader Martin Luther King Jr. to push through a bill outlawing racial discrimination in housing.

JOHNSON'S REMARKS IN THE ROSE GARDEN ON PROJECT HEAD START, MAY 18, 1965

We set out to make certain that poverty's children would not be forevermore poverty's captives. We called our program Project Head Start. . . . Today we are able to announce that we will have open, and we believe operating this summer, coast-to-coast, some 2,000 child development centers serving as many as possibly a half million children.

This means that nearly half the preschool children of poverty will get a head start on their future.

Five- and six-year-old children are inheritors of poverty's curse and not its creators. Unless we act these children will pass it on to the next generation, like a family birthmark.

DECODED President Johnson began a wide variety of programs to help low-income Americans. The Head Start program was designed for preschool children from poor families. Head Start tried to meet the children's educational, social, emotional, and physical needs so that they could be competitive in school with kids who had more advantages.

Martin Luther King Jr.

JOHNSON'S SPECIAL MESSAGE TO CONGRESS, MARCH 15, 1965

At times history and fate meet at a single time in a single place to shape a turning point in man's unending search for freedom. So it was at Lexington and Concord. So it was a century ago at Appomattox. So it was last week in Selma, Alabama. . . .

Many of the issues of civil rights are very complex and most difficult. But about this there can and should be no argument. Every American citizen must have an equal right to vote. There is no reason which can excuse the denial of that right. There is no duty which weighs more heavily on us than the duty we have to ensure that right. . . .

But even if we pass this bill, the battle will not be over. What happened in Selma is part of a far larger movement which reaches into every section and State of America. It is the effort of American Negroes to secure for themselves the full blessings of American life.

Their cause must be our cause too. Because it is not just Negroes, but really it is all of us, who must overcome the crippling legacy of bigotry and injustice.

And we shall overcome.

DECODED Johnson gave this address after a civil rights march in Selma, Alabama, in which Alabama state troopers, some on horses, tear-gassed and beat marchers, injuring more than sixty people, some seriously. That day became known as Bloody Sunday. Johnson's use of the words "we shall overcome" sent a powerful signal. That was an anthem of the Civil Rights Movement; to hear those words said by the most powerful American—and a white Southerner—showed a shift in American thought. The Civil Rights Movement was gaining powerful protectors.

After finishing JFK's term, Johnson ran for a term of his own in 1964, and he won by the biggest popular vote margin in US history. By the end of his term he was so unpopular that he wouldn't run again.

There were 20,000 US troops in Vietnam when Kennedy died. Johnson increased US involvement as part of the global competition with the Soviets, fearing a communist takeover of the area. The great escalation of the war came during his administration. In 1964, after it appeared that US Navy ships had come under attack, Congress overwhelmingly passed the Gulf of Tonkin Resolution. The sweeping resolution gave the President power to "take all necessary measures." Johnson never asked for a formal declaration of war; the Gulf of Tonkin Resolution served as one in its absence.

Johnson campaigned on a platform of less involvement in Vietnam, but three weeks after his inauguration in 1965, he authorized Operation Rolling Thunder, which consisted of heavy bombing of North Vietnam. By mid-April 1965, the United States was fully at war, with significant numbers of ground troops in Vietnam. At the end of Johnson's term, the United States would have 535,000 troops in Vietnam. American opposition to the war surged. Before 1969, men between the ages of eighteen and twenty-six were eligible for the draft, but the older they were the more likely they were to be drafted. That meant that younger men faced several years where it was hard to make plans, including whether to marry or start a family, because they didn't know if they would be drafted. Faced with a vigorous antiwar movement, Johnson announced that he wouldn't run again.

Letter from Lyndon Johnson to Ho Chi Minh, March 21, 1967

[Released March 21, 1967. Delivered February 8, 1967]

Dear Mr. President:

I am writing to you in the hope that the conflict in Vietnam can be brought to an end. That conflict has already taken a heavy toll–in lives lost, in wounds inflicted, in property destroyed, and in simple human misery. If we fail to find a just and peaceful solution, history will judge us harshly.

DECODED Ho Chi Minh was president of North Vietnam. The United States would stay involved in the Vietnam War until 1973.

Legacy

Lyndon Johnson had sharply different legacies in domestic and foreign policy. At home, he secured landmark civil rights legislation and social programs that helped needy Americans. At the same time, he greatly increased American involvement in Vietnam, which hurt US prestige abroad and divided Americans. Johnson was one of the presidents who left a very mixed legacy.

RICHARD MILHOUS NIXON

BORN: 1913

DIED: 1994

IN OFFICE:
January 20, 1969–
August 9, 1974

FROM: California

VICE PRESIDENT:
Spiro Agnew (for
the first term and
the second term
through October 10,
1973), Gerald Ford
(from December 6,
1973, through Nixon's
resignation)

PARTY: Republican

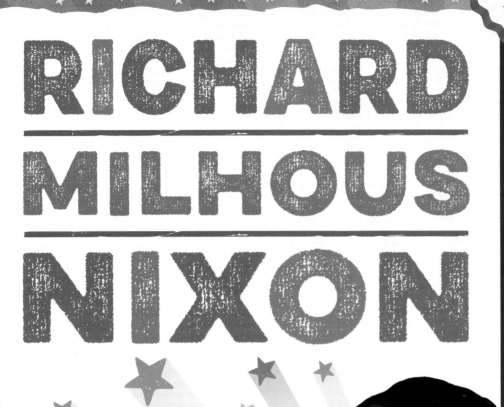

DID YOU KNOW?

- Nixon is the only president to have resigned.

- Nixon went to law school during the Depression. He was so poor his first year that he lived (without permission) in a tool shed in the woods on campus. The school was in North Carolina, which was good because the shed didn't have heat.

- While he was in law school, Nixon broke into a professor's office through a little window above the door. He rifled through the professor's records to find out where he ranked in the class.

Life Before the Presidency

R ichard Nixon was born in California. He went to Whittier College, majored in history, and was active in student government. He went on to Duke University Law School where he was third in his class. Nixon returned to California, worked as a lawyer, and was briefly a partner in a frozen orange juice business that failed.

During World War II, Nixon got a job in the tire-rationing section of the Office of Price Administration in Washington, DC. He later joined the navy and served in the South Pacific. When the war ended, Nixon ran for a seat in the US House of Representatives and beat the incumbent Democrat, partly because he made vague allegations that the incumbent was a communist sympathizer. He became known nationally for his work with the House Un-American Activities Committee (HUAC), the congressional body trying to identify Americans who might be communists. Nixon helped expose Alger Hiss, a former State Department official accused of passing secrets to the Soviets. The case helped make Nixon's reputation as a strong anticommunist.

In 1950, Nixon ran for Senate and used the strategy that had been effective in his House race—he accused his opponent of being soft on communism. Nixon was an early innovator in "negative campaigning," which is making personal attacks on an opponent instead of debating issues. He won the Senate seat. In 1952, he was Eisenhower's vice presidential running mate. When a story broke that Nixon had a secret slush fund of donations, Eisenhower considered dropping him. Nixon gave a televised speech admitting that the fund existed but claiming that he hadn't misused it. He pointed out that his family wasn't wealthy, and he ended by saying he had accepted one gift—a cocker spaniel for his daughter. Nixon wriggled out of trouble and Eisenhower kept him on the ticket.

When he ran against Kennedy in the presidential election of 1960, a televised debate hurt Nixon and he lost a close race. The next year he wrote a book, *Six Crises*, and the year after that, he ran for governor of California and lost badly. Nixon had a bitter, brooding edge, and after the loss he told reporters, "You don't have Nixon to kick around any more."

He joined a law firm in New York City, but then he decided to run for president in 1968 and got the Republican nomination. It was a chaotic year for the country—the Democratic convention was disorderly, antiwar protests were strong, Martin Luther King Jr. was assassinated in April, and Robert Kennedy, who was running for the Democratic nomination, was assassinated in June. Nixon campaigned with the "Southern Strategy," fueling the fears of white Southerners that Black political power was increasing, to get them to vote for Republicans. The 1954 *Brown v. Board of Education of Topeka* decision requiring schools to desegregate was deeply unpopular among white Southerners. The Republican Party championed a slow approach, stalling on desegregation and creating alternatives like private schools for white children. They also appointed conservative judges to stall the progress of civil rights. As the Democratic Party embraced the Civil Rights Movement, the Republican Party became the champion of people who opposed it. The Southern Strategy helped Nixon win in 1968.

Mr. President

One of the most stunning moments in American history occurred during Nixon's presidency: Astronauts landed on the Moon. President Kennedy had called for NASA to try to reach the moon by the end of the decade, but he didn't live long enough to see the landing.

Nixon inherited the war in Vietnam. Working very closely with his national security advisor, Henry Kissinger, Nixon followed a

President's Daily Diary, July 20, 1969

11:45 11:50 P [p.m.] *The president held an interplanetary conversation with Apollo 11 Astronauts, Neil Armstrong and Edwin Aldrin on the Moon.*

DECODED What an astonishing entry! The president's daily diary lists his activities and this notes his conversation with astronauts who were on the moon. Edwin Aldrin is usually called "Buzz."

policy of "Vietnamization"—turning over the fighting to South Vietnamese forces while expanding the war. Nixon ordered the bombing of Cambodia in 1969 and kept it a secret from Congress and the people, even to the extent of altering pilots' flight reports.

In 1969, the military draft changed to a lottery system so that instead of drafting men at the higher end of the age range first, everyone had an equal and random chance of being drafted, at least in theory. Anxiety and anger about the draft fueled antiwar protests.

In 1970, Nixon sent US ground troops into Cambodia to destroy communist strongholds there. He ran a secret war in Laos as well. (Cambodia and Laos lie on Vietnam's western border.) The antiwar movement protested the bombings in Cambodia. A protest at Kent

State University ended in tragedy when the Ohio National Guard opened fire on students, killing four people. In 1971, the *Pentagon Papers*, a top secret study by the Defense Department of US involvement in Vietnam, starting before the Nixon administration, was published. It revealed that the government had lied to the American people about what was going on in Vietnam, revelations that increased suspicion of the government and frustration with the war.

In January 1973, a peace agreement was reached between the United States, North Vietnam, and South Vietnam that included an immediate cease-fire and American withdrawal from Vietnam. The Vietnam War had been an embarrassment for the United States and had aroused large-scale resistance at home,

Vietnam

Laos

Cambodia

including many protests on college campuses and efforts to resist the draft.

China had had a communist revolution in 1949, and the United States had not recognized the new government. Nixon sent Henry Kissinger to China for talks that were kept secret because the countries had no diplomatic relations and these first attempts to establish communication were very sensitive. Then in 1971, China invited a US table tennis team to visit, and the next year a Chinese team came to the United States. The press called it "ping-pong diplomacy." In February 1972, Nixon visited China, the first visit by an American president while in office. It was a significant breakthrough in relations. In May 1972, Nixon traveled to Moscow and signed the SALT I (Strategic Arms Limitation Talks) agreement that limited specific weapons, reducing the Soviet and American arsenals. It ushered in an era of détente, or better relations, in which the nations communicated more.

WAR POWERS RESOLUTION, 1973

The President in every possible instance shall consult with Congress before introducing United States Armed Forces into hostilities . . . and after every such introduction shall consult regularly with the Congress until United States Armed Forces are no longer engaged in hostilities or have been removed from such situations. . . .

Within sixty calendar days after a report is submitted. . . the President shall terminate any use of United States Armed Forces . . . unless the Congress . . . has declared war. . . .

[DECODED] President Nixon bombed two neutral countries and didn't tell Congress or the American people. Upset at the lack of transparency and angry that its constitutional role had been ignored, Congress passed the War Powers Act, which allows presidents to send troops into conflict but requires them to get congressional approval to leave troops in place. (The Constitution says that Congress declares war, not the president.)

In his domestic agenda, Nixon proposed a program that would have given poor families a guaranteed annual income, or a "negative tax," as he put it. In 1969, a family of four would have had a guaranteed income of $1,600 a year. Nixon ran a test program to see if the people who received the funds would work less, but they didn't. The Senate rejected his proposal, but discussion of the measure eventually helped people accept similar bills, such as cost of living increases for people getting Social Security. Nixon also proposed expanding the food stamp program, although he was hoping it would fail and he could blame that on Democrats. And he put in the first affirmative action programs, which he called "set asides." On construction projects financed with federal money, a certain percentage of jobs would be given to minorities. He increased funding for some civil rights agencies, although he opposed busing as a way to integrate schools. And he proposed the Occupational Safety and Health Administration (OSHA), an agency to oversee workplace safety.

Nixon barely mentioned environmental issues while campaigning, but the environmental movement rose up at this time and both Democratic and Republican voters cared about the issue. Nixon responded by creating the Environmental Protection Agency (EPA) in 1970. He signed the Clean Air Act, which allowed federal and state governments to limit air pollution from both factories and cars. Congress passed the Clean Water Act over his veto; it regulated how much of a pollutant could be dumped into the water and established standards for what counted as safe water.

In 1973, he signed the Endangered Species Act, which tried to protect animals in danger of dying out, and in 1974, he signed the Safe Drinking Water Act, which set guidelines for safe drinking water, including water treatment. At the same time, he angered environmentalists by requiring economic analyses that highlighted the costs of environmental legislation. Seeing the costs increased opposition to environmental measures.

The economy was sluggish. High inflation and unemployment prompted Nixon to freeze wages and prices, which means to lock them in place, something normally only done during war. The controls helped, but once they were lifted inflation rose sharply.

In 1973, Vice President Spiro T. Agnew was investigated on charges of bribery, extortion, and income tax evasion. Agnew argued that a vice president couldn't be indicted while still in office and refused to resign. But President Nixon had a scandal of his own brewing, and after a court ruled that sitting vice presidents can be indicted, Agnew resigned. The prosecutor worked out a deal for Agnew that saved him from a lengthy prison term.

Nixon immediately nominated Gerald R. Ford, a Republican congressman from Michigan, to replace him, and both houses of Congress confirmed the appointment.

Spiro Agnew   Gerald Ford

The Nixon administration is best known for the Watergate burglary and cover-up. On June 17, 1972, police caught five White House operatives in the process of illegally bugging phones and photographing documents in the Democratic National Headquarters at the Watergate Building. There was an election coming up in 1972, and what the burglars were up to would likely benefit Nixon's campaign. President Nixon said the White House had nothing to do with it. The *Washington Post* investigated and discovered that Nixon's reelection campaign had paid the burglars thousands of dollars. Further revelations showed that Nixon had arranged for the burglars to get "hush money," which

means a payment not to talk. And he tried to get the CIA to stop the FBI from investigating the crimes. The question became whether the president was personally involved. As Republican senator Howard Baker of Tennessee asked, "What did the president know, and when did he know it?"

In 1973, the Watergate burglars were found guilty. A special prosecutor, Archibald Cox, was appointed to look into the affair. When Cox discovered that Nixon had taped conversations in the Oval Office, he ordered the tapes to be turned over. Nixon said no and ordered Attorney General Elliot Richardson to fire Cox. Richardson refused and resigned.

TRANSCRIPT of a Recording of a Meeting Between the President and H. R. Haldeman in the Oval Office on June 23, 1972, from 10:04 to 11:39 a.m.

Haldeman: Now, on the investigation, you know, the Democratic break-in thing, we're back to the—in the, the problem area because the FBI is not under control, because Gray doesn't exactly know how to control them, and they have, their investigation is now leading into some productive areas, because they've been able to trace the money, not through the money itself, but through the bank, you know, sources—the banker himself. And, and it goes in some directions we don't want it to go.

Nixon then ordered Deputy Attorney General William Ruckelshaus to fire Cox, and he also refused and resigned. That all happened in one evening, which became known as the "Saturday Night Massacre." (No one was killed. "Massacre" just refers to the people losing their jobs.) Finally the acting attorney general, Robert Bork, followed Nixon's order and fired Cox. Republicans as well as Democrats thought that the president shouldn't have fired the person investigating him.

In May 1974, the House began impeachment proceedings against Nixon, and in July, the Supreme Court ruled unanimously that he had to hand over the tapes. Nixon had claimed executive privilege, which means the right of the president to keep some things private to preserve national security. The Supreme Court ruled that there is no absolute right to executive privilege and that it can be overridden by the need to make sure the law is obeyed. Nixon turned the tapes over—although his secretary had erased an eighteen-minute segment on one of them. The House passed three articles of impeachment against Nixon: obstruction of justice, misuse of power, and contempt of Congress. Nixon announced his resignation on August 8, and the next day, Gerald Ford was sworn in as president.

DECODED This is the "smoking gun" tape. *Smoking gun* means proof that somebody committed a crime. This tape showed that President Nixon was trying to use the CIA to stop an FBI investigation, and led the House to draw up impeachment charges against him. "Gray" is L. Patrick Gray, acting director of the FBI, and H. R. Haldeman was White House chief of staff. The "Democratic break-in thing" was the burglary at the Democratic National Headquarters at the Watergate Building.

Legacy

After resigning, Nixon wrote several books, including his autobiography and books on foreign policy. He traveled widely as a private citizen, including to China and the Soviet Union.

Nixon's administration had a number of real achievements in environmental protection, opening communication with China, and improving relations with the Soviet Union. He is remembered for the Watergate scandal, however, and as the only president to have resigned. Nixon's scandals shocked the nation and increased suspicion of the government.

GERALD FORD

BORN: 1913

DIED: 2006

IN OFFICE:
August 9, 1974–
January 20, 1977

FROM: born in in
Nebraska; grew up in
Michigan

VICE PRESIDENT:
Nelson Rockefeller

PARTY: Republican

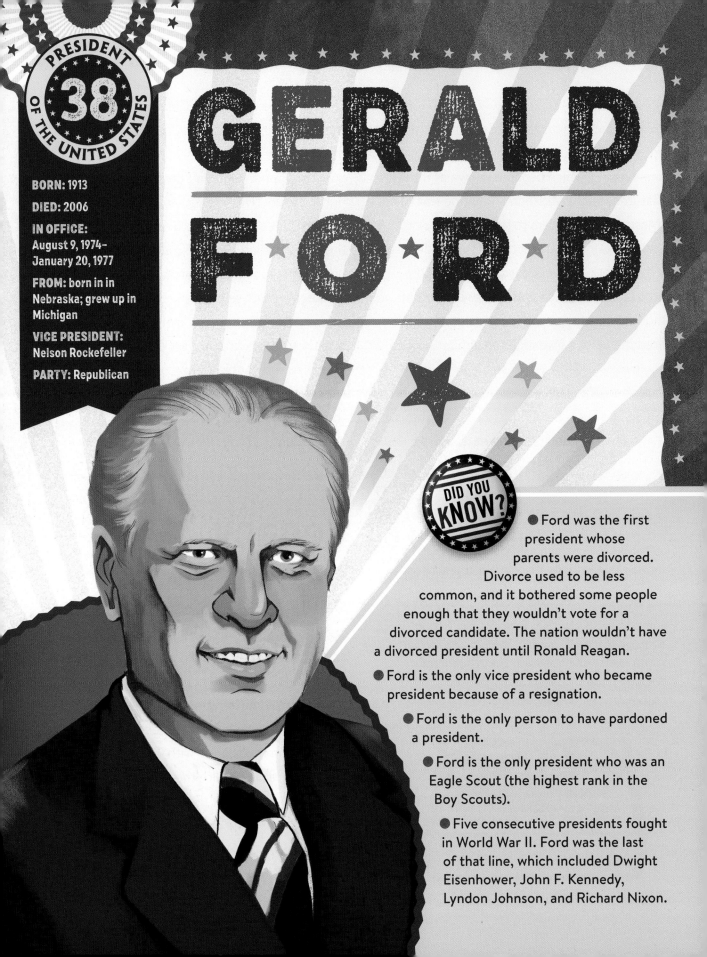

DID YOU KNOW?

- Ford was the first president whose parents were divorced. Divorce used to be less common, and it bothered some people enough that they wouldn't vote for a divorced candidate. The nation wouldn't have a divorced president until Ronald Reagan.

- Ford is the only vice president who became president because of a resignation.

- Ford is the only person to have pardoned a president.

- Ford is the only president who was an Eagle Scout (the highest rank in the Boy Scouts).

- Five consecutive presidents fought in World War II. Ford was the last of that line, which included Dwight Eisenhower, John F. Kennedy, Lyndon Johnson, and Richard Nixon.

Life Before the Presidency

Gerald Ford was born Leslie Lynch King Jr. His mother left his abusive father, moved to Grand Rapids, Michigan, and married Gerald Rudolff Ford. He adopted young Leslie and changed his name to Gerald Rudolff Ford Jr. (The future president later changed the spelling of his middle name.) Ford played football in high school and at the University of Michigan, where he was the team's most valuable player his senior year. He was a good student and turned down pro football contracts to go to law school.

After Pearl Harbor, Ford enlisted in the navy and served for four years. He won ten battle stars for service in the Pacific theater. After the war, he practiced law in Grand Rapids. He won a seat in the House of Representatives, and in 1965, he became the House minority leader. He developed a reputation for honesty and conservatism, meaning that he favored small government. Ford, a Republican, opposed Lyndon Johnson's domestic programs and wanted him to increase American involvement in Vietnam.

When Richard Nixon became president in 1969, Ford supported his policies. Vice President Spiro Agnew resigned while under investigation for taking bribes. Nixon, too, was in trouble as his involvement in the Watergate burglary came to light. Nixon nominated Ford to be his vice president, and Congress confirmed him with an overwhelming vote. He was sworn in on December 6, 1973.

At first Ford thought that Nixon was innocent, but on August 5, 1974, Ford said that taped evidence made it clear that Nixon could be impeached. Nixon announced his resignation on August 8, and Ford took the oath of office the next day. He is the only US president never to have been elected president or vice president by the American people. His vice president, Nelson Rockefeller, was also appointed rather than elected.

FORD'S INAUGURAL REMARKS, AUGUST 9, 1974

The oath that I have taken is the same oath that was taken by George Washington and by every President under the Constitution. But I assume the Presidency under extraordinary circumstances never before experienced by Americans. This is an hour of history that troubles our minds and hurts our hearts.

Therefore, I feel it is my first duty to make an unprecedented compact with my countrymen. Not an inaugural address, not a fireside chat, not a campaign speech—just a little straight talk among friends. And I intend it to be the first of many.

I am acutely aware that you have not elected me as your President by your ballots, and so I ask you to confirm me as your President with your prayers. And I hope that such prayers will also be the first of many. . . .

Our Constitution works; our great Republic is a government of laws and not of men.

DECODED Ford came to office in a unique way—and he knew it. His final point, that the United States is a "government of laws and not of men," is a basic point that John Adams made during the Revolution. Americans are loyal to the law, not the leader. In other words, no one is above the law.

Mr. President

When Ford took office the nation was shocked by Nixon's scandals and divided over social issues. The economy was sputtering, plagued by inflation, high unemployment, and high energy prices. The most immediate issue was the aftermath of Watergate. Most Americans had wanted to see Nixon punished. But Ford pardoned Nixon for his crimes to spare Nixon from jail, allow the country to move forward without having to focus on scandals, and give himself the chance to govern without being overshadowed by the spectacle of a trial. Ford's press secretary resigned in protest over the pardon and Ford's popularity, as measured by polls, fell by almost half. Some people thought that Nixon and Ford must have made a deal—that Nixon had agreed to resign in return for a pardon. There was no evidence of this and Ford denied it, but a House committee briefly investigated. Ford testified before the committee and the matter was dropped.

GERALD FORD'S REMARKS ON PROCLAMATION 4311, SEPTEMBER 8, 1974

I have come to a decision which I felt I should tell you and all of my fellow American citizens, as soon as I was certain in my own mind and in my own conscience that it is the right thing to do. . . . I have promised to uphold the Constitution, to do what is right as God gives me to see the right, and to do the very best that I can for America. . . .

There are no historic or legal precedents to which I can turn in this matter, none that precisely fit the circumstances of a private citizen who has resigned the Presidency of the United States. But it is common knowledge that serious allegations and accusations hang like a sword over our former President's head, threatening his health as he tries to reshape his life, a great part of which was spent in the service of this country and by the mandate of its people. . . .

The facts, as I see them, are that a former President of the United States, instead of enjoying equal treatment with any other citizen accused of violating the law, would be cruelly and excessively penalized either in preserving the presumption of his innocence or in obtaining a speedy determination of his guilt in order to repay a legal debt to society.

During this long period of delay and potential litigation, ugly passions would again be aroused. And our people would again be polarized in their opinions. And the credibility of our free institutions of government would again be challenged at home and abroad.

As President, my primary concern must always be the greatest good of all the people of the United States whose servant I am. As a man, my first consideration is to be true to my own convictions and my own conscience.

DECODED President Ford here explains to the American people why he pardoned Richard Nixon. It wasn't a step he took lightly, and he understood there would be outrage that the former president escaped accountability. Ford thought it was best for the country to move on instead of being bogged down in a trial, and likely appeals, that would take at least months and possibly years.

Letter from Gerald R. Ford to Betty Ford, September 1974, after Her Diagnosis with Breast Cancer

No written words can adequately express our deep, deep love. We know how <u>great</u> you are and we, the children and Dad, will try to be as strong as you. Our faith in you and God will sustain us. Our total <u>love</u> for you is everlasting. We will be at your side with our love for a wonderful Mom. XXXX, Jerry

DECODED Betty Ford had surgery for breast cancer a month after President Nixon resigned and her husband took over as president. It was a tumultuous time for the Ford family, as well as for the country. Women were often private about breast cancer diagnoses at the time, but Betty Ford used her illness as an opportunity to spread awareness of the disease, helping other women.

Ford had no vice president when he came to office since he himself had been the VP. The Constitution (according to the Twenty-Fifth Amendment, ratified in 1967) required him to name one and he chose Nelson Rockefeller, a moderate Republican, upsetting the party's conservatives. Ford also had problems with Congress, where Democrats had a large advantage and picked up seats in the 1974 midterm elections because voters were tired of scandal and angry that Nixon was pardoned.

The economy was weak, with both high inflation and high unemployment, a condition economists called "stagflation" (a combination of *stagnation*, which means lack of growth, and *inflation*). Ford wanted a tax hike and reduced government spending.

As economic problems worsened and unemployment hit 9 percent, Ford switched over to calling for a tax cut rather than a tax hike. He had focused on trying to reduce inflation, but with midterm elections coming up and unemployment rising, Republicans didn't want to campaign on a tax hike. Democrats pointed out that he was changing his position.

Ford signed an energy bill that reduced oil prices—something Democrats wanted—but also allowed him to phase out price controls on oil. Increasing oil prices were a big part of the economic problems of the 1970s, and they grew out of conflict in the Middle East. In 1967, Israel fought against Egypt, Syria, and Jordan in the Six-Day War. Fighting flared again in October 1973, when Egypt and Syria attacked Israel. Since it began on the Jewish holy day of Yom Kippur, this conflict was called the Yom Kippur War. The Soviet Union backed and supplied Egypt, Syria, and Jordan, and the United States backed and supplied Israel. The United Nations pressured the two sides to stop fighting, and Israel signed a cease-fire with Egypt in November 1973 and with Syria in May 1974. The Yom Kippur War had interrupted oil production in the Middle East. In addition, oil-producing states that opposed US involvement in the Yom Kippur War made it harder for the United States to get oil to punish it for having supported Israel in the Yom Kippur War. This led to a decreased supply and higher prices, which hurt the US economy and made things harder for President Ford.

The *Brown v. Board of Education of Topeka* decision in 1954 had called for desegregating schools but it was met with resistance by many white people, and not just in the South. Many northern cities had residential segregation—that is, people of different races or ethnicities lived in separate neighborhoods. Because schools serve children from a specific neighborhood, the schools remained segregated. In 1974, Boston was ordered to integrate its schools by busing in students from outside a neighborhood in order to make the schools more racially diverse. White resistance to busing in Boston led to violence and calls for the president to intervene, but he refused. Ford thought the government should end legal segregation, but not segregation that occurred because of social or economic circumstances.

In foreign affairs, Ford continued to try to lessen tension with the Soviet Union and he signed the Helsinki Accords, which recognized the borders of all European countries as drawn at the end of World War II. The Helsinki Accords included an important statement on human rights, like the freedom to travel and the free flow of information between countries. The Soviet Union and the United States interpreted the human rights clauses differently, and that was a source of friction between the two nations.

In 1975, the city of Saigon, the capital of South Vietnam, fell to North Vietnamese troops. American troops had left in 1973, but there were still Americans in Vietnam. These people left in helicopters that took off from city rooftops, with South Vietnamese allies desperately trying to get on board. The evacuation was embarrassing.

Legacy

After he lost the 1976 election, Ford retired to California, golfed, wrote books, and lectured. Ronald Reagan considered him for his running mate in 1980 but chose someone else. President Clinton awarded him the Congressional Medal of Freedom in 1999 for helping to heal the nation after Watergate.

Ford was only in office for two and a half years and the most important thing he did was to pardon Richard Nixon for crimes committed while in office. He was an honest and decent person who helped restore some trust in government after the Nixon years, but that process would take longer than the time he had in office.

JAMES EARL ★ CARTER

PRESIDENT
39
OF THE UNITED STATES

BORN: 1924

IN OFFICE:
January 20, 1977–
January 20, 1981

VICE PRESIDENT:
Walter Mondale

FROM: Georgia

PARTY: Democratic

DID YOU KNOW?

● President Carter's mother, Lillian, became a Peace Corp volunteer at the age of sixty-eight and served in India. When her son was president, he sent her to the 1977 funeral of Indian president Fakhruddin Ali Ahmed, making her the first mother of a president to go on a diplomatic mission. Earlier the same year the First Lady, Rosalynn Carter, went on a foreign policy trip to Latin America, the first time a First Lady took that type of trip.

STATES OF AMER

Life Before the Presidency

Jimmy Carter was the first president to be born in a hospital. He grew up on a Georgia farm that grew peanuts and cotton. His mother was a nurse but stayed home to raise her four children. Carter, the eldest, attended the US Naval Academy at Annapolis (1943–1946), the only president to do so. In 1946, Carter finished at the Naval Academy and became a submarine officer. He served during the Korean War but not in combat. Instead he helped design nuclear propulsion plants for naval vessels and taught nuclear engineering to the crew of the USS *Seawolf*, a submarine. It looked like he would have an impressive career in the navy, but when his father died in 1953 he returned home to run the family farm.

Carter entered politics in 1955, getting elected to the county board of education. After the Supreme Court ordered the desegregation of public schools with *Brown v. Board of Education* in 1954, serving on a school board in the South became a difficult job. An anti-integration organization called the White Citizens Council formed groups across the South, including in Plains, Georgia, Carter's hometown. He was the only white man in Plains who refused to join. When other people in town boycotted his business, he still refused to join. Eventually the boycott ended, and when Carter ran for a seat in the state senate in 1963, he won. In 1971, he became Georgia's governor. He served one term before running for president of the United States in 1976.

Mr. President

Jimmy Carter was elected after the scandals of the Nixon administration and Gerald Ford's "caretaker" presidency, meaning an administration that doesn't make many new policies but mostly tries to keep things together to hand off to the next person. Carter, then a Southern Baptist, was a very religious man and said he wanted to bring honesty back to the White House. He also tried to advance human rights internationally: He wanted all countries to respect people's basic rights, like the right to food and shelter, and political rights, like voting, and for all people to have freedom from the government violating their rights, like jailing people for political speech.

Carter's biggest challenges were a bad economy and rising energy costs. He hoped to beat inflation by putting off tax cuts and limiting spending, but inflation and unemployment both rose. Gasoline prices almost doubled between 1973 and 1976, the year that Carter was elected, creating an energy crisis. Instead of using less energy, Americans began to use more—which only drove the prices higher

and made it necessary to import, or bring in, more oil from other countries.

Faced with rising energy prices and the drag they put on the American economy, Carter tried to promote sustainable energy sources like solar energy.

CARTER'S "MORAL EQUIVALENT OF WAR" SPEECH,
APRIL 18, 1977

Good evening.

Tonight I want to have an unpleasant talk with you about a problem that is unprecedented in our history. With the exception of preventing war, this is the greatest challenge that our country will face during our lifetime.

The energy crisis has not yet overwhelmed us, but it will if we do not act quickly. It's a problem that we will not be able to solve in the next few years, and it's likely to get progressively worse through the rest of this century. . . .

Two days from now, I will present to the Congress my energy proposals. . . .

Many of these proposals will be unpopular. Some will cause you to put up with inconveniences and to make sacrifices. . . . This difficult effort will be the "moral equivalent of war," except that we will be uniting our efforts to build and not to destroy.

DECODED Carter called for conserving, or using less, energy and for Americans to make sacrifices. But the idea that the world was running out of fossil fuels and people would need to be more careful about their energy use and the environment was extremely unpopular.

CARTER'S SOLAR ENERGY REMARKS ANNOUNCING ADMINISTRATION PROPOSALS,
JUNE 20, 1979

We import now about half of all the oil we use from overseas. And this dependence on foreign sources of oil is of great concern to all of us. . . .

Today, I am sending to the Congress legislative recommendations for a new solar strategy that will move our Nation toward true energy security and abundant, readily available energy supplies.

In the year 2000, the solar water heater behind me, which is being dedicated today, will still be here supplying cheap, efficient energy. A generation from now, this solar heater can either be a curiosity, a museum piece, an example of a road not taken, or it can be just a small part of one of the greatest and most exciting adventures ever undertaken by the American people: harnessing the power of the Sun to enrich our lives as we move away from our crippling dependence on foreign oil.

DECODED In June 1979, Jimmy Carter gave this speech announcing that thirty-two solar panels had been put on the White House roof. He hoped that they would cause other Americans to take actions to help the environment, especially using solar power. But the next president, Ronald Reagan, had the panels removed. Some of them are now in the Smithsonian, so they are museum pieces and examples of the road not taken.

The United States was heavily dependent on oil as a fuel, much of which it imported. During Carter's term in office, the biggest oil-producing nations raised the price of oil so that it was almost three times as expensive as it had been before.

Carter hoped to increase production of sustainable fuels, which don't get used up the way oil does. But gas prices and inflation remained high, and Americans had what Carter called a "crisis of confidence" in the government and the future.

Carter had a strong record in environmental protection. He signed a bill in 1977 that limited strip mining, in which coal or iron ore is reached by removing the layers of earth above it instead of tunneling after it. He also signed the Superfund law, which required cleanup of hundreds of abandoned hazardous waste sites. And he set aside fifty-six million acres of public land in Alaska.

In 1978, Carter deregulated the airline industry, along with trucking and railroads. That meant that the government had far fewer rules for the transportation industry. Rates fell, but airlines stopped flying many routes to small communities, which meant that it could be much harder for people who lived there to find flights.

In 1979, there was a revolution in Iran. The shah (ruler) of Iran was overthrown and Ayatollah Khomeini became the new ruler. Khomeini and his followers, who were religious conservatives, wanted the government to be religiously based. The shah was dying of cancer, and Carter let him come to the United States for medical treatment. That outraged Muslim fundamentalists in Iran. In November 1979, student militants who supported Ayatollah Khomeini attacked the US embassy in Tehran, Iran's capital. They took sixty-six Americans hostage (and held fifty-two of them), trying to force the shah to return to Iran so they could put him on trial. Carter tried negotiations, which failed. He then authorized a secret military mission to free the hostages, but one of the helicopters crashed, killing eight US soldiers, and the mission failed. At the very end of his term, Carter made an agreement to release Iranian funds in the United States that had been frozen in response to the Iranian Revolution. Iran in turn released the hostages. It happened on the day that Ronald Reagan was inaugurated. Reagan had nothing to do with the release, but it benefited him, and the yearlong hostage drama badly damaged Carter's prestige.

Carter's greatest impact may have been helping to reduce conflict in the Middle East. In September 1978, President Carter hosted Egypt's president, Anwar el-Sadat, and Israel's prime minister, Menachem Begin, at Camp David. Sadat and Begin

Syria
Israel
Iran
Egypt

Legacy

After leaving office, Jimmy and Rosalynn Carter started the Carter Center, a nonprofit organization to promote human rights and democracy, improve public health, and help people improve the way they farm. Carter continued to work for human rights around the world, and he even picked up a hammer to help build homes for low-income people. He was one of the most active ex-presidents. In 2002, Carter won the Nobel Peace Prize for his work trying to find peaceful ways to solve social justice problems.

tried to bring peace to their countries after the Yom Kippur War of 1973, when Egypt and Syria had fought Israel. In 1978, the two nations, along with the United States, signed the Camp David Accords, which were agreements in which Israel and Egypt recognized each other's governments. Israel also agreed to pull out of the Sinai Peninsula. It was a big deal when Sadat and Begin shook hands. There's still fighting in the Middle East, but the Camp David Accords were an important step toward peace.

He is remembered as a president troubled with rising energy prices, a poor economy, and a hostage crisis that he couldn't solve, and he had trouble working with Congress. He was also an active advocate of human rights and a leader in the search for a peace settlement in the Middle East.

Anwar el-Sadat

Menachem Begin

RONALD REAGAN

BORN: 1911

DIED: 2004

IN OFFICE:
January 20, 1981–
January 20, 1989

FROM: born in Illinois;
lived in California

VICE PRESIDENT:
George Herbert Walker
Bush

PARTY: Republican

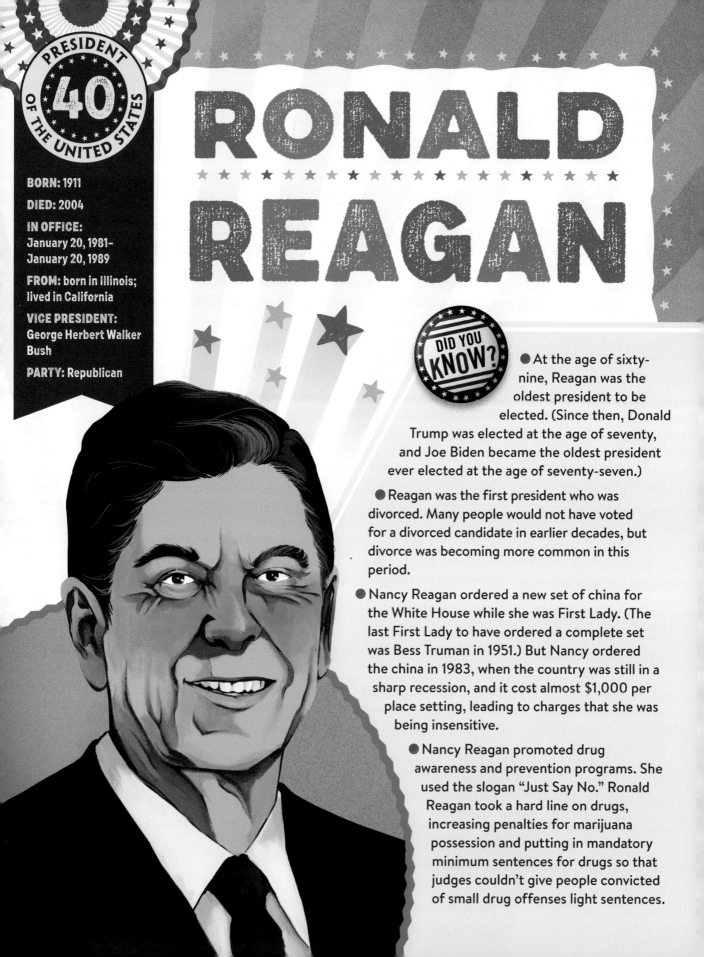

DID YOU KNOW?

● At the age of sixty-nine, Reagan was the oldest president to be elected. (Since then, Donald Trump was elected at the age of seventy, and Joe Biden became the oldest president ever elected at the age of seventy-seven.)

● Reagan was the first president who was divorced. Many people would not have voted for a divorced candidate in earlier decades, but divorce was becoming more common in this period.

● Nancy Reagan ordered a new set of china for the White House while she was First Lady. (The last First Lady to have ordered a complete set was Bess Truman in 1951.) But Nancy ordered the china in 1983, when the country was still in a sharp recession, and it cost almost $1,000 per place setting, leading to charges that she was being insensitive.

● Nancy Reagan promoted drug awareness and prevention programs. She used the slogan "Just Say No." Ronald Reagan took a hard line on drugs, increasing penalties for marijuana possession and putting in mandatory minimum sentences for drugs so that judges couldn't give people convicted of small drug offenses light sentences.

Life Before the Presidency

Reagan was born in tiny Tampico, Illinois, and grew up in nearby Dixon. He was a good athlete who worked as a lifeguard as a teenager and swam and played football in college. He was an average student. After college he became a sports radio announcer.

In 1937, he took a screen test in Hollywood and was offered an acting contract. Reagan made more than fifty movies.

He worked as a spokesman for the General Electric Company and got his first taste of politics while serving as president of the Screen Actors Guild (SAG) for seven years. As president of SAG, he testified before the House Un-American Activities Committee about possible communists in Hollywood in 1947.

Reagan had been a Democrat as a young man, but while working for General Electric he came to see government power and regulation as a threat to individual liberty. In 1964, he gave a televised campaign speech for Republican Barry Goldwater (who would lose to Lyndon Johnson in the presidential election that year). Reagan was an excellent public speaker when he had notes, but he tended to forget details if he had to speak without a prepared speech. He impressed the audience, and when he ran for governor of California in 1966 he won in a landslide. As governor, Reagan took money from the state and gave it to cities instead, letting them decide what to do with it. He tried to lower property taxes, sharply reduced the number of people who could get welfare, and reduced government regulation of businesses. He also criticized the antiwar protest movement of the 1960s.

In 1976, Reagan challenged President Ford for the Republican nomination. He didn't get the nomination, but he gained national prominence. He appealed to the religious right, which was becoming a powerful force. Democrat Jimmy Carter won in that 1976 election, but in 1980, Reagan got support from some Democrats as well as Republicans and won the election in a landslide.

Mr. President

Iran released the American hostages it had taken during Jimmy Carter's presidency as soon as Reagan came to office in 1981. The hostage release was a response to negotiations Carter had made, but Reagan got the political benefit, so it was a good start for his administration. A month after taking the oath, Reagan asked Congress for sweeping budget cuts on social programs and income tax cuts. Congress responded by cutting taxes by $750 billion over five years.

It also cut welfare by $25 billion. Reagan argued that lowering taxes for the wealthy would lead them to use the extra money to create new businesses or hire new workers for established businesses. As the wealthy got wealthier, they would grow the economy and the good times would "trickle down" to poorer people, he said. The policy became known as "trickle-down economics."

The plan suffered from Reagan's astonishing increase in defense spending. He insisted on raising the defense budget by a trillion dollars over five years, the largest peacetime military buildup in US history, to counter what he saw as an increasing threat from the Soviet Union. Congress gave Reagan what he wanted—a large tax cut and a massive increase in military spending. Reagan's plan hinged on the economy booming because of the tax cuts—and it didn't. The result was an enormous increase in the budget deficit. (A deficit occurs when more money is going out than coming in.) Reagan also cut regulations on businesses and worker safety because he thought that government regulations put an unfair burden on businesses. And when air traffic controllers went on strike in 1981, demanding better working conditions and pay, he came down hard, firing more than eleven thousand striking workers when they violated an order to return to work.

The combination of the tax cuts, spending cuts, and military buildup drove the economy into the worst recession since the Great Depression. It began to recover in 1983.

During Reagan's first term in office the HIV/AIDS epidemic began. Reagan was silent in the face of the epidemic, which began the year he took office; it took him four years to mention the disease in public.

PRESS CONFERENCE, SEPTEMBER 17, 1985

Q. Mr. President, the Nation's best-known AIDS scientist says the time has come now to boost existing research into what he called a minor moonshot program to attack this AIDS epidemic that has struck fear into the Nation's health workers and even its schoolchildren. Would you support a massive government research program against AIDS like the one that President Nixon launched against cancer?

The President. I have been supporting it for more than four years now. It's been one of the top priorities with us, and over the last four years, and including what we have in the budget for '86, it will amount to over a half a billion dollars that we have provided for research on AIDS in addition to what I'm sure other medical groups are doing.

DECODED   This press conference was the first time President Reagan said "AIDS" in public. It was four years after the epidemic began.

And Reagan appointed the first female Supreme Court justice, Sandra Day O'Connor, fulfilling a campaign promise to appoint a woman to the Supreme Court.

Sandra Day O'Connor

Shortly after he took office, a gunman shot at Reagan on the street while the president was walking to his car. A Secret Service special agent, Timothy McCarthy, and police officer Thomas Delahanty were hit. Press Secretary James Brady was shot in the head, permanently disabling him. Reagan was seriously injured when a bullet bounced off his car and hit him under his left armpit. The bullet stopped less than an inch from Reagan's heart. He was in the hospital for twelve days—but he became the only US president to survive injury in an assassination attempt while president.

In foreign policy, Reagan sent 1,500 American marines to Beirut, Lebanon, in 1982, hoping to provide some order to the city during a war in that country. In October 1983, Islamist terrorists who were angry about US involvement blew up the Beirut marine compound with a truck bomb and killed 241 soldiers. Reagan announced that US soldiers would remain in Beirut—and then withdrew them because of congressional opposition and continued threats to their safety. Immediately after the Beirut bombing Reagan ordered the invasion of

Grenada, a tiny Caribbean island most Americans had never heard of before. Grenada had a left-wing government after a revolution. Reagan said that invading and overthrowing the Grenadian government was necessary for the safety of Americans in the area. There were nearly

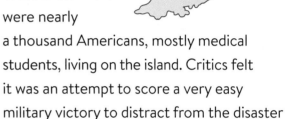

Grenada

a thousand Americans, mostly medical students, living on the island. Critics felt it was an attempt to score a very easy military victory to distract from the disaster in Lebanon.

Reagan won reelection in a landslide in 1984. His opponent was Walter Mondale, who was running with Geraldine Ferraro, the first female vice presidential candidate on a major ticket. Reagan won forty-nine of the fifty states and had the highest electoral vote count in history.

As part of his massive military buildup, Reagan proposed the Strategic Defense Initiative (SDI), popularly called "Star Wars." It would use lasers to destroy Russian missiles should the two countries go to war. The program would be very costly—and the economy was already suffering through a recession. The president met considerable opposition to his plan but eventually got Congress to approve a smaller version.

Russia had been called the Soviet Union since 1922. The Soviets and Americans had fought on the same side in World War II, but their differences led to a postwar Cold War. Both nations saw the other as a threat to peace, and they competed for allies as they built military blocks against each other. (It was called a "cold" war because they weren't fighting each other but were competing against each other diplomatically.) The Soviets struggled to keep up with Reagan's massive military buildup—and in the end they couldn't. It was one of the factors that contributed to the fall of the Soviet Union in 1991 and the end of the Cold War. Russian reformer Mikhail Gorbachev and President Reagan met several times in person, and in 1987, Reagan famously stood by the Berlin Wall, which divided West Berlin from Soviet-controlled East Berlin, and said, "Mr. Gorbachev, tear down this wall!" The Soviets lost control over the countries they had dominated in Eastern Europe—and over the republics that made up their own country. In 1989, the Berlin Wall came down. Americans felt that they had won the Cold War—and they had, at least for a time.

Reagan was especially concerned about Latin America, which led to the Iran-Contra scandal. Its roots lay in Reagan's support for a right-wing dictatorship in El Salvador

REAGAN'S SPEECH AT THE BRANDENBURG GATE, BERLIN, GERMANY, JUNE 12, 1987

Behind me stands a wall that encircles the free sectors of this city, part of a vast system of barriers that divides the entire continent of Europe. . . . Standing before the Brandenburg Gate, every man is a German, separated from his fellow men. Every man is a Berliner, forced to look upon a scar. . . . As long as this gate is closed, as long as this scar of a wall is permitted to stand, it is not the German question alone that remains open, but the question of freedom for all mankind. . . .

Mr. Gorbachev, tear down this wall!

DECODED This is perhaps the most famous of Reagan's speeches. In 1961, East Germany built a wall through the city to keep people in the Soviet-dominated eastern half of Berlin from going to the American-dominated western half. Reagan was making an historic call to reunite Berlin—and Germany.

that had murdered thousands of civilians. But the Salvadoran government was also fighting communists—and because it was anticommunist, Reagan felt it was the side to back.

Reagan provided money and supplies to a right-wing group in Nicaragua called the Contras. They were fighting the group that was in power, the Sandinistas, because the Sandinistas were providing aid to rebels in El Salvador who opposed the government Reagan backed. And in Iran, the Reagan administration secretly sold around five hundred antitank missiles to Iran in exchange for the release of some American hostages in Lebanon. By the time Reagan had shipped 1,500 missiles to Iran, the terrorists had released only three hostages—and had taken three more to replace them. At the same time, Reagan wanted to support the Nicaraguan Contras in their fight against the Sandinistas, but Congress had passed a law preventing him from sending any money to them. So he arranged to overcharge Iran for the weapons in the secret sales, then sent the extra money to the Contras. That kept the money transfer—which was illegal— off the books.

Eventually news of the secret arms-for-hostages deal leaked and President Reagan appointed an independent commission to investigate. The Tower Commission, named for John Tower who headed it, concluded that the President had shown poor management

but hadn't done anything illegal. Congress ran its own investigation and came to harsher conclusions but didn't begin impeachment proceedings. In the end, fourteen people were charged with crimes related to the Iran-Contra scandal. Reagan weathered the storm. His humor, charm, and charisma helped him escape scandals that might have brought down a different president.

Legacy

After leaving office, Reagan wrote his autobiography, *An American Life*. Then in 1994 he wrote a letter to Americans telling them that he had been diagnosed with Alzheimer's disease, an incurable dementia that would kill him ten years later. He died at the age of ninety-three—the longest a president had lived at that time.

Reagan is a hero to conservatives who like the idea of trickle-down economics. His toughness with the Soviet Union helped end the Cold War, and his personal charisma and humor charmed many Americans, even those who didn't agree with his policies. And after the economic and social problems of the 1970s, the Reagan '80s provided a welcome sense of optimism. The Iran-Contra scandal was one of the worst American political scandals, but it has done little to tarnish his legacy.

BORN: 1924

DIED: 2018

IN OFFICE:
January 20, 1989–
January 20, 1993

FROM: born in
Massachusetts; raised
in Connecticut; lived
in Texas

VICE PRESIDENT: Dan
Quayle

PARTY: Republican

GEORGE H. W. BUSH

DID YOU KNOW?

● Bush was the last president to have fought in World War II.

● The bomber Bush flew in World War II had the name *Barbara* painted on the side, after his girlfriend and future wife.

Barbara

● Bush's inauguration was two hundred years after George Washington's. While taking the oath of office, Bush put his hand on the same Bible that Washington had used.

Life Before the Presidency

George Herbert Walker Bush was born in Massachusetts and grew up in Connecticut, where he went to prestigious private schools. His father was a banker and a US senator. Bush became a navy pilot at the age of eighteen—the youngest one in the navy—and during World War II he flew fifty-eight bomber missions in the Pacific. In 1944, he was shot down and crashed in the Pacific Ocean, where an American submarine rescued him. He won the Distinguished Flying Cross for bravery in action.

Bush began working for an oil company after he graduated from Yale, a job his father lined up for him. He ran for the US Senate from Texas in 1964 and lost, in part because he was seen as a Northerner and an outsider, and in part because 1964 was the year that Lyndon Johnson, also from Texas, ran for president and won in a landslide. It was a good year for Texas Democrats—and a hard year to be a Republican. Bush rebounded and was elected to the House of Representatives in 1966. In 1973, Bush became chairman of the Republican National Committee as the Watergate burglary was becoming public knowledge. He defended Nixon until the release of the secret tapes of White House conversations, which changed his mind on Nixon's guilt. Bush served as a diplomat in China and as director of the Central Intelligence Agency (CIA), which collects and analyzes information about national security.

In 1980, Bush ran for president. Ronald Reagan got the Republican nomination—and chose Bush to be his running mate. They won by a landslide in 1980—and again in 1984.

In 1988, Bush ran for president with Senator Dan Quayle as his running mate, on the promise of no new taxes, saying, "Read my lips: no new taxes!"

BUSH'S SPEECH ACCEPTING THE REPUBLICAN NOMINATION FOR PRESIDENT, AUGUST 18, 1988

And I'm the one who will not raise taxes. My opponent now says he'll raise them as a last resort or a third resort. When a politician talks like that, you know that's one resort he'll be checking into. My opponent won't rule out raising taxes, but I will, and the Congress will push me to raise taxes, and I'll say no, and they'll push, and I'll say no, and they'll push again, and I'll say to them, "Read my lips: no new taxes." . . .

I want a kinder and gentler nation.

DECODED Bush draws a comparison between himself and Democratic nominee Michael Dukakis, saying that Dukakis would raise taxes only if he really had to, but that Bush wouldn't raise them under any circumstance. Nevertheless, when Bush became president he raised taxes. He thought raising taxes was necessary for the country and the right thing to do, even though it hurt him politically. Bush's phrase of "a kinder and gentler nation" was one of his best-known lines.

Mr. President

Bush was an active and interventionist president internationally, which means that he got involved in situations with other countries. After a US soldier was killed by Panamanian forces in 1989, Bush sent in US troops to overthrow Panama's corrupt leader, Manuel Noriega, an action that was condemned by the United Nations.

In August 1990, Saddam Hussein, the leader of Iraq, sent troops to invade Kuwait to seize its oil supply and access to ports on the Persian Gulf. Kuwait had loaned several billion dollars to Iraq during the Iran-Iraq War (1980–1988); Hussein wanted Kuwait to forgive the loans and Kuwait refused. President Bush and Soviet leader Mikhail Gorbachev issued a joint statement demanding Iraq's withdrawal from Kuwait, and the United Nations passed a resolution authorizing removing Hussein's forces from Kuwait by any means necessary. On January 17, 1991, the United States led a multinational force in the Persian Gulf in a campaign called Operation Desert Storm.

It took about four days for the American-led forces to push Iraqi troops out of Kuwait. Bush could have destroyed Hussein's army and removed him from power, but he chose not to and simply put things back the way they had been before. Some people thought that Hussein was a dangerous tyrant and Bush should have ended his regime while he could, but Bush thought that would have been an overreach by the United States and he never considered it.

Bush also signed a nonaggression pact with Soviet leader Mikhail Gorbachev, which essentially ended the Cold War. Countries that had been aligned with the United States and countries that had been aligned with the Soviet Union agreed not to be the first to use force against another country. The end

BUSH'S SPEECH, AUGUST 8, 1990

Less than a week ago, in the early morning hours of August 2d, Iraqi Armed Forces, without provocation or warning, invaded a peaceful Kuwait. Facing negligible resistance from its much smaller neighbor, Iraq's tanks stormed in blitzkrieg fashion through Kuwait in a few short hours.

A puppet regime imposed from the outside is unacceptable. The acquisition of territory by force is unacceptable. No one, friend or foe, should doubt our desire for peace; and no one should underestimate our determination to confront aggression.

[DECODED] A "puppet regime" means a government that is really controlled by outside forces, the way a puppet is controlled by the person holding the strings. Here, Bush announces that Iraq invaded Kuwait. This was the beginning of the First Gulf War and lasted from August 1990 to February 1991.

of the Cold War and the breakdown of the Soviet Union occurred at about the same time, in 1989 to 1991. The Soviet Union had been made up of fifteen republics, of which Russia was the largest. Gorbachev was planning to sign a treaty giving the republics more freedom, and some members of his government, who wanted to preserve the Soviet Union with its former power, tried to overthrow him. Their coup failed and the backlash led to the complete breakup of the Soviet Union in December 1991.

President Reagan had cut income taxes and the federal deficit was getting much larger. Bush had campaigned on the promise not to raise taxes—he'd said it over and over. He raised taxes anyway; while it was embarrassing, he thought it was necessary for the country. Bush also negotiated the North American Free Trade Agreement (NAFTA) with Canada and Mexico, which made it much easier for the three nations to trade. The agreement was signed after Bush left office.

George H. W. Bush ran for reelection in 1992. The Gulf War that spring had ended successfully and Bush had very high poll numbers. But his foreign policy successes proved not to be as important to voters as the economy, which was sluggish. His Democratic opponent, Bill Clinton, had charisma and a common touch that left Bush looking stiff in contrast. In addition, there was a third-party challenger in 1992, a rarity on the American political scene. Businessman Ross Perot ran as an independent and got 19 percent of the popular vote, although he didn't win any electoral votes. In the end, Bush lost because of Clinton's appeal to the voters and because of the defections of some conservatives who were angry that he had raised taxes.

Legacy

After his term ended, George and Barbara Bush lived in Houston, Texas, and in Kennebunkport, Maine, where they had a second home. Bush joined with his successor, Bill Clinton, in international disaster relief work. And he was an informal advisor to two sons who went into politics: Jeb, who became governor of Florida (1999–2007), and George W. Bush, who became governor of Texas (1995–2000) and then the forty-third president (2001–2009). He also helped set up his presidential library on the campus of Texas A&M University in College Station, Texas. He is buried there beside his wife, Barbara, and daughter Robin.

George H. W. Bush brought quiet, competent leadership to Washington. He is often overlooked, sandwiched between Reagan and Clinton, both of whom were charismatic presidents. But issues that were important during his presidency would continue to be significant, such as conflict in the Persian Gulf.

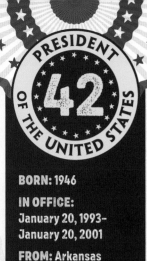

WILLIAM JEFFERSON CLINTON

BORN: 1946

IN OFFICE:
January 20, 1993–
January 20, 2001

FROM: Arkansas

VICE PRESIDENT:
Albert Gore

PARTY: Democratic

DID YOU KNOW?

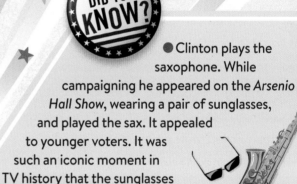

● Clinton plays the saxophone. While campaigning he appeared on the *Arsenio Hall Show*, wearing a pair of sunglasses, and played the sax. It appealed to younger voters. It was such an iconic moment in TV history that the sunglasses he wore are now in the Clinton Presidential Library.

● Clinton, at the age of forty-six, and Al Gore, at forty-four, are the youngest running mates to have won the White House.

● Clinton was the first president from the Baby Boomer generation. Baby Boomers were born between 1946 and 1964 in the post–World War II era, when many returning soldiers married and started families. It was a large generation.

● After Clinton left office, his wife, Hillary Rodham Clinton, ran for and won a New York Senate seat, making her the first First Lady to win national office.

Life Before the Presidency

Bill Clinton was born in Hope, Arkansas. He was an excellent student and had a good memory. At seventeen he was a delegate to Boy's Nation, an American Legion–sponsored mock political convention. It was held in Washington, DC, and while he was there, Clinton visited the White House and shook President Kennedy's hand in the Rose Garden. (You can find a photograph of the handshake online.) He participated in student government in college and worked as an aide to Arkansas Democratic Senator J. William Fulbright, an opponent of the Vietnam War. Clinton won a prestigious Rhodes Scholarship to study in England and got a draft notice while he was there. He returned to Arkansas and agreed to enter an Army ROTC (Reserve Officers' Training Corps) program the next fall in return for being able to finish the year in England as a Rhodes Scholar. Being in the ROTC program almost certainly would have kept him out of Vietnam, but Clinton changed his mind and made himself eligible for the draft again the next year. When his birthdate was called in the draft lottery it got a high number, which meant there was almost no chance he would be drafted. He took part in antiwar protests while he was in England—and that became a campaign issue when he ran for president, along with his initial attempt to avoid the draft.

Clinton went on to study at Yale Law School, where he met Hillary Rodham; they married in 1975 and their daughter, Chelsea, was born five years later. In Arkansas he lost a race for Congress (1974), won the race for state attorney general (1976), and then became governor at the age of thirty-two (1978). He supported competency tests for students and teachers, and dropout rates fell and test scores rose while he was governor. He also supported changes in welfare to help people reenter the workforce and affirmative action programs to help minorities.

Clinton won the 1992 Democratic nomination for president and ran for president against incumbent George H. W. Bush. Clinton was charismatic, young, exceptionally bright, and articulate—with a reputation for giving long-winded speeches. A third-party candidate, Ross Perot, made an impact that year, helping to split the Republican vote, and Clinton and running mate Al Gore won the election.

Mr. President

Clinton put together an economic package that increased taxes on the wealthy while cutting spending on welfare and defense. No Republican in either chamber of Congress voted for it, but it passed anyway. It lowered the deficit by almost one-third in two years. In 1992, the US deficit was $290 billion and rising. In 1994, it was down to $203 billion, and by 1999 the United States had a $124 billion surplus, or extra money. Unemployment, inflation, and interest rates were very low, and the economy boomed. In fact, Clinton oversaw the longest period of sustained economic growth in US history to that time. The economy grew for 120 straight months.

A centrist, Clinton replaced traditional welfare, which included cash assistance to families, with block grants to the states so the states got the money and could decide what to do with it. Clinton's changes included creating the Temporary Assistance for Needy Families (TANF) program and limiting how long a person could get that assistance. The reforms made legal immigrants unable to receive welfare for five years after coming to the United States but allowed children of illegal immigrants to attend school. Republicans had tried to block that; they felt that letting those children go to school put too much of a burden on local communities that funded the schools. Clinton also secured passage of the Family and Medical Leave Act, which allowed people with newborn or adopted babies to take up to twelve weeks of unpaid leave.

Clinton pushed passage of the North America Free Trade Agreement (NAFTA), which President Bush had negotiated. NAFTA made trade between the United States, Canada, and Mexico easier by ending nearly all tariffs between those nations. And he got the 1994 Violent Crime Control and Law Enforcement Act passed, which called for more than $30 billion for hiring police officers and constructing prisons. (The number of people in jail rose sharply under President Clinton, including many people sentenced for drug offenses.) The act banned many assault weapons for civilian use. The law had loopholes, but it banned more than a dozen specific guns and also certain features, like clips that could hold more than ten bullets. The ban lasted for ten years—but it expired in 2004 when Congress didn't renew it.

In 1993, Clinton nominated Ruth Bader Ginsburg to the Supreme Court. Ginsburg had long been an advocate for gender equality—that is, equality under the law for men and women. She herself had faced discrimination in her career, including being paid less than male colleagues. She was the first female Jewish justice.

Ruth Bader Ginsburg

Medical costs had been skyrocketing in part because of technological improvements that made better—and more expensive—tests available. Medical expenses were a drag on the economy. Clinton wanted every American to have access to affordable health insurance and was troubled that the United States was the only industrialized nation that didn't provide health care for all its citizens. Americans paid the most for health care of anyone in the world,  but many Americans didn't have access to doctors because they couldn't afford them or didn't have medical insurance. Thousands of people died every year who would have survived if they'd been able to get the care they needed. Republicans fought bitterly. The plan was complex and confusing, and they supported small government and knew that once a plan to provide health care to everyone was in place, it would be hard to eliminate it. Clinton—like FDR and Harry Truman before—failed in passing legislation.

Clinton overturned the ban on gay people serving in the military, which was supported by people who thought that the presence of gay people in military units would hurt troop morale. He put in a "don't ask/don't tell" policy—the military wouldn't ask its service members if they were gay, and the service members weren't supposed to tell anyone. In other words, the military wouldn't discriminate against gay service people as long as they hid the fact that they were gay. The policy was widely criticized as wishy-washy.

Clinton won reelection in 1996, although he was plagued with scandal throughout his second term. The Clintons had invested in land on the White River in Arkansas with another couple in 1978; the other couple complained that they had made more of the payments on the debt for the land. The Clintons sold their share when Bill became president, but critics wondered

CLINTON'S SPEECH ON HEALTH CARE REFORM, SEPTEMBER 22, 1993

This health care system of ours is badly broken, and it is time to fix it. Despite the dedication of literally millions of talented health care professionals, our health care is too uncertain and too expensive, too bureaucratic and too wasteful. It has too much fraud and too much greed.

Millions of Americans are just a pink slip away from losing their health insurance and one serious illness away from losing all their savings. Millions more are locked into the jobs they have now just because they or someone in their family has once been sick and they have what is called the preexisting condition. And on any given day, over 37 million Americans, most of them working people and their little children, have no health insurance at all.

DECODED Clinton here points out that in most developed countries, being diagnosed with a serious illness doesn't cause a person's family to go bankrupt, but in the United States people could lose their life's savings if they were diagnosed with a serious illness. He also mentions preexisting conditions, meaning a disease or health condition that's already been diagnosed. Most people got their health insurance through their job. If they switched jobs, they had to apply for new health insurance. But many insurance companies wouldn't give a new health care policy to a person with a preexisting condition.

if there was anything inappropriate in the land deal. Clinton's attorney general, Janet Reno, appointed an independent counsel, Robert Fiske, to investigate. When he found no wrongdoing by the Clintons, a panel of three federal judges removed Fiske and replaced him with Kenneth Starr, a conservative attorney. Starr conducted an investigation of every aspect of the Clintons' finances and history, not confining himself to the real estate sale in question. Starr also investigated Clinton's inappropriate relationship with a White House intern, Monica Lewinsky, although it had broken no laws.

Kenneth Starr

Starr spent more than four years investigating the Clintons—at a cost to taxpayers of more than $70 million. Eventually Starr sent his report to Congress, and the House wrote two articles of impeachment against Clinton for perjury and obstruction of justice. The charges involved the affair with Lewinsky, even though that was not a government matter, but the senators who voted to convict Clinton felt that the president's conduct should be above reproach, including in private matters. They didn't have enough votes to convict and Clinton was acquitted in February 1999. Clinton remained popular with the public—while Republican poll numbers went down.

HOUSE RESOLUTION 611 (IMPEACHMENT CHARGES)

Resolved, That William Jefferson Clinton, President of the United States, is impeached for high crimes and misdemeanors, and that the following articles of impeachment be exhibited to the United States Senate:

ARTICLE I

In his conduct while President of the United States . . . William Jefferson Clinton willfully provided perjurious, false and misleading testimony to the grand jury. . . .

ARTICLE II

In his conduct while President of the United States, William Jefferson Clinton . . . has prevented, obstructed, and impeded the administration of justice. . . .

DECODED House Resolution 611 brought impeachment charges against Clinton for lying under oath and obstruction of justice. According to the Constitution, the House of Representatives is the only body that can impeach; the Senate hears the trial. The Senate found Clinton not guilty on both counts.

Clinton's foreign policy was overshadowed by the booming prosperity and fight for health care on the domestic front, but he intervened in Bosnia in 1995. Bosnian Serbs were committing genocide—that is, they were trying to wipe out Bosnian Muslims and Croatians. Americans launched air strikes against the Serbs, trying to force them into peace talks. NATO sent a peacekeeping force that included thousands of US troops to try to prevent the slaughter of the Bosnian Muslims and Croatians.

Clinton also worked out an agreement with North Korea designed to shut down its nuclear weapons program while allowing it to develop nuclear energy as a power source. And he gave $20 billion in loans to Mexico when it was on the verge of economic collapse. (Mexico ended up paying off most of that loan ahead of schedule.) Vice President Al Gore played an important role in writing the Kyoto Protocol, an international agreement to reduce greenhouse gas emissions in order to minimize climate change. Clinton signed the protocol in November 1998, but the Senate refused to ratify it.

Legacy

After his presidency ended, Clinton wrote a memoir, attended the dedication of his presidential library in Little Rock, Arkansas, and twice teamed with former president George H. W. Bush to raise money for relief for victims of a tsunami in Asia (2004) and then for the victims of Hurricane Katrina in New Orleans (2005).

He started the Clinton Global Initiative in 2005 to help with climate change, disease prevention, and economic issues in the United States and abroad and wrote more books. He campaigned for his wife, Hillary, in 2008 when she lost the Democratic nomination to Barack Obama and again in 2016 when she became the first female presidential nominee of a major party, losing in the election to Donald Trump.

Hillary Clinton

The Clinton years are remembered for their peace and extraordinary prosperity. And although he remained popular, in many ways Clinton's second term was wasted because of the impeachment battle, which occupied the president and his advisors.

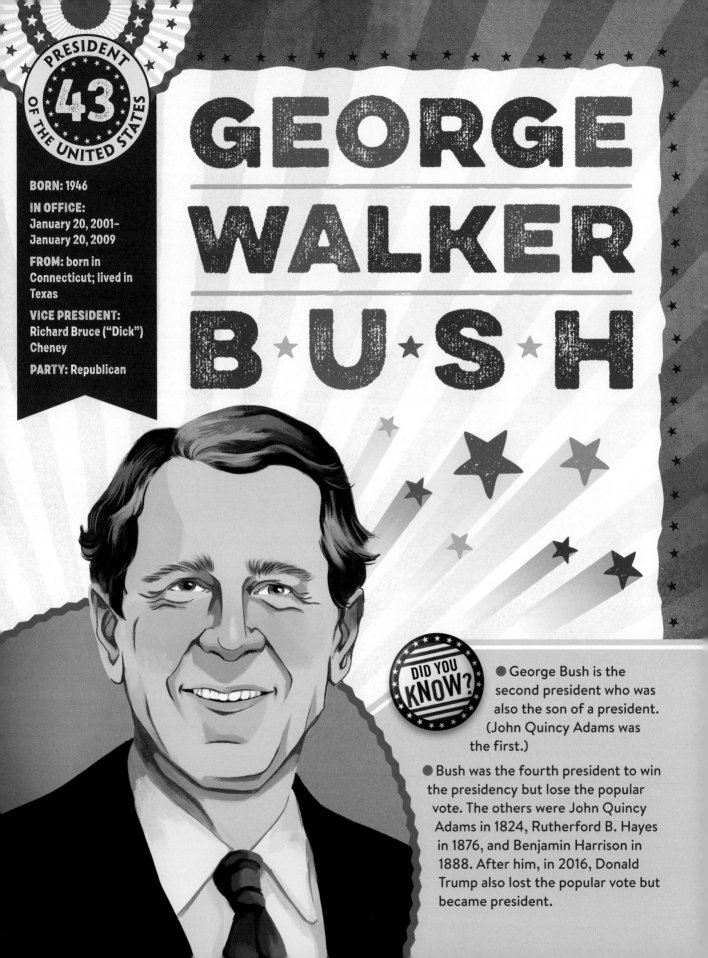

GEORGE WALKER BUSH

BORN: 1946

IN OFFICE:
January 20, 2001–
January 20, 2009

FROM: born in
Connecticut; lived in
Texas

VICE PRESIDENT:
Richard Bruce ("Dick")
Cheney

PARTY: Republican

DID YOU KNOW?

● George Bush is the second president who was also the son of a president. (John Quincy Adams was the first.)

● Bush was the fourth president to win the presidency but lose the popular vote. The others were John Quincy Adams in 1824, Rutherford B. Hayes in 1876, and Benjamin Harrison in 1888. After him, in 2016, Donald Trump also lost the popular vote but became president.

Life Before the Presidency

George W. Bush was born in Connecticut and moved to Texas with his family when his father, the future president George H. W. Bush, went into the oil business. He attended a prestigious private school, where he worked hard to do better in his classes, and then went to Yale, where he got a degree in history and was an average student. He served a year in the Texas Air National Guard. At that point the National Guard was unlikely to be called up for service overseas and so was a safe option for young men who wanted to avoid the draft. As such, it was very hard to get in without political connections. Bush got a spot in the national guard through the Speaker of the Texas House of Representatives even though he scored the minimum grade on the entrance exam. In addition, Bush got permission to leave before his term was fulfilled and received an honorable discharge. Political opponents felt that he had taken advantage of his father's connections to avoid service. Eventually Bush got an MBA at Harvard, and then he returned to Texas to work in the oil business.

Bush ran for a US House seat in 1978 and lost. He occupied himself for several years with his oil business, making several mergers that made him wealthy. When his father ran for president in 1988, the younger Bush helped with the campaign.

He ran for governor of Texas in 1994, won and was reelected in 1998. As governor, Bush supported legislation that limited lawsuits that were filed mostly to harass the other party and limited the amount of damages that workers and customers could get if they won a case against a business. He increased funding to schools and tied teacher salaries to student scores on standardized tests. He also cut property taxes. He shot down a hate crimes bill that had made it halfway through the Texas legislature; Bush opposed it because it protected gay people as well as racial minorities. In 2000, he ran for president, quickly leading the field of Republican contenders and getting the nomination. Bush chose Dick Cheney to be his running mate; Cheney was older, he had more experience in government than Bush did, and best of all, Bush liked to quip, Cheney didn't want his job.

Dick Cheney

Bush and Cheney ran against Democratic senators Al Gore and Joe Lieberman. The race would be incredibly close. The election came down to Florida—whoever won the state would win the election because Florida had so many electoral votes. But there were thousands and thousands of votes in dispute. The Florida ballot was laid out in a confusing way, and it relied on voters using a stylus to punch out an oval hole in the paper ballot. The punched-out paper oval could look like it had been removed cleanly from the front—but still be dangling on the back of the ballot. These "hanging chads," as they were called, were a nightmare for election officials, who had to decide if ballots should count if they weren't cleanly punched. Al Gore's team was particularly concerned because Bush's brother, Jeb, was Florida's governor, and the Florida secretary of state who would certify the vote, Katherine Harris, had helped run Bush's campaign in the state. Under the circumstances, Gore wanted a careful recount.

Katherine Harris

The vote-counting machines couldn't deal with the hanging chad issue, so any ballots with a hanging chad needed to be counted by hand. The issue wound up in the Florida Supreme Court, which ruled unanimously that the manual recounts could continue. Bush was ahead by just 537 votes when Secretary of State Harris refused to include hand recounts from Palm Beach County and certified the vote. The issue went to the US Supreme Court, which issued its ruling in *Bush v. Gore* on December 12 and ordered recounts stopped. The court said that counties had used different standards for deciding whether a ballot was legitimate and that there wasn't time to put in uniform standards. Therefore the count had to stop where it was—with Bush ahead by the slimmest of margins. Bush had lost the popular vote, but winning Florida gave him the White House—by one electoral vote.

Mr. President

George W. Bush took office with a nation at peace and the economy in good shape—but the country was deeply divided over the election and politics continued to be sharply partisan. Bush appointed a racially diverse cabinet that included some extreme conservatives, upsetting liberals who thought he should be more moderate since he had lost the popular vote.

Bush moved swiftly to enact his domestic agenda. He succeeded in getting a $1.35 billion tax cut over the objection of Democrats, who complained that it helped wealthy people the most. He vetoed or canceled environmental regulations in order to help industry. The relaxed rules allowed an increase in arsenic levels in water and carbon dioxide emissions, a culprit in the growing problem of climate change. (During the campaign Bush had said he favored reducing carbon dioxide emissions.) He wanted industries to regulate themselves on environmental issues. And he rejected the Kyoto Treaty, designed to combat climate change, because he thought it might hurt the US economy, particularly the coal industry. Environmentalists were especially angry that in rejecting the treaty, the administration indicated that it felt the science on climate change was uncertain, suggesting that the 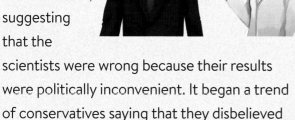 scientists were wrong because their results were politically inconvenient. It began a trend of conservatives saying that they disbelieved science.

The president moved to allow federal money to go to faith-based (religious) organizations, believing that at the local level they were often best placed to do relief work.

In another nod to Christian conservatives, who were very powerful within the Republican Party, Bush stopped some medical research with stem cells. Stem cells can become part of a number of different organs. That flexibility makes them extremely useful in medical research, and they help researchers search for new cures for diseases. They're taken from destroyed embryos, though, and abortion opponents thought it was wrong to use those cells or tissues. Under Bush's new rules, no new stem cells could be taken from embryos in the future, but research using stem cells already available could continue.

On September 11, 2001, President Bush was in Florida reading to a group of elementary students when he got word of terrorist attacks in New York City. Members of al-Qaeda, an Islamist terrorist group headed by Osama bin Laden, had hijacked four airplanes. They had flown two of them into the World Trade Center buildings in New York City, bringing both towers down. They crashed a third plane into the Pentagon, and a fourth went down in a field in Pennsylvania after the passengers fought the hijackers. Almost three thousand people were killed in the attacks. In an unprecedented move, the Department of Transportation shut down air traffic over the entire country to prevent further attacks. Bush flew back to Washington on the only plane in the sky.

In the national grief after the attacks, Bush's popularity soared. In late September 2001, Congress passed a joint resolution authorizing force against the people behind the September 11 attacks. In October, the United States invaded Afghanistan in order to strike at the Taliban, the fundamentalist Islamist group that had ruled Afghanistan since 1996 and had sheltered al-Qaeda. The Afghan government toppled in a month, overwhelmed by American military strength, and was replaced with a pro-American government. However, Osama bin Laden remained at large.

BUSH'S ADDRESS TO THE NATION, OCTOBER 7, 2001

On my orders the United States military has begun strikes against al-Qaeda terrorist training camps and military installations of the Taliban regime in Afghanistan.

These carefully targeted actions are designed to disrupt the use of Afghanistan as a terrorist base of operations, and to attack the military capability of the Taliban regime.

We are joined in this operation by our staunch friend, Great Britain. Other close friends, including Canada, Australia, Germany and France, have pledged forces as the operation unfolds.

DECODED President Bush addressed the nation, announcing military action against the Taliban and stressing that other nations were sending troops to help.

In 2001, Bush pushed through the PATRIOT Act, which allowed law enforcement extremely broad powers in combating terrorism, including arresting anyone who wasn't a citizen without charge and holding them indefinitely, denying them an attorney, and keeping their arrest secret. Foreigners accused of terrorism were held without trial at Guantánamo Bay, Cuba, popularly known as "Gitmo." People who felt that the PATRIOT Act violated civil liberties wanted to see Gitmo closed. They also objected to a number of other provisions in the PATRIOT Act, such as those that dealt with searching homes without telling the people who lived there, tracking people's online activity, and requiring libraries to show records of what books people have checked out. (This is why many libraries stopped keeping track of what people have read; if anyone ever asks for the records, the libraries won't have them.) In addition, the United States began using torture in the interrogation of people suspected of terrorism.

As part of the war on terror, President Bush announced the Bush Doctrine, which said that the United States could launch a preemptive strike against any nation (or group) that threatened American interests. In other words, he didn't have to wait for someone to attack the United States or its interests—he would be justified in attacking them first. Bush felt that this policy would let him respond quickly and flexibly to events. Conservatives liked the Bush Doctrine, thinking it was common sense, but many other countries bristled at the hit-first strategy, wondering what would happen if everyone adopted it.

Bush was concerned that Iraq might be building weapons of mass destruction (WMDs). If Iraq had WMDs, it could launch a catastrophic attack on the United States.

Bush decided to invade Iraq and remove Saddam Hussein as the leader. He wanted other nations to help and to get the approval of the United Nations if he could. His administration told the public that Iraq had WMDs, building a case for war. This turned out not to be true. The president asked Congress for authorization to go to war with Iraq, and after intense debate, Congress approved the use of force if Bush felt it was needed. On March 19, 2003, the United States and Great Britain invaded Iraq. Saddam Hussein was later executed.

The United States had quickly won the war in Iraq but found it difficult to win the peace. With the government toppled and Hussein dead, squabbles among different groups in Iraq turned violent. The situation became chaotic. In 2007, Bush ordered a "surge," which is a significant increase in US troops in Iraq for a short time to get the situation under control and prepare Iraqis to take over when the Americans left. It worked and the situation became more stable. When Democrats in Congress tied a military funding bill to troop withdrawals from Iraq, Bush vetoed it and got what he wanted—money for the war with no timeline for leaving. Eventually he would plan for the United States to withdraw from Iraq at the end of 2011, three years after he had left office.

On the domestic front, President Bush signed the No Child Left Behind Act in 2002, which required elementary and secondary schools to test students every year in math and reading and show progress in test scores. Teachers also had to meet higher standards. Some test scores rose, but critics complained that the law forced schools to focus on material that students would be tested on and didn't leave time for subjects like music, art, and literature.

DICK CHENEY'S SPEECH TO THE VETERANS OF FOREIGN WARS (VFW) CONVENTION, NASHVILLE, TENNESSEE, AUGUST 26, 2002

The case of Saddam Hussein, a sworn enemy of our country, requires a candid appraisal of the facts. . . . The Iraqi regime has in fact been very busy enhancing its capabilities in the field of chemical and biological agents. And they continue to pursue the nuclear program they began so many years ago. These are not weapons for the purpose of defending Iraq; these are offensive weapons for the purpose of inflicting death on a massive scale, developed so that Saddam can hold the threat over the head of anyone he chooses, in his own region or beyond. . . .

Simply stated, there is no doubt that Saddam Hussein now has weapons of mass destruction. There is no doubt that he is amassing them to use them against our friends, against our allies, and against us.

[DECODED] Vice President Cheney builds the case for going to war with Iraq and replacing Saddam Hussein by convincing Americans that Iraq had weapons of mass destruction (WMDs). In 2004, it was concluded that Iraq had not had WMDs.

When Hurricane Katrina hit New Orleans in 2005, causing massive damage, Bush authorized federal aid but expected state and local agencies to take the lead because of his belief in small government. They were slow in their responses, hampered by the loss of power, flooding, and sheer size of the disaster. More than 1,800 people died, more than half a million had to leave their homes, at least temporarily, and the hurricane caused $100 billion in property damage. It was a catastrophe that left local, state, and federal officials pointing fingers at each other, but Bush was widely criticized for not taking the lead.

In 2008, the stock market crashed because of the inappropriate lending of mortgages to people who couldn't afford them. Banks repossessed thousands of homes—that is, they took them back from homeowners who couldn't make their payments. Some banks began to fail, or go out of business, because they didn't have enough money to meet their obligations. In the face of a cascading crisis—which appeared to be headed toward a depression—Bush allowed the federal government to take over two giant mortgage companies, Fannie Mae and Freddie Mac, to keep them from crashing. Together they held $5 trillion in mortgages; if they had gone bankrupt, it would have staggered the economy.

Bush signed an act that set up the Troubled Asset Relief Program (TARP), which helped. TARP money was used to stabilize banks so they didn't crash and to save the American auto industry, particularly Chrysler and GM. But the combination of tax cuts, high military expenses, and the housing market crisis led to soaring deficits and a major drop in the economy that was called the Great Recession. The recession lasted from December 2007 through June 2009. Millions of jobs were lost, and the economy was the worst it had been since the Great Depression of the 1930s.

Legacy

After leaving office, Bush returned to Texas and bought a home in Dallas. He stayed out of the national news, but after an earthquake rocked Haiti, President Obama asked Bush and former president Bill Clinton to co-chair a charitable fund for Haiti.

Many people found Bush likable, but his presidency is remembered for the Great Recession and the wars in Afghanistan and Iraq, which were staggeringly expensive and became increasingly unpopular. Bush had inherited a prosperous nation that was at peace; he left it at war and with an economy in tatters.

BARACK ★ OBAMA

PRESIDENT
44
OF THE UNITED STATES

BORN: 1961

IN OFFICE:
January 20, 2009–
January 20, 2017

FROM: Hawaii

VICE PRESIDENT:
Joseph R. Biden, Jr.

PARTY: Democratic

DID YOU KNOW?

- Obama was the first president to be born in Hawaii.

- Obama doesn't like ice cream. He doesn't hate it, but his first job was at an ice cream shop and he hasn't cared for it since.

- Obama was *Time* magazine's Person of the Year two times.

- Obama won the 2009 Nobel Peace Prize.

Life Before the Presidency

Barack Obama was born in Hawaii to a white mother and a Black Kenyan father. His father left the family when Barack was a toddler, and his mother remarried to an Indonesian man, Lolo Soetoro. His mother and stepfather moved to Indonesia, where Barack lived from the ages of six to ten. His mother sent Barack back to Hawaii to live with his grandparents because she thought he would get a better education in the United States.

He came to the mainland for college, ending up with a political science degree from Columbia. After graduation, Obama took a job as a community organizer in Chicago. He thought he could have gotten more done as an organizer if he'd had a law degree—so he got one. Obama attended Harvard Law School where he was elected president of the *Harvard Law Review*. He wrote a memoir in 1995, and began to teach law at the University of Chicago Law School.

In 1996, Obama ran for a seat in the Illinois state senate and won the election. He later said that he didn't feel especially successful as a state legislator, but he got nearly three hundred laws passed, mostly bills helping the poor, children, the elderly, and labor unions. In 2000,

Obama ran for a US House seat and was badly beaten. He rebounded, winning a 2004 race for US Senate by the largest margin in the history of Illinois Senate races. Obama was only the fiftieth Black person in the nation's history to serve in the Senate, and upon his election he became the highest-ranking Black official in the country.

When Obama ran for president in 2008, his campaign created a huge internet database of volunteers and donors called Obama for America. Despite rumors that he hadn't been born in the country and would therefore be ineligible to be president (a smear campaign called "birtherism" that began in 2008), Obama and running mate Joe Biden beat Republican nominee, John McCain, and his running mate, Sarah Palin, 365 to 173 in the electoral college.

OBAMA'S ELECTION NIGHT VICTORY SPEECH,
NOVEMBER 5, 2008

If there is anyone out there who still doubts that America is a place where all things are possible; who still wonders if the dream of our founders is alive in our time; who still questions the power of our democracy, tonight is your answer. . . .

This is our chance to answer that call. This is our moment. This is our time—to put our people back to work and open doors of opportunity for our kids; to restore prosperity and promote the cause of peace; to reclaim the American Dream and reaffirm that fundamental truth that out of many, we are one; that while we breathe, we hope, and where we are met with cynicism, and doubt, and those who tell us that we can't, we will respond with that timeless creed that sums up the spirit of a people: Yes, we can.

DECODED President-elect Obama opens his speech noting the historic nature of the night—the nation's first Black president had been elected that day. He ends with the phrase he used throughout his campaign: Yes, we can.

Mr. President

The economy was in crisis when Barack Obama took office in 2009; it was in a severe recession, and economists feared it could tip into depression. The unemployment rate was almost 10 percent and many banks were in danger of collapsing. President Bush had put the Troubled Asset Relief Program (TARP) in place to try to save banks, and President Obama kept it. He sent an extra $60 billion of TARP money to automobile manufacturers General Motors and Chrysler to save the American car industry, which was in danger of collapse. Some people objected to the bailouts, but President Obama thought letting them go out of business would have ripple effects in other industries and be too great a blow to the economy overall. TARP worked; GM, Chrysler, and the large banks survived and repaid most of their loans.

The president asked Congress for the American Recovery and Reinvestment Act, which provided funds to a variety of projects, including middle-class tax cuts, infrastructure projects like bridges, and development of solar and wind power. No Republican in the House voted for the Recovery Act and only three Republican senators did; they thought the program was too expensive. There were enough Democrats in Congress that the measure passed anyway in February 2009. The economy responded well, and instead of sliding into a depression, unemployment fell by half, the federal budget deficit fell dramatically, and the stock market went up, continuing to increase for 128 months until early 2020.

Obama fulfilled a campaign promise in 2010, when he signed the Affordable Care Act (ACA), giving more people access to health insurance. Provisions included allowing children to stay on their parents' insurance until the age of twenty-six and guaranteeing coverage of preexisting conditions. Republicans called the ACA "Obamacare," hoping it would fail and voters would blame the president.

Republicans gained seats in Congress in the midterm elections and voted to repeal the ACA, but the president vetoed the attempt in January 2016. Congressional Republicans tried multiple other times to repeal the bill, even when there was no possibility of doing so, and Americans held strong—and conflicting—opinions on it. For many Republicans, it was an example of expensive government overreach and intrusion into people's lives. For Democrats, it was a life-saving measure that reduced expenses, in part by giving people access to doctors so they didn't have to go to emergency rooms for routine health care. But some people who had had insurance wound up with a new plan that was more expensive, and while people got tax adjustments to help them afford the new plans, that didn't reduce the immediate expense.

Obama also got passage of the Lilly Ledbetter Fair Pay Act (2009), which outlawed paying men and women differently for the same work. He also replaced the unpopular No Child Left Behind Act with the Every Student Succeeds Act (2015), which reduced the federal government's role in education and gave more power back to the states. It tried to help students who were sometimes overlooked, like low-income students, minorities, special education students, and those with limited English skills.

He also oversaw passage of the Dodd-Frank Wall Street Reform and Consumer Protection Act (2010). Dodd-Frank was designed to protect against the kind of economic problems like those Obama inherited when he took office, when the country was on the verge of sliding into a depression.

He also began a program called Deferred Action for Childhood Arrivals (DACA), which allowed prosecutors to choose not to deport undocumented immigrants who were brought to the United States as children and had been living in the States for at least five years. It didn't permanently fix their immigration status or make them citizens, and it had to be renewed every two years. But DACA let young people, many of whom didn't know any country besides the United States, go about their lives without worrying constantly that they might be deported.

In foreign affairs, Obama inherited a war in Iraq and one in Afghanistan. By 2012, he had withdrawn almost all American troops from Iraq, fulfilling another campaign promise. At the same time he increased the number of US troops in Afghanistan in order to prevent the Taliban from taking over there. At one point in 2011, almost one hundred thousand US troops were in Afghanistan; in his second term he reduced that number considerably. Obama ordered a raid on a suspected hideout of Osama bin Laden, the terrorist behind the September 11 attacks, and Navy SEALs killed him. It was considered a high point in the war on terror.

In November 2012, President Obama won reelection in a race against Republican Mitt Romney. The electoral college vote was 332 to 206.

In December 2012, a twenty-year-old man walked into the Sandy Hook Elementary School in Newtown, Connecticut, and shot and killed twenty-six people, including twenty first-grade students. It was part of an epidemic of mass shootings in American schools, theaters, malls, and churches. On June 17, 2015, a white gunman entered Emanuel African Methodist Episcopal Church in Charleston, South Carolina, and killed nine Black people at a Bible study. Americans were deeply split on whether such tragedies could be prevented by passing laws reducing the number of guns and bullets anyone could buy.

After the fall of the Soviet Union, Vladimir Putin eventually came to power in Russia. Democratic government declined and a few wealthy business people used public resources (like mineral deposits) to enrich themselves. Putin wanted to restore Russia to the power it had had during the Cold War. In 2014, Russian forces seized parts of Ukraine. The United States put economic sanctions, or penalties, on Russia to try to stop it from further aggression in Europe, but they had no immediate effect.

OBAMA'S EULOGY FOR REVEREND CLEMENTA PINCKNEY, CHARLESTON, SOUTH CAROLINA, JUNE 26, 2015

What a good man. Sometimes I think that's the best thing to hope for when you're eulogized—after all the words and recitations and resumes are read, to just say someone was a good man. . . .

Amazing grace. Amazing grace.

(Begins to sing)—Amazing grace—(applause)—how sweet the sound, that saved a wretch like me; I once was lost, but now I'm found; was blind but now I see. (Applause.)

Clementa Pinckney found that grace.

Cynthia Hurd found that grace.

Susie Jackson found that grace.

Ethel Lance found that grace.

DePayne Middleton-Doctor found that grace.

Tywanza Sanders found that grace.

Daniel L. Simmons, Sr. found that grace.

Sharonda Coleman-Singleton found that grace.

Myra Thompson found that grace.

Through the example of their lives, they've now passed it on to us. May we find ourselves worthy of that precious and extraordinary gift, as long as our lives endure. May grace now lead them home. May God continue to shed His grace on the United States of America. (Applause.)

DECODED President Obama gave the eulogy for slain pastor Clementa Pinckney, and at the end of his remarks he began to sing "Amazing Grace." Obama is the only president known to have sung in public (except as part of a crowd during the national anthem). Many Americans found the president's grief moving.

At the end of 2014, President Obama reestablished relations with Cuba, which had been cut off under Eisenhower. In late 2015, the United States signed the Paris Agreement, which intended to slow climate change.

In 2009, President Obama appointed Sonia Sotomayor to the Supreme Court, and in 2010, he appointed Elena Kagan. Then in February 2016, conservative Supreme Court justice Antonin Scalia died suddenly. About an hour after the news broke, Senate Majority Leader Mitch McConnell, a Republican from Kentucky, announced that the Senate wouldn't consider a nomination to fill the vacancy because it was an election year. It was the first time in US history that the Senate refused to hear a Supreme Court nomination (although it had denied confirmation before). The Supreme Court went almost fourteen months without a ninth justice.

Elena Kagan

Sonia Sotomayor

Legacy

President Obama's biggest legacy is the Affordable Care Act, or Obamacare, which tried to bring health care to all Americans and reduce health care costs. He also prevented a slide into economic depression and began the longest sustained period of economic growth in American history.

President Obama was the first Black president. Despite an Ivy League education and political experience at the local, state, and federal level, he faced a campaign of "birthers" who challenged his right to hold the highest office based on vague, and completely false, accusations. Political opponents also spread rumors that Obama was Muslim in an era of anti-Muslim sentiment, even though he was a Christian. It was a way of painting him as somehow different and unqualified for office without saying that the reason was his race.

Obama was also one of the youngest presidents and was just fifty-five when he finished his second term. He has occupied his post-presidential life with work on his presidential library, which will be located in Chicago. Both he and Michelle Obama wrote their memoirs, and he frequently gives speeches. Obama is also active in charity work, including personally funding a job-training program in Chicago and cooperating with former Presidents Clinton and George W. Bush on relief for Haiti after a natural disaster. He also campaigned for the 2020 Democratic presidential nominee, Joe Biden, his former vice president and a close friend.

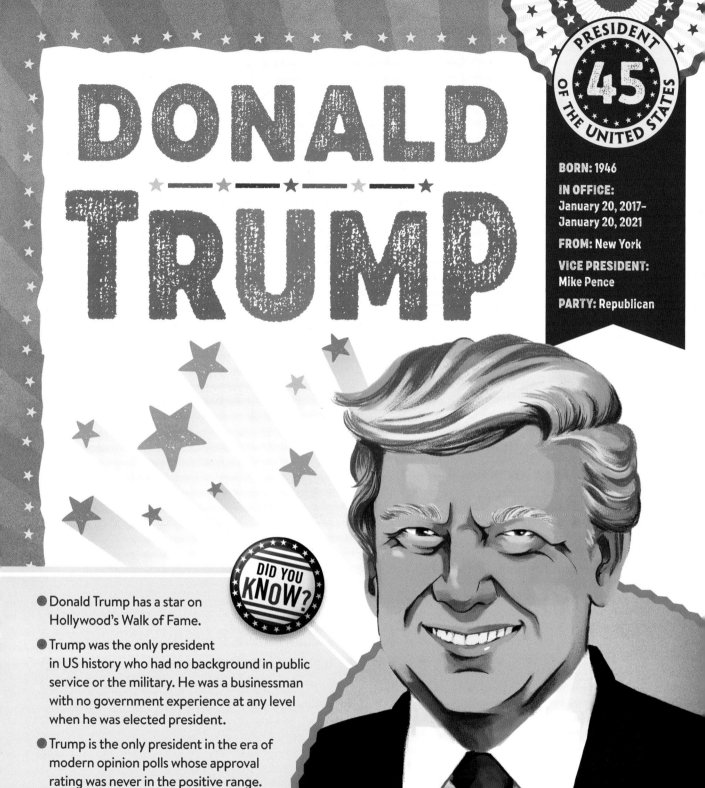

DONALD ★ ★ ★ TRUMP

PRESIDENT 45 OF THE UNITED STATES

BORN: 1946

IN OFFICE:
January 20, 2017–
January 20, 2021

FROM: New York

VICE PRESIDENT:
Mike Pence

PARTY: Republican

DID YOU KNOW?

- Donald Trump has a star on Hollywood's Walk of Fame.

- Trump was the only president in US history who had no background in public service or the military. He was a businessman with no government experience at any level when he was elected president.

- Trump is the only president in the era of modern opinion polls whose approval rating was never in the positive range. That means that at no time during his presidency did the majority of voters approve of his job performance.

- Donald Trump is the only president to have been impeached twice.

Life Before the Presidency

Donald Trump was born in Queens, New York. His parents sent him to New York Military Academy, a private boarding school, when he was thirteen. After graduating in 1964, Trump attended Fordham University; two years later he transferred to the Wharton School of the University of Pennsylvania and got a bachelor's degree in economics. At that time, attending college allowed a young man to avoid the Vietnam draft and Trump got four deferments for attending college, but he would lose that protection when he graduated. Right before that happened, he was diagnosed with bone spurs in his feet, which kept him from being drafted.

In 1971, he took over the family real estate business and renamed it the Trump Organization. He began to develop real estate in more expensive neighborhoods than his father had. One of his best-known projects was Trump Tower, located in Manhattan, New York. He built casinos in Atlantic City, but they failed. Trump maintained his real estate empire, which focused especially on hotels, and built a string of successful golf courses, including his Mar-a-Lago resort in Florida. Students filed a class action suit against Trump University, claiming that they were defrauded; a federal court ordered Trump to pay the students $25 million. In addition to his commercial real estate ventures, he also wrote a book, *The Art of the Deal*.

Trump appeared on *The Apprentice*, a reality TV show in which contestants competed for a job and Trump said, "You're fired!" to the unsuccessful candidates. It was a hit.

Trump ran for president in 2016. In a crowded Republican field, he stood out. Not only was he the only candidate with no background in government, he also didn't watch what he said the way a seasoned politician would. He didn't release his past tax returns, although it was customary (but not legally required) for presidential candidates to do so.

Trump had exceptionally loyal supporters who stuck with him no matter what personal or professional scandals emerged. He held rallies that were well attended and enjoyed the crowds who came to see him. He ran on the slogan "Make America Great Again," which was shortened to MAGA on merchandise, especially red baseball caps.

In 2016, Trump lost the popular vote by almost three million votes to former Secretary of State Hillary Clinton, but he beat her 306 to 232 in the electoral college.

In addition to winning the Electoral College in a landslide, I won the popular vote if you deduct the millions of people who voted illegally.

DECODED In the 2016 election, Trump lost the popular vote by almost three million votes but won the electoral college. There was no evidence of widespread voter fraud.

Mr. President

As president, Trump was more active in domestic than foreign policy. A week after taking office he issued an executive order, nicknamed the "Muslim ban," that stopped entry into the United States of people from seven mostly Muslim countries: Iran, Iraq, Libya, Somalia, Sudan, Syria, and Yemen. The ban would last for ninety days, and Trump said it was necessary to prevent terrorism. It also stopped refugees from entering the United States for 120 days and kept Syrian refugees out indefinitely. Opponents of the Muslim ban felt that Trump was equating Muslims with terrorism and were outraged. In his first year in office he also stopped accepting deferments for undocumented young people under the DACA program; in 2020 the Supreme Court ruled against him.

President Trump also lifted environmental regulations, including pulling the United States out of the Paris Agreement against climate change, although the agreement was legally binding so the withdrawal may not have been legal. He relaxed regulations on industry and cut back on enforcement of fair housing laws. He pushed a $1.5 trillion tax cut through Congress, though Democrats complained that it benefited the wealthiest people and corporations rather than average Americans and contributed to the extreme concentration of wealth in the hands of the richest people. The economy was good when Trump took office and continued to boom until 2020, when the COVID-19 pandemic led to the single sharpest contraction in modern history.

President Trump followed an isolationist and America-first policy, which appealed to his supporters and caused him to withdraw from a variety of international agreements. He pulled out of the Trans-Pacific Partnership, a 2016 trade agreement President Obama had negotiated between several nations on the Pacific Ocean, including the United States, in order to increase US exports to Pacific-area nations. President Trump also pulled the United States out of the North American Free Trade Association (NAFTA) and a deal with Iran to contain its nuclear program, and he even questioned the need for the North Atlantic Treaty Organization (NATO), the West's military alliance and the centerpiece of its security. He also pulled out of an international arms treaty.

EXECUTIVE ORDER 13783, MARCH 28, 2017

[I]t is the policy of the United States that executive departments and agencies (agencies) immediately review existing regulations that potentially burden the development or use of domestically produced energy resources and appropriately suspend, revise, or rescind those that unduly burden the development of domestic energy resources. . . .

The heads of agencies shall review all existing regulations, orders, guidance documents, policies, and any other similar agency actions (collectively, agency actions) that potentially burden the development or use of domestically produced energy resources, with particular attention to oil, natural gas, coal, and nuclear energy resources.

DECODED President Trump issued Executive Order 13783, which rolled back clean energy and climate policies of the Obama administration, including the Clean Power Plan, which tried to reduce pollution from electric power production. Trump thought it would help the coal industry.

President Trump began a trade war with China, sharply raising tariffs. China retaliated, reducing American imports, which slowed US economic growth. Increased tariffs on goods from China sharply raised some prices for American consumers. When farmers lost markets, the federal government gave them billions of dollars to make up for their losses. The United States and China reached an agreement in January 2020, on essentially the same terms China had offered before the trade war.

Donald Trump had campaigned on a promise to stop illegal immigration and build a wall across the southern border, between Mexico and the United States. As president he tried to have one built, even waiving environmental assessments for a wall. He ran into opposition over the cost of the proposed project, which approached $20 million a mile. He also got significant criticism for the policy of separating immigrant family members at the border and keeping them in chain-link enclosures that critics called cages. Trump did not begin the policy of border separations, but previously they weren't used routinely. It was a humanitarian disaster, and his critics hammered on it—but his supporters were strongly in favor of a harsh border policy, hoping to reduce Mexican and Central American immigration.

TRUMP AT HIS CAMPAIGN LAUNCH, JUNE 16, 2015

Mark my words, I would build a great wall, and nobody builds walls better than me, believe me, and I'll build them very inexpensively, I will build a great, great wall on our southern border.

DECODED President Trump campaigned on more restrictive immigration policies, especially for immigrants coming from Mexico. He promised to build a wall across the southern border—and get Mexico to pay for it. Mexico paid for none of the wall, but Trump did succeed in getting about 450 miles built, more than 80 percent of which replaced barriers that already existed.

On August 11 and 12, 2017, right-wing groups held a Unite the Right rally in Charlottesville, Virginia, which brought together different white supremacist, white nationalist, anti-Semitic groups, and the Ku Klux Klan to try to prevent a statue of Confederate General Robert E. Lee from being removed. A number of cities were removing Confederate monuments at the time because they were coming to be seen as symbols of racism and treason. In Charlottesville, many marchers carried torches and chanted phrases from Hitler's fascist Germany. A number of marchers gave Nazi salutes. On August 12, 2017, the protestors and counterprotestors fought several times and a Unite the Right rally attendee drove a car into counterprotestors, injuring twenty people, including thirty-two-year-old Heather Heyer, who was killed. White nationalist sentiment rose dramatically during President Trump's time in office.

President Trump had several scandals—for example, his campaign manager, deputy campaign manager, an advisor, national security advisor, foreign policy advisor, and personal attorney were convicted of crimes including conspiracy to commit wire fraud, campaign violations, obstruction, making false statements, and witness tampering, among others. But the issue of his ties to Russia and Russian interference in the 2016 election wouldn't go away. Russian leader Vladimir Putin openly favored Donald Trump in the election, and Russia hacked into the voting machines in all fifty states during the 2016 election, although there's no evidence that they changed any votes. Russian disinformation campaigns—that is, spreading false information—focused on helping Trump; they were widespread and influenced voters, especially through false information spread on social media sites like Facebook.

A special prosecutor, Robert Mueller, was appointed to investigate the Trump campaign's ties (or lack of ties) to Russia. He investigated for months and finally issued a report in April 2019 that said Russian election interference was "sweeping and systemic." Mueller refused to say that Trump himself had done nothing wrong, saying instead that if he could have cleared the president, he would have done so. In the meantime, the Department of Justice issued a ruling that a sitting president cannot be indicted for a crime. (The Constitution is clear that a president can be charged after leaving office.)

Mueller's report was followed by charges that Trump had pressured the Ukrainian president to try to get him to start an investigation of Democrat Joe Biden, who would be Trump's opponent in the 2020

Robert Mueller

election, suggesting that US aid to Ukraine depended on it. An investigation would look bad for Biden even if it didn't turn anything up. Pressuring Ukraine was especially unfortunate since Russia had invaded in 2014, and Ukraine desperately needed help.

The House drew up articles of impeachment against the president, charging him on December 18, 2019, with abuse of power and obstruction of Congress. After a trial in the Senate, he was found not guilty of both counts on February 5, 2020.

In early 2020, a new virus, SARS-CoV-2, spread across the globe. This is the virus that causes COVID-19. President Trump compared COVID-19 to the flu and suggested it would simply go away on its own. By mid- to late March, the pandemic had caused many states and cities to shut down businesses and ask people to stay home as much as possible, hoping to stop the spread of the disease. People were asked to wear masks to prevent the spread of the virus. But President Trump avoided wearing a mask in public, and health officials complained that he was setting a bad example. By the time he left office, four hundred thousand Americans had died from the disease.

As the economy ground to a halt and twenty-two million Americans lost their jobs in the pandemic, President Trump signed executive orders providing economic help, including extending unemployment benefits, suspending student loan payments, and preventing people from being evicted from their homes.

In May 2020, security officer George Floyd, who was Black, was killed by a white police officer in Minneapolis, Minnesota, when the officer knelt on his neck for more than nine minutes. Black Lives Matter (BLM) protests erupted in many cities.

When liberal Supreme Court Justice Ruth Bader Ginsburg died shortly before the 2020 election, Senate Majority Leader Mitch McConnell moved forward with President Trump's nominee to fill her seat. That outraged Democrats because in 2016, he had blocked President Obama from filling a Supreme Court seat that came open in February of an election year saying the election was too close. Justice Ginsburg's replacement, Amy Coney Barrett, took the oath one week before the 2020 election.

In foreign policy, Trump moved the American embassy in Israel from Tel Aviv to Jerusalem in early 2018, thereby recognizing Jerusalem as Israel's capital. (The United Nations doesn't recognize Jerusalem as the capital.) The move was controversial. Trump and North Korean dictator Kim Jung-un insulted each other until they exchanged letters, and later met in person.

President Trump ran for reelection in 2020, and on Election Day a record number of voters turned out. Many states allowed voters to vote by mail, and more voters did so that year because of the COVID-19 pandemic. The Democratic nominee, Joe Biden, running with Senator Kamala Harris, won with 81 million votes to Trump's 74 million. The electoral college result was 306 to 232. Trump claimed that he had lost because of voter fraud but had no evidence. After the election he appeared to pressure officials to get them to throw out the election results.

On January 6, 2021, Vice President Mike Pence met with both the House of Representatives and the Senate to open the electoral college votes and count them. President Trump's supporters claimed that Pence could overturn the election result by not counting the electoral college vote. (The Constitution does not say this.) The president spoke to a group of his supporters who had come to Washington, DC, to protest counting the electoral ballots; it included white supremacists and other far-right groups with extreme nationalist, racist, and religious fundamentalist views, and antigovernment groups that wanted to overthrow the US government and Constitution. Then Trump

TRUMP'S PHONE CALL TO GEORGIA SECRETARY OF STATE BRAD RAFFENSPERGER, JANUARY 2, 2021

All I want to do is this: I just want to find 11,780 votes, which is one more than we have because we won the state.

DECODED President Trump called Georgia Secretary of State Brad Raffensperger, a Republican, after losing the state in the 2020 election. Here he appears to be pressuring Raffensperger to come up with enough votes to change the result of the state election.

Trump Tweet, January 1, 2021, 2:53 p.m.

The BIG Rally in Washington, DC, will take place at 11:00 a.m. on January 6th. Locational details to follow. StopTheSteal!

Trump Tweet, January 6, 2021, 6:01 p.m.

These are the things and events that happen when a sacred landslide election victory is so unceremoniously & viciously stripped away from great patriots who have been badly & unfairly treated for so long. Go home with love & in peace. Remember this day forever!

DECODED "Stop the Steal" was the name of a movement to overthrow the results of the 2020 presidential election and install Donald Trump in office. It refers to the widespread belief among Trump loyalists that he had won and Democrats had prevailed only through voter fraud. Trump's campaign filed—and lost—dozens of lawsuits related to the election.

urged his supporters to march on the Capitol while Congress was inside certifying the electoral college results (to *certify* the count means to confirm it).

The mob approached the Capitol building, erected a gallows outside it, and broke into the building, overwhelming Capitol and regular police officers and injuring more than 140 of them. They went through the building smashing windows, defecating in the halls, and chanting "Hang Mike Pence." They came very close to members of Congress who barricaded doors to hide in their offices or fled.

The insurrection was ultimately unable to overthrow the results of an American presidential election, and law enforcement painstakingly tracked down the rioters. In the aftermath of an unprecedented attack on American democracy, the House of Representatives impeached Donald Trump again, charging him with incitement of insurrection. Ten Republicans crossed party lines to vote for impeachment, but Trump was found not guilty of the charge on February 13.

Legacy

After losing the 2020 election, Trump retired to his Mar-a-Lago estate in Florida, where he remained politically active, consulting with Republican politicians who flew down to see him. He announced that he would run for president again in 2024.

Donald Trump's years in office were tumultuous, and the president seemed to enjoy that. Trump is best remembered for his disruptive style, starting a trade war with China, and his hardline policy on immigrants at the southern border. His verbal attacks on journalists and on government institutions undermined faith in American institutions, and his foreign policy support for traditional adversaries while criticizing traditional allies caused international concern, especially his softness toward Russia while it attacked another European country and interfered in an American election.

The most significant aspect of his legacy, and the one likely to have the longest impact, was his refusal to hand over power peacefully when he lost the 2020 election. The forty-four presidents preceding him all left office quietly (or died while president), understanding that an orderly political process that respects the voters' will is the United States' great strength.

Trump also faced many investigations into his actions, including his failure to return classified documents to the National Archives after leaving office, his role in the January 6, 2021 attempt to overturn the presidential election, criminal investigations of his business in New York, and defamation lawsuits. On March 30, 2023, he was indicted in New York on multiple counts of business fraud. He was the first former president to face criminal charges.

JOSEPH ROBINETTE BIDEN, JR.

PRESIDENT 46 OF THE UNITED STATES

BORN: 1942

IN OFFICE: January 20, 2021–

FROM: born in Scranton, Pennsylvania; lives in Delaware

VICE PRESIDENT: Kamala Harris

PARTY: Democratic

DID YOU KNOW?

- Joe Biden won the 2020 election with eighty-one million votes—by far the most ever cast for a presidential candidate.

- Biden is the oldest president. He was seventy-seven when he was elected and seventy-eight when he took the oath of office.

- Vice President Kamala Harris is the first woman, first Black person, and first person of Asian descent to hold that office.

- Biden had a stutter as a child.

- Jill Biden is the first First Lady to have a doctorate degree.

- Jill Biden is the first First Lady to hold a job while her husband was president. She teaches English at a community college.

Life Before the Presidency

Joe Biden grew up in an Irish Catholic family in Scranton, Pennsylvania. He had a severe stutter as a child and was bullied for it for years. Other kids called him "Dash" because they thought his stutter sounded like the dashes in Morse code.

The family moved from Scranton to Delaware in 1953 after his father lost his job, a traumatic experience for the family and one that made Biden aware of the struggles of working-class Americans. He was a football star in high school and worked as a lifeguard during the summer as a student at the University of Delaware.

Biden met Neilia Hunter when they both went to the Bahamas on spring break; they married in 1966 and had two boys and a girl. Biden went to Syracuse University Law School and became a public defender. He won election to the New Castle County Council (in Delaware), and then in 1972, he ran for a seat in the US Senate and won. He was twenty-nine, and one of the youngest people ever elected to the Senate. (The Constitution requires a senator to be thirty years old—and Biden turned thirty before he took the oath of office.)

A week before Christmas 1972, Neilia Biden's car was hit by a semitruck. The three Biden children were with her. Neilia and daughter, Amy, were killed, and both boys, Beau and Hunter, were seriously injured. When Biden took the Senate oath, he did so in the chapel at his sons' hospital. In 1975, he met Jill Jacobs when his brother set them up on a blind date. She provided a loving presence to him and his sons, and he began to think that it was possible to have a future after tragedy. They married in 1977 and had a daughter, Ashley. Biden frequently took the train home to Delaware, which is close to Washington, DC, when he was in Congress. He was nicknamed "Amtrak Joe" after the passenger train line.

Biden served thirty-six years in the Senate. He criticized President Nixon's violations of trust and President Ford's decision to pardon him. He served many years on the Senate Judiciary Committee, which oversees the Justice Department and acts on judicial nominations, among other things. He chaired the confirmation hearings of five Supreme Court justices, including Clarence Thomas's hearing. When a law professor, Anita Hill, came forward to say that Thomas had sexually harassed her, Biden didn't allow other witnesses to confirm her story and drew criticism from women's groups. He has said since then that he should have proceeded differently.

Anita Hill

HEARINGS BEFORE THE COMMITTEE ON THE JUDICIARY, ON THE NOMINATION OF CLARENCE THOMAS TO BE ASSOCIATE JUSTICE OF THE SUPREME COURT OF THE UNITED STATES, OCTOBER 11, 12, AND 13, 1991

THE CHAIRMAN: So, in your view, you are here as a result of some unexpected events—

MS. HILL: Definitely.

THE CHAIRMAN: [continuing] —and events that turned out not to be within your control?

MS. HILL: Definitely.

THE CHAIRMAN: Do you consider yourself part of some organized effort to determine whether or not Clarence Thomas should or should not sit on the bench?

MS. HILL: No, I had no intention of being here today, none at all. I did not think that this would ever—I had not even imagined that this would occur.

DECODED Ms. Hill is Anita Hill, the law professor who testified in Clarence Thomas's Supreme Court confirmation hearing that Thomas had sexually harassed her. The chairman is Joe Biden, chair of the Senate Judiciary Committee. Hill is saying that she hadn't wanted to be subjected to public questioning, but the committee goes on to question her motivations, including whether she was trying to get a book deal out of the situation.

In 1994, Biden wrote a crime bill that put more police officers on the street, built new prisons, and increased jail sentences in response to spiking crime rates. It passed with bipartisan (meaning both parties) support; at the time, getting tough on crime was a popular cause among both Democrats and Republicans. In recent years, however, that bill has been seen as contributing to the United States' huge prison population because even minor drug crimes led to prison sentences. Biden also wrote the Violence Against Women Act, which passed in 1994. Among other things, it required law enforcement officials to take domestic violence seriously and led to a sharp decline in domestic violence rates.

Biden was known for his compassion, springing out of the loss of his wife and daughter. And he has often helped young people who have a stutter, as he did—and occasionally still does.

Letter from Joe Biden to Branden Brooks, June 9, 1994

Dear Branden,

It was a pleasure meeting you yesterday. You are a fine, bright young man with a great future ahead of you if you continue to work hard. Remember what I told you about stuttering. You can beat it just like I did. When you do, you will be a stronger man for having won. Also remember, every time you are tempted to make fun of someone with a problem, how it feels when you are made fun of. Treat everyone with respect and you will be respected yourself.

Your friend,
Joe Biden

DECODED Brooks's eighth-grade class made a field trip to Washington, DC, in 1994, and he met Joe Biden there. Brooks had a stutter, which caught Biden's attention because of his own struggle with stuttering. Biden spoke with him about it at the event, trying to encourage him, and followed up with this note a week later.

Biden ran for the Democratic presidential nomination twice, in 1988 and 2008, and lost both times. The 2008 presidential candidate, Barack Obama, chose Biden as his running mate, and they went on to win in the general election. Unlike many vice presidents, Biden had a prominent role in the administration. He often traveled on official business and represented the administration. And almost to their surprise, the two men became close personal friends. Shortly before he left office, President Obama awarded the Medal of Freedom to Joe Biden in a surprise ceremony.

Biden's son Beau died of brain cancer in 2015. President Obama's second term was ending and Biden had a good shot at getting the Democratic nomination, but he decided not to run for president that year because the family was grieving.

In 2020, Biden ran for president again in a very crowded field of Democratic hopefuls. He did very poorly in the first few primaries, which choose who will be the nominee, then in a surprising turnaround won South Carolina when he received strong support from Black voters. When he got the nomination, he named California senator Kamala Harris as his running mate. The COVID-19 pandemic made campaigning tricky. Joe Biden tried to campaign without spreading the virus. He wore his mask in public, for which Trump mocked him, and appeared virtually more than in person.

Voter turnout was extremely high—almost two-thirds of eligible voters went to the polls (or voted by mail, which was a popular option during the pandemic). Biden received

BARACK OBAMA'S EULOGY FOR BEAU BIDEN, JUNE 6, 2015

It's no secret that a lot of what made Beau the way he was was just how much he loved and admired his dad. He studied law, like his dad, even choosing the same law school. He chased public service, like his dad, believing it to be a noble and important pursuit. From his dad, he learned how to get back up when life

knocked him down. He learned that he was no higher than anybody else, and no lower than anybody else— something he got from his mom, by the way. And he learned how to make everybody else feel like we matter, because his dad taught him that everybody matters.

He even looked and sounded like Joe, although I think Joe would be first to acknowledge that Beau was an upgrade—Joe 2.0.

DECODED Biden and his son Beau were very close. Biden asked his friend, President Barack Obama, to give Beau's eulogy, which is a talk at a funeral about the person who has died.

eighty-one million votes, the most votes ever cast for a candidate in any American election, beating Trump by seven million votes. It was 306–232 in the electoral college.

Trump claimed falsely that he had won the election, and on January 6, 2021, rioters attacked the Capitol building while the electoral college votes were being counted (see pages 229 and 230). Trump did not attend President Biden's inauguration ceremony.

Mr. President

President Biden came to office two weeks after the Capitol insurrection. The economy had sharply contracted, the COVID-19 pandemic had killed four hundred thousand Americans, and people were sharply divided in their political beliefs, in part because they got their news from different sources and disagreed on the facts of many issues and events.

In Biden's first year in office he had a major embarrassment when the United States pulled its troops out of Afghanistan, on a timeline set down by President Trump, and the country fell almost immediately to the Taliban. The war in Afghanistan had been America's longest, lasting from 2001 to 2021, and it seemed to have produced no lasting result. In addition, people desperate to get out of the country crowded the airport, reminding many people of the US exit from Vietnam. Biden's poll numbers fell in response.

He scored a major legislative victory in a highly partisan Congress when he got passage of an infrastructure bill that provided funds to improve roads, bridges, and airports, as well as the electric and water systems. He also signed the American Rescue Plan, which provided money to Americans to help the economy recover from the impact of the COVID-19 pandemic.

The economy had staggered in 2020 due to the pandemic, and President Biden inherited serious economic problems. He was able to slash unemployment rates to their lowest level since the 1960s, but inflation angered consumers. He announced student loan debt forgiveness for many college graduates, but some states fought back to require people to repay the loans.

Under President Biden, the US rejoined the Paris Agreement, an international effort to reduce climate change. (President Trump had withdrawn from the agreement.)

JOE BIDEN'S REMARKS ON THE SIGNING OF THE INFRASTRUCTURE BILL,
OCTOBER 28, 2021

Good morning. Today, I am pleased to announce that after—after months of tough and thoughtful negotiations, I think we have a historic—I know we have a historic economic framework.

It's a framework that will create millions of jobs, grow the economy, invest in our nation and our people, turn the climate crisis into an opportunity, and put us on a path not only to compete, but to win the economic competition for the 21st century against China and every other major country in the world.

It's fiscally responsible. It's fully paid for. Seventeen Nobel Prize winners in economics have said it will lower the inflationary pressures on the economy.

And over the next 10 years, it will not add to the deficit at all; it will actually reduce the deficit, according to the economists.

I want to thank my colleagues in the Congress for their leadership. We've spent hours and hours and hours over months and months working on this.

No one got everything they wanted, including me, but that's what compromise is. That's consensus. And that's what I ran on.

DECODED Biden celebrates not just getting money to build roads and bridges, but the fact that he could get anything through a divided Congress.

A number of climate-related disasters alarmed activists, including a major drought in the summer of 2022 and a longer wildfire season on the West Coast. In addition, Hurricane Ian caused massive damage in Florida. (Storms crossing warmer oceans can develop higher winds and produce more rain when they make landfall, adding to the already destructive nature of hurricanes.) President Biden also signed an executive order designed to reduce deforestation (the cutting of trees across a wide area without replacing them). The measure protected forests, especially old growth forests, which absorb carbon dioxide and help to lower the amount in the atmosphere, reducing global warming. The order also contained measures to fight the increase in fires in the western United States that resulted from drought and increased temperatures.

Biden had several foreign policy successes, including the death of terrorist and al-Qaeda leader Ayman al-Zawahiri. But the biggest challenge was Russia. Russian president Vladimir Putin had ordered an invasion in 2014 and taken over parts of eastern Ukraine and the Crimean peninsula, which hangs down into the Black Sea and is important for shipping and security. On February 24, 2022, Russian troops began a massive attack on Ukraine. Putin thought he could quickly defeat Ukraine's much smaller military, but Ukrainian resistance was fierce, and the Russian military was hampered by lack of supplies and poor maintenance of vehicles because of corruption in the Russian system. Ukrainian defenders held out long enough that western nations were able to send military and financial aid—and slap economic sanctions on Russia that were intended to punish it for attacking a peaceful neighbor and make it harder for Russia to replace military equipment it lost in the fighting. Biden sent wave after wave of American military aid to Ukraine and increased sanctions on Russia several times. Russia continued to bomb civilian infrastructure, including targeting hospitals and the energy grid, and numerous atrocities were discovered in areas liberated from Russian control. And in February 2023, Biden visited Kyiv, the Ukrainian capital. It was a bold move. Biden was the first US president to visit a war zone that didn't have American troops stationed nearby, and the trip underscored American commitment to protecting Ukraine's freedom from foreign domination.

President Biden strengthened ties with US allies and with NATO, the American security alliance, and in the wake of the Russian invasion, Sweden and Finland began the process of joining NATO.

Legacy

President Biden faces multiple challenges. The American public is divided and increasingly vulnerable to disinformation campaigns, both domestic and foreign. Political violence and threats have increased. Congress itself is sharply divided. And major foreign policy challenges will test American resolve. How Biden's presidency is evaluated will likely depend on his success in ending the Russian threat to Europe; how he handles the economy, which staggered during the COVID-19 pandemic; and his ability to restrict the growth of political extremism, which threatens democracy itself.

CONCLUSION

Forty-five people have held the highest office in the land. Some of them have acted with wisdom, like Abraham Lincoln. Some have been popular with a wide range of voters, like Ronald Reagan. Others have irritated a lot of folks, like John Tyler, who got kicked out of his own party while he was president, and Millard Fillmore, who made people so angry that they vandalized his house years after he left office. President Biden and his successors can choose to follow the best examples of the forty-five presidents who came before him. Wait, should that be forty-four? Still a problem, Grover. Still a problem.

Presidents wield great power, but there are limits. The Constitution contains checks and balances to prevent any president from becoming too strong. John Adams compared the branches of government limiting one another to two kids cutting a piece of cake in half: One would choose how to cut the cake and the other would choose which piece they wanted.

Maybe one day you'll run for president. Until then, what advice do past presidents have for you? Study. Ulysses S. Grant told a group of Civil War veterans that "The free school [will] preserve us as a free nation." John F. Kennedy said, ". . . [N]o free society can possibly be sustained, unless it has an educated citizenry . . ." And a week before his assassination, he told a group of students, "[W]e expect something of you . . . [W]e ask the best of you."

So do your homework; the nation is depending on you. And when you're old enough—vote. As Dwight Eisenhower said, "The future of this Republic is in the hands of the American voter." That's you. *You're* the future that will hold the nation in your hands.

SUGGESTIONS FOR FURTHER READING

Barber, James. *Presidents*. New York: DK Publishing, 2021. 72 pp. ISBN 978-1-4654-5770-7

Bausum, Ann. Foreword by Barack Obama. *Our Country's Presidents: All You Need to Know about the Presidents, from George Washington to Barack Obama*. Washington, DC: National Geographic Society, 2013. 224 pp. ISBN 978-1-4263-1089-8

Bausum, Ann. *Our Country's Presidents: A Complete Encyclopedia of the US Presidency*. Washington, DC: National Geographic Society, 2017. 224 pp. ISBN 978-1-4263-2685-1

Davis, Kenneth C., and Pedro Martin. *Don't Know Much about the Presidents*. New York: HarperCollins Publishers, 2014. 64 pp. ISBN 978-0-0602-8615-6

Hajeski, Nancy J. *The Big Book of Presidents: Fascinating Facts and True Stories about U.S. Presidents and Their Families*. New York: Skyhorse Press, 2021. 148 pp. ISBN 978-1-5107-6024-0.

Krull, Kathleen, and Kathryn Hewitt. *Lives of the Presidents: Fame, Shame (and What the Neighbors Thought)*. Boston: Harcourt Children's Books, 2011. 104 pp. ISBN 978-0-5474-9809-6

Parker, Philip, and Shannon Reed. *The Presidents Visual Encyclopedia*. New York: DK Publishing, 2021. 208 pp. ISBN 978-0-7440-3710-4

Rubel, David. Foreword by James M. McPherson. *Encyclopedia of the Presidents and Their Times*. New York: Scholastic, 1994, updated 2013. 248 pp. ISBN 978-0-545-49985-9

Yenne, Bill. *Complete Book of US Presidents*. New York: Crestline, 2021. 272 pp. ISBN 978-0-7858-3923-1

DOCUMENTS USED THROUGHOUT COURTESY OF THE FOLLOWING SOURCES:

The American Presidency Project

American Rhetoric

Atomic Heritage Foundation

The Avalon Project Brooklyn Public Library

Cato Institute

Charlottesville: University of Virginia Press, Rotunda

Cox Media Group

House Divided: The Civil War Research Engine at Dickinson College

Indiana Historical Society

Iowa State University Library Special Collections and University Archive

Library of Congress

Massachusetts Historical Society

Miller Center

National Archives

National Public Radio (NPR)

Princeton University Library

Records Administration, Ohio History Connection

Rutherford B. Hayes Presidential Library & Museum—Memoirs of Thomas Donaldson

The Shapell Manuscript Foundation

Theodore Roosevelt Center at Dickinson State University

Truman Library Institute

United States Government Publishing Office (GovInfo)

University of North Carolina Press

University of Rochester Frederick Douglass Project

The White House

Yale Law School

Excerpt from transcript of forum entitled "LBJ: From Senate Majority Leader to President, 1958–1964" with Robert Caro © John F. Kennedy Library Foundation, Inc.

ABOUT THE AUTHOR

KATIE KENNEDY has taught college history and American government for more than thirty years. She currently teaches in Iowa. She and her husband have a daughter and a son. She is the author of *The Constitution Decoded: A Guide to the Document That Shapes Our Nation*, and two young adult novels, *Learning to Swear in America* and *What Goes Up*. She used to have finches named Bess and Harry, after the Trumans. Then Harry Truman laid an egg.

ALSO AVAILABLE

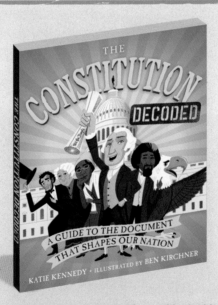

Don't miss the companion volume from Katie Kennedy— *The Constitution Decoded: A Guide to the Document That Shapes Our Nation!*